COMMENDATIONS

Rev. Dr. Alistair Petrie
—Pastor, Author and Executive Director, Partnership Ministries

Marie and I have been devouring the pages of this fantastic book. It is absolutely outstanding! I thoroughly recommend it for anyone who wants to experience the fulness and promise of what it means to be created in God's image! But be prepared – this book will be life changing – even for the seasoned leader! It will unveil the depths of a God of love who touches and heals, bringing revelation and understanding to every level of life – spirit, soul and body! This book will be a profound tool in the hand of the Lord!

And Marie Petrie adds:

This beautifully written book, weaves real life struggles and breakthroughs with the earthing of God's loving plan for us all, bringing hope and encouragement. Wonderfully blended with Scripture and easy to read, it answers the *'why'* and *'how to'* for those who pray for healing for others, but have not yet discovered creativity as a tool for breakthrough.

Bishop Graham Dow
—former Bishop of Carlisle, UK

This is a wonderful book for those whose heart is to see people healed. For over twenty years Fiona and her team have watched the Holy Spirit use messy painting, outdoor walks, and all kinds of creative play to bring far reaching healing and restoration. Affirming strongly that every human being is created in God's image and, therefore, good, creative play releases aspects of the person that have been suppressed and shut away.

Through creativity God finds the real person in us that has been lost. Jesus enters into our suffering, assures us of complete forgiveness and recreates us in his love. The book is soaked in moving personal testimony. Later chapters illustrate many practical ways through which these ground-breaking insights bring healing to the wide range of human pain. It is a magnificent and comprehensive guide.

Rev. Dr. David Kyle Foster
—Founder of Mastering Life Ministries

The Church needs this book, and badly! Why? Because our head-centered western focus has disconnected us from a God-centred heart, turning us into human *doings* rather than human *beings*. We've lost that intimate walk with the Lord and replaced it with knowledge *about* Him, setting us adrift from the very purpose of life, which is relationship *with* Him.

Someone once said that the longest distance in all of life is the one between the head and the heart! *Healing Through Creativity* will help you connect with God again. It takes you on a journey of healing and discovery that is salve to the soul for anyone who has been struggling with intractable brokenness and performance-based living. These principles have set me on a path to wholeness in ways I could never have imagined!

Arie de Waard
—Retired Psychiatrist (Netherlands)

Prayer for healing is an adventure. Knowing about God is not the same as knowing God and having a special relationship with Jesus, His son. This brings healing to all relationships, especially the one we have with ourselves. The testimonies in this book tell us in plain language how the depth of God's love is beyond our understanding. I was moved to tears reading some of these stories. As a retired psychiatrist, and now a member of the Ellel Ministries Netherlands prayer team, I am privileged to regularly witness the changes God brings to people through discovering our creativity. Fiona explains the essence of God's purpose for our lives and encourages others to share in this special work of God. I recommend you read it for yourself!

Diane Daune
—Retired University Lecturer and Textile Designer

This comprehensive resource demonstrates that although creativity is not an end in itself, it forges a powerful connection to ourselves, others and most importantly to God, bringing healing and restoration. For 15 years I have been part of Fiona Horrobin's creativity team. I have been able to combine my gifting in textile crafts, a professional background in health care and the arts, as I helped people embark on their personal journey of healing through creativity. I have seen how the Lord comes close to the broken-hearted and saves those who are crushed in spirit *(Psalm 34 v 18)*. Fiona presents profound truths in a straightforward and understandable way. By taking the time and space to allow God to touch your heart as you read, He will use the ordinary to do the extraordinary. The potential for blessing is limitless.

Zoltán Dörnyei
—Professor of Psycholinguistics, University of Nottingham and author of "Vision, Mental Imagery and the Christian Life."

Creativity can mean various things in psychology, from intellectual originality to artistic talent. In this fascinating and inspiring book, the essence of human creativity is understood as a reflection of God the Creator. But, as Fiona explains, in many of us the creative side has, sadly, been *"crushed along life's way,"* to the detriment of our health and well-being. The good news, however, is that our creative gifting can be rediscovered and released, so that *"God is able to bring His presence and healing"* into our lives. She offers convincing biblical principles, tried and tested experience and shares real-life 'success stories' that all point to the same conclusion – that when we tap into our inner font of creativity, it leads to divine restoration.

This is a uniquely useful book. It glorifies God, the Creator and Healer, and offers hope and practical pathways not only to people who are struggling, but, also, to anybody who wants to get closer to God through their own God-given creativity. I concur with the author in saying, *"I cannot think of anyone for whom it would not be relevant."*

'Sarah'

God has done an amazing work of healing in my life. I was a psychiatric patient taking maximum dosages of psychiatric drugs in my desperate struggle to stay alive. I had been sexually abused since the age of three. I was trapped in a well of darkness and there was no way out.

Yet through creativity, in ways I could never have thought or imagined, God reached the 'real me' on the inside. The healing He brought has been totally life-transforming for me and my family. I'm no longer suicidal, have been free of all medication for many years now and no longer need my lifetime Government disability pension!

I thank God for the psychiatric care which kept me alive and safe, but ultimately it was only God who could transform my life. I will never cease to thank Him for my healing. I don't think I would be alive today if it wasn't for all that God taught Fiona Horrobin and the Ellel Ministries' team about *Healing Through Creativity*. The principles Fiona describes so powerfully are life-changing and life-giving.

I know – for through them God saved me and gave me my life back!

HEALING
through
Creativity

HEALING
through
Creativity

A Bridge from the Head to the Heart
How simple creativity can bring
deep healing from our Creator

FIONA
HORROBIN

Sovereign World Ltd
Bringing together the Word & the Spirit

Published by
Sovereign World Ltd
Ellel Grange
Bay Horse
Lancaster
LA2 0HN
United Kingdom

www.sovereignworld.com
Twitter: @sovereignworld
Facebook: www.facebook.com/sovereignworld

Published November 2020
Copyright © 2020 Fiona G Horrobin

Hardback ISBN 978-1-852408-37-4
Kindle ISBN 978-1-852408-38-1

British Library Cataloguing-in-Publication Data.
A catalogue record for this book is available from the British Library.

Commercial Image Copyright Sources: Freepik, Creative Market, Design Cuts,
Unsplash, Paul Stanier, Ellel Ministries.
With thanks to all the individuals who gave permission for their images to be used
in this book, the copyright of which is held by them.

Book cover and interior design by Paul Stanier, Zaccmedia.com

MIX
Paper from
responsible sources
FSC® C118234
FSC
www.fsc.org

CONTENTS

Part 1

PRINCIPLES OF HEALING THROUGH CREATIVITY

PART 2

PRACTICAL HEALING THROUGH CREATIVITY

FOREWORD

I cannot look at a flower, a sunset or the intricacies of the natural world without marvelling at the creative genius of our amazing God. And mankind is made in the image and likeness of God. Creativity is a gift of God to His creation. As a result, mankind is also exceedingly creative – always pushing the creative boundaries of science, technology and the arts.

But, as with all gifts, creativity can be used or abused. It can be used for the purposes which God intended or, as history teaches us, in the hands of an evil person those self-same gifts can be used to cause untold suffering and, even, bring devastation to mankind.

The pain of abuse, rejection and personal suffering at the hands of others has the effect of crushing the creative instinct. The creative core of humanity goes into hiding, often broken on the inside of the personality, limiting the potential of God's creative power to be at work restoring and healing the inner man or woman.

For the past twenty years now, I have watched as Fiona and her team have worked with some of the most devastated and broken individuals to bring God's healing to them. In the early days of the ministry, we learnt many other healing keys, embracing such vital topics as forgiveness, the consequences of ungodly relationships, the need for deliverance and various inner healing issues. But, important though these keys still are, it was when Fiona's team discovered the power of God to heal from within, through the release of His creativity, that they began to see major breakthroughs in the healing of both the very broken and also those struggling with, seemingly, lesser issues. It is not over-dramatising what happened to say that miracles began to take place.

This book is not only a good read – the story of what God did - but it will also be a revelation, both to those who are trying to help others and to those who are struggling to find their own breakthrough. It tells how the release of God's creativity brings the presence and power of God into the most hidden areas of damage. I have seen first-hand how the teaching this book contains is totally life-transforming. It brings hope and healing to those who have been cruelly devastated by others with evil intent, as well as those who are struggling with less obvious but, nevertheless, life-limiting issues.

I am not just commending this book to you because it is written by my wife! But because all that Fiona and the team have experienced has brought the presence of God into the heart of men and women in a way that both brings Scripture to life and demonstrates the truth of the Gospel message in an extraordinary way. It illustrates how the power of the cross can transform every broken life. I have seen it and I know it to be true.

My prayer is that this book will travel far and wide, bringing revelation, hope, healing and equipping to many.

Peter Horrobin
Founder, Ellel Ministries International
October 2020

PREFACE

Why *Healing Through Creativity* and why *A Bridge from the Head to the Heart* you may ask? The answer is simple: I have discovered that God uses creativity to break into places where we need healing – bringing life-giving streams from the Father to His children, restoring back to them what has been robbed from their lives.

Streams of living water flowing over God's children

Nobody was more surprised than me, when I found myself playing on the floor with glue, glitter and some dirty old shells. No, I wasn't with my grandchildren or anyone else's! Our small team and I were with a lady who had come to our centre in desperate need of help. She was on the highest dosage of psychiatric drugs and came direct from the psychiatric hospital. Her story weaves its way through the first part of this book.

It was a breakthrough moment which I will never forget. As we played with the lady on the floor, she began to receive life from the dead. God was showing us how He, as Creator, does not look on the outward appearance but He sees the need of the heart and He has ways of reaching beneath the rubble and the mess to find the beauty He created, where the key to healing lies.

There is no-one who has been created 'bad', since each of us was originally made in God's image and likeness. Yet we are all human and have human needs, frailties, weaknesses and sinfulness which are now part of our human nature. We are all in the same situation, yet God loves and accepts each one of us. The lady who came for help believed that she was intrinsically 'bad' and resisted with all she was worth, any redemptive message until as she simply but profoundly put it, "God found me!"

The phrase 'bridge from the head to the heart' simply means that what we know in our head and what we experience in our heart can be two different things, which cause many hidden struggles and conflicts. It is in the heart area where we are most vulnerable and need to be found.

Creativity in its broadest sense is not something we do, but it is an expression of who we are. And through the release of our creative gifting, God is able to bring His presence and healing. It is His design for wholeness and wellbeing. He is Creator and knows us better than we know ourselves. After many years of experience and seeking to understand the healing ministry, we were learning something new and vital about the way God can reach the human heart.

> " No one is created bad

Working at the Coal Face

Working at the coal face of prayer ministry with those in need, we began seeking God in prayer for His restoration plan for broken lives. If He was Creator and His Word was the plumb line by which those He created could align their lives and find healing, then we needed to know His plan.

God's Word was our guiding light and gradually we received understanding as we learnt how to apply His truth, resulting in profound changes and lasting healing. Excitement grew as we discovered, through prayer and much practical experience, dependency on God and His way forward. Out of those pioneering years has come a wellspring which continues to flow with life-giving water around the world, to countless individuals, beyond anything we could have ever imagined.

I will tell more about our adventures at the Ellel Grange Centre where Ellel Ministries was first established in 1986, for it was here that the life-changing principles contained within Luke 9:11: 'Jesus welcomed them and spoke to them about the kingdom of God, and healed those who needed healing' were first applied. The message of *Welcome, Teach and Heal* has been at the heart of the ministry ever since and has been a key foundation of discovering how God heals through discovering our creative selves.

"You must write the book!"

The excitement generated by our pioneering course on *Healing Through Creativity* invariably prompted the response, "You must write the book!" – not just from one person but from many, many people. I knew in my heart that the book needed writing. But it took me nearly twenty years to reach the place where I was ready and able to sit down and write.

In the meantime, the *Healing Through Creativity* vision has reached many different nations and people groups. And yes, at last, the book has emerged. It is my hope and prayer that it will bring the heart and healing of the Creator to many more people, in the same way as has happened on our courses.

Healing Through Creativity is both inspirational and practical in its application. However, right at the outset, I would like to express the foundational truth that the healing principles originate in God, the Creator. They are not my good ideas, they come out of having a relationship with Him as outlined in His Word, and the application of the divine laws and principles that God set forth in Creation. That which is created cannot be separated from the Creator, as expressed in these words from Psalm 8:

That which is created cannot be separated from the Creator

O LORD, our Sovereign, how majestic is your name in all the earth! You have set your glory above the heavens ... When I look at your heavens, the work of your fingers, the moon and the stars that you have established; what are human beings that you are mindful of them, mortals that you care for them? You have made them a little lower than GOD and crowned them with glory and honor. You have given them dominion over the works of your hands; you have put all things under their feet, all sheep and oxen, and also the beasts of the field, the birds of the air, and the fish of the sea, whatever passes along the paths of the seas. O LORD our Sovereign, how majestic is your name in all the earth!

(PSALM 8: 1, 3-9 NRSV)

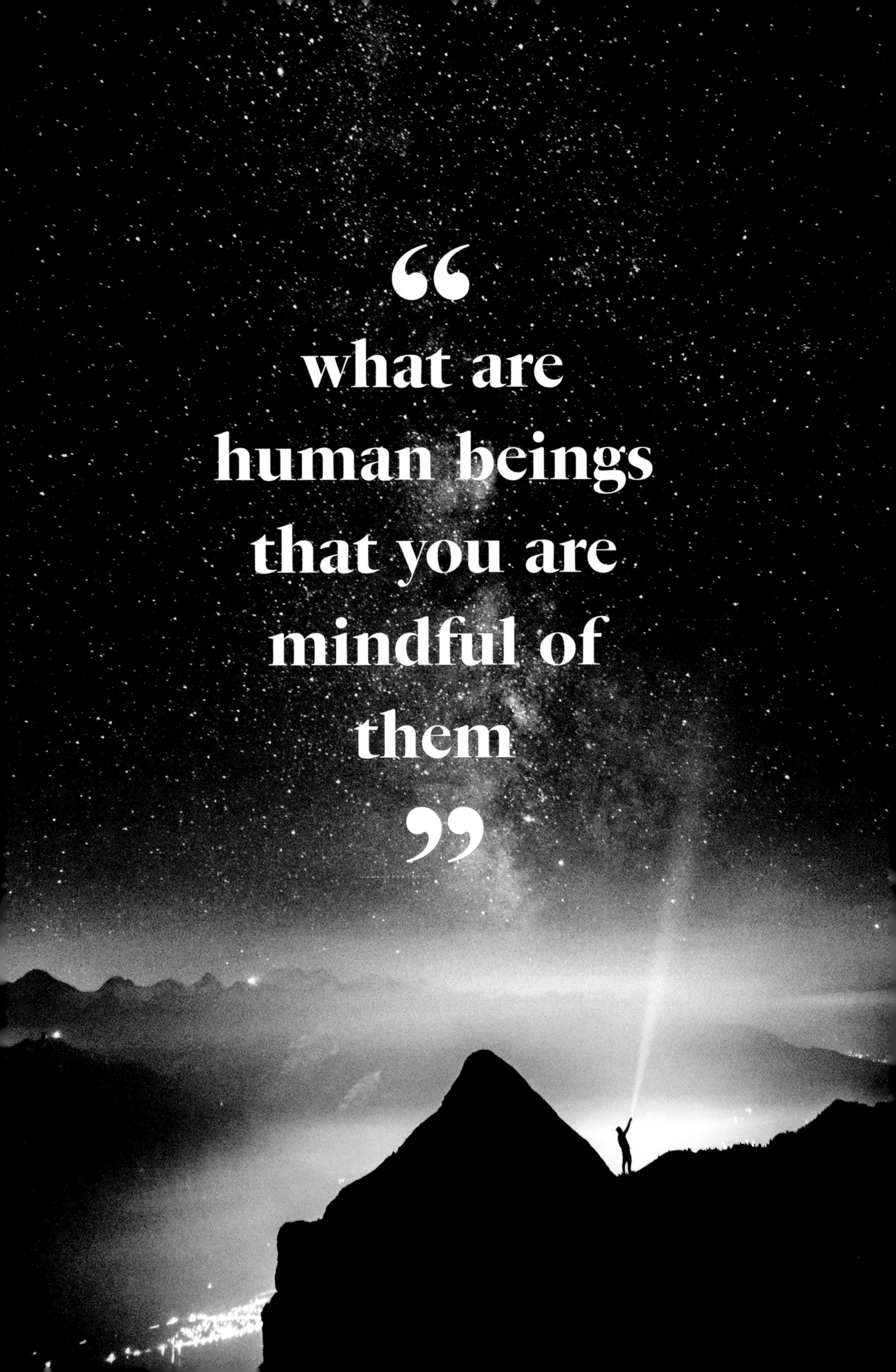
“what are human beings that you are mindful of them”

I pray you will see and experience through the pages of this book something of the genius of Almighty God. He formed us in His own image and likeness (Genesis 1:31) with beauty and creativity, and the capacity to express these qualities in ways that reflect who He is. He has embedded spiritual and physical laws into the whole universe amongst all created things – laws which cannot change, whether we acknowledge Him or not. He invites us to explore all this for ourselves and to discover our own personal God-made identity and destiny.

Creativity is not something we do, it is an expression of who we are. From the first moment of life at our conception, we demonstrate His creativity. We will discover later in the book just how our innate creativity is in both who we are and who we are becoming.

"
An expression
of who we are

Creativity is not something we do, it is an expression of who we are

Being creative and being artistic are not necessarily one and the same thing; we are all creative, but we are not all artistic. Nevertheless, I have been amazed at how many gifted artists have been released into artistic freedom, simply through having a creative relationship with God freshly established in their hearts. And for some, when the burden and memories of harsh 'artistic' critique have been lifted, they have literally come alive!

Equally, many who come from a scientific or engineering background have experienced immense freedom when creative truth has brought a release from the bondage of head knowledge. And then there are countless others who have expressed the joy and release of being healed through creativity in its broadest sense.

As adults, living in a complex, stressful and demanding world, it is easy to live in our heads with what is rational. Intuitive creative expression can, at best, be ignored and, at worst, buried. Whatever our culture, the pressure to perform, carry great responsibilities, work, cope, exist and survive takes its toll. Without realising it, it is easy to become 'machine like', subconsciously overriding a God-given part of ourselves to the detriment of our health and well-being.

I have often heard people say, "I know all about God's love in my head, but I don't feel it in my heart." To one degree or another, belief in God has become a head exercise rather than a relationship. God, the Creator seeks out a relationship with us, born of natural trust and dependency. We see a reflection of this through the musician with an instrument, a cook with ingredients, a potter with clay and a scientist with an experiment. And it is expressed in God's Word:

> Woe to you who quarrel with their Maker, earthen vessels with the potter! Does the clay say to the one who fashions it, "What are you making?" or "Your work has no handles"?
> (ISAIAH 45:9 NRSV)

> Yet you, LORD, are our Father. We are the clay, you are the potter; we are all the work of your hand.   (ISAIAH 64:8)

As we progress through this book, we will see how the creativity in us all needs expression. So often, it has been crushed along life's way and, as a result, part of our human identity, including our spirituality, has suffered. We ignore at our peril the truth that, in our humanity, we are primarily spiritual beings. We only need to watch a football match and see the players kneeling, looking skywards or crossing themselves, to witness innate spirituality. The human need to look to a higher being or person is apparent to all.

The first cry when an accident is about to occur is usually something like, "Oh God!" When someone dies, the first response is usually a spiritual one, the deceased loved one is sometimes referred to as a star in the sky or is presumed to be still watching over those they have left behind. The Bible describes that spirituality as having a sense of 'eternity in our hearts' (Ecclesiastes 3:11). But what, and where, is eternity?

"
We are primarily spiritual beings

19

What does it mean? How can we know what it is? Whatever race or creed, all human life is wired to respond to their Maker and Creator and needs to know Him.

Of course, it is possible to put all this down to simply being 'superstitious', 'irrational' or 'religious.' Yet, even the most determined and hardened atheist worships something – even if it is their own atheistic, wholly rational self-belief which trusts and believes in science above all other beliefs. The biblical reality, however, is that God is the God of science. The very word 'science' simply means knowledge – and one of the characteristics of God is His omniscience – He has all knowledge, He knows all things! God's perfect created order originates in who He is. The history of science is God's story of an indescribably creative journey of discovery, which He gave to human beings as a gift.

> God's perfect created order originates in who He is

Whatever extremities there have been in a person's life, and whatever they believe or don't believe, their need of a relationship with their Creator screams out to be met. The core of every human being cries out, "Who am I and why am I here?" These profoundly creative and spiritual questions cannot be ignored. The spiritual side of life needs to be examined to see how this pertains to the physical realm, and specifically, to our human life and its needs, which are of critical significance.

"Why should it be me writing this book?!"

I do ask, "Why me?" I don't have any professional, psychological or secular counselling training. But I do have over thirty years' experience of seeing lives transformed through entering into a relationship with God. Simply put, along with our team I have been seeking God's way of restoring broken lives, and throughout the journey, have learnt to trust and rely fully on Him and His Word, where I am convinced the answers lie for every human condition.

Every human being has a human spirit – a spirit that is created by God to be the source of energy and life. The human spirit contains all that pertains to the beauty, uniqueness and value God has placed in every single individual. We can see from the Bible that the human spirit has within it the gift of life expressed through our creativity, but that this can become crushed, broken or even defiled. God's principles for restoration and healing of the human spirit release the energy of life into every area of our being.

> The LORD, who stretches out the heavens, who lays the foundation of the earth, and who forms the human spirit within a person. (ZECHARIAH 12:1)

> The human spirit is the lamp of the LORD that sheds light on one's inmost being. (PROVERBS 20:27)

> The LORD is close to the brokenhearted and saves those who are crushed in spirit. (PSALM 34:18)

I greatly respect psychiatry and psychology, for they contain vital God-given knowledge, understanding and principles for human wellbeing. But, outside of a relationship with God, they have limitations. Helpful and lifesaving though medication can be, it can never be a fully satisfactory substitute for spiritual reality and divine restoration. Only in a relationship with the Creator can the spiritual needs and condition of the heart be fully met, as is illustrated so powerfully throughout the Bible.

A Book of Two Parts

There are two parts to *Healing Through Creativity*. Part One contains the principles of healing through creativity and establishes how, as God's created beings, our innate human creativity is part of our core identity and, as such, has needs that cannot be ignored.

The second part expresses the more practical outworking of the healing principles outlined in Part One.

The illustrations, stories and pictures throughout will help bring understanding and application of the principles of healing through creativity. I pray that you, and others through you, will be touched and blessed, renewed and restored, and yes, even transformed by the power of God's truth in the face of life's circumstances. This is healing. Jesus is the one who radically declared in His Word, "I have come that you may have life and have it more abundantly" (John 10:10). Enjoy, and may God bless you in your journey.

Thank You

This book could never have been conceived or written without the involvement of hundreds of other people. I want to express my personal deep gratitude to everyone who has been part of the Ellel teams down the years, and who has pioneered with me to bring hope and healing to all who have come through our doors. You have all played a vital and massive part in the journey – thank you.

I also want to give my special thanks to my dear friend, Anna Wood, who has walked with me in countless hours, bringing God's heart to the most broken. Without her encouragement and unflinching faith, this book would not have been possible.

Along with Anna, there are those I affectionately call 'The Creativity Gang' through whose dedication and volunteering, Ellel Ministries has been able to pioneer the *Healing Through Creativity* vision. And grateful thanks go to Angie Whitaker for the pictures of her stunning pottery sculptures.

I cannot miss out thanking my husband, Peter, who is my best cheerleader and faithful support. His sacrificial love in releasing me into my calling and being a constant rock in my life is immense. He has believed in me, urged me on and given me the confidence to keep going. Not least he has encouraged me into writing this book and been a constant hand through the process.

Then a heartfelt thank-you to our family, all now grown up and married, but who have played their part in encouraging me and supporting me, especially Lindsey, who herself has been part of the developing vision – how blessed I am. And thank you, Paul, for designing the book. Your creative and artistic gifting is second to none!

It has been impossible to write this book without also telling the story of how the vision was born and illustrating it with real-life stories of deep and profound healing. I am so very grateful for the many people who have been part of our *Healing Through Creativity* story, but I especially want to thank 'Sarah', who came to our Centre for help in the depth of severe suicidal brokenness, and through whom we discovered how healing through creativity is God's wonderful gift.

Sarah's story is interwoven throughout these pages, providing many insights into how God brings healing and restoration. She has told her remarkable story in her own book, "S*arah – From an abusive childhood and the depths of suicidal despair to a life of hope and freedom"* (Shaw S, available from Sovereign World, 2014).

Above all, I want to give thanks to the Lord Jesus, who paid the price to save, heal and restore us all, and through whom the heart of our Creator and Father God is known. He left His inexpressible gift of the Holy Spirit to inspire, strengthen and empower us along the way. He has graciously trusted us to work with Him to bring healing – even when we were ignorant and had so much to learn. To God be all the glory for everything He has done. This is His work and the fruit belongs to Him.

Fiona Horrobin
October 2020

"

Our Father who art in Heaven, hallowed be your name

"

INTRODUCTION

I came into the Christian healing ministry with a compassionate heart to help people in need. My own secure home background and Christian upbringing taught me much about God's love: that He is not distant and uncaring, and that His desire is to have a close personal relationship with us. I grew up understanding that the Bible teaches us about a living God, who seeks out our hearts, and who longs to impart security, healing and abundant life – so much so, that He invites us to call Him, Father.

The Great Britain of the fifties and sixties, was known and recognised as a Christian nation. At school every day, we sang hymns and spoke out loud together the prayer Jesus taught us to pray:

> *Our Father who art in Heaven, hallowed be your name, Your kingdom come, Your will be done on earth as it is in Heaven. Give us this day our daily bread and forgive us our trespasses as we forgive those who trespass against us. And lead us not into temptation but deliver us from evil ...*

"
He invites
us to call
Him, Father

I inherited an understanding that God as Creator was also our Father, and as such He was good. And His nature was to provide for the needs of His children. He created us, loves us and knows what we need more than any human being ever could. It was natural for me, therefore, to turn to God as my Heavenly Father whenever I encountered difficulties or experienced people in great need. I knew that, although human help was necessary, it would not be enough without a relationship of trust in God Himself. He was the answer to the needs of the human heart.

When the doors of the Ellel Grange Healing Centre (Ellel is the village where the Grange is situated) first opened, it was this core belief, coupled with a love for people, that motivated and inspired me to help them. From my own sheltered and, to a certain extent, naïve background, I was not prepared for what I was about to face.

It felt like the Red Cross in a war zone as people with all kinds of conditions and problems came through the doors. During our residential *Healing Retreats*, people were pouring out long-held, dark secrets, many of which related to sexual abuse, child cruelty and violence, which had taken place years ago, but which had left behind painful and unhealed scars.

A Changed Society

In those days, newspapers, the media and various publications, had only just begun to expose stories of illicit affairs, sexual abuse, paedophilia and rape. Nowadays magazines, the soaps on TV, along with endless media exposure and coverage of true-life stories, have left people with no illusions about man's potential depravity and inhumanity to man.

Alongside all this, there has been an explosion of new age practices, personal gurus, horoscopes, relaxation techniques and much, much more. Witchcraft practices and the dark arts have become popularised. Things that in the past were considered, at best, 'hokey pokey' and, at their worst, the dangerous 'occult', were now being embraced and followed avidly. Eastern religions began replacing traditional Christian beliefs as people turned to these religions and their gods for wellbeing, healing and relaxation.

A spiritual awakening was taking place within society with the increase of globalisation. People were beginning to find release for what was hitherto held firmly in a very private box labelled 'guilt and shame'. Dark secrets, long hidden, were being released. And once these were out of the box, the roots had to be faced with all the consequential pain that this caused.

During this time, there was a steady movement away from traditional Christianity until, as we see today, our western lifestyle and secularism have largely abandoned such things as being irrelevant to modern society.

Yet, in the middle of all of this, God still had a plan. His Holy Spirit is waking up a sleeping church to some unpalatable truths. Those hitherto unspoken, denied and minimalised stories are true. The voice of the abused and the oppressed can no longer be silenced and disregarded. God is raising His voice in our day in answer to the cries He hears. He has an answer for those in need, through the healing that is there for us all, through belonging to Him and living as part of His family.

> God has an answer for those in need

No one, back in 1986 when the work of Ellel Ministries began, could have imagined the exposure there is now, of man's depraved behaviour in the form of sexual abuse by people in high positions of trust. These include close family members, people within the media, entertainment industry, police, education, social care system and yes, the church. It is as if God has lifted a huge stone, exposing the reality that lies underneath, and all the worms are crawling out to try and find other places to hide.

We are seeing Godly justice arising. Yet, alongside the good aspects of people being hungry for help and being free to be open about their problems, the relentless turning from traditional Christian beliefs has left a spiritual vacuum, causing people to search for spiritual answers in places that can never satisfy the human condition, because they lead people even further away from the Living God.

A Wake-Up Call

Thirty years ago, as a relative 'rookie', I stepped out in faith to pray for people in need. From my place of ignorance, I had no idea what situations would be encountered. Stories of abuse and violence poured out: people who had been sired in an occult ritual, people abused and raped by their own fathers, domestic violence, paedophilia, self-harming, suicide attempts, childhood battering and cruelty, addictions to alcohol, eating disorders and, not to mention, the mental and physical health issues, which were often a consequence of such suffering. The list was endless. It is out of these years of seeking Father God for His answers through His Word and finding Him to be the best psychiatrist and doctor of the soul, that I became passionate about the truths that this book contains.

Around twenty years ago, following many years of watching God at work, I experienced a direct intervention of God whilst attempting to help Sarah, an extremely broken lady. The story of this intervention is threaded through this book, and the moment it occurred is told in Chapter One. But, without doubt, it was this particular incident that has resulted in countless changed lives and has brought about a connection to the heart of God, which in all my years of Christian living (I am now, as I write this, 70 years old), I could not have imagined.

Sarah first came to Ellel Grange straight from a psychiatric unit. Her vicar urged us to help her. Her husband was desperate. She had been in hospital for many months, she was on the highest dosage of psychiatric drugs to control her symptoms of extreme depression and desire to die.

Her diagnosis was one of Obsessive-Compulsive Disorder, Severe Clinical Depression and Suicidal Tendencies. The only medical way forward was for Sarah to receive electro-convulsive therapy. Sarah also had an extreme eating disorder and was self-harming.

Having been sexually, mentally, emotionally and physically abused by her own parents from a young age until the age of eighteen, Sarah's life was hanging by a very vulnerable thread. Now married to a marvellous husband and with two lovely children, she desperately needed to hold everything together, but the inside agenda was in serious overload, and for a while had been dangerously close to taking over completely. When that happened, she suffered a complete breakdown resulting in her immediate need for residential psychiatric care.

God's Response

As a healing ministry, we see so many people who have gone through similar experiences. Sarah came from an extreme background of childhood cruelty, and other people's stories all too commonly include parallel events in their abusive pasts. Our role, as those who are helping people to receive healing, is to allow God's Holy Spirit to use us as human channels of His love and grace and to facilitate a divine heart exchange. The prophetic words from Isaiah 61, telling of the healing that Jesus Christ would bring when He came into our broken world, say it all:

> The Spirit of the Sovereign LORD is on me, because the LORD has anointed me to proclaim good news to the poor, He has sent me to bind up the brokenhearted, to proclaim freedom for captives and release for the prisoners; to proclaim the year of the LORD's favor and the day of vengeance of our GOD,

To comfort all who mourn, to provide for those who grieve in Zion – to bestow on them a crown of beauty instead of ashes, the oil of joy instead of mourning, and a garment of praise instead of a spirit of despair.

Instead of your shame you will receive a double portion, and instead of disgrace you will rejoice in your inheritance. And so you will inherit a double portion in your land, and everlasting joy will be yours.

For I, the LORD, love justice; I hate robbery and wrongdoing. In my faithfulness I will reward my people and make an everlasting covenant with them (Isaiah 61: 1-3, 7-8).

Who is sufficient except Creator God in the face of all the injustices people suffer? What could anyone say to Sarah, whose life had been robbed of an innocent, fun-loving childhood, growing up with extreme fear, panic and terror? I knew that God was real and that only He could be the answer. The medical profession had given her their very best. But Sarah could not control her desire to die. Yet, as a Christian, she hung on to God and came to Ellel Grange in a last-ditch attempt to find some chink of hope.

A Steep Learning Curve

As a backdrop to Sarah's visit, and also the many others who have come to Ellel Grange from a wide spectrum of painful experiences, God had much to teach me and our team. None of us were trained professionals, we were ordinary folk with a heart to serve God and help others in need.

One wintry, February day with the wind and rain lashing, I reluctantly took our dog out for what dogs need to do! I was at Ellel Grange which, with its beautiful grounds, is an ideal spot for a dog to be unleashed into the highest form of reward, that of hunting for rabbits and squirrels, never to be quite caught, of course! On this particular day I did not want my dog to go chasing off so I kept him firmly on the lead, so that I could get back into the warmth as soon as possible.

As I was passing an old oak tree in the adjoining farmer's field, I glimpsed a grey bundle at the foot of the tree. Realising this was a lamb, I looked for its mother. No other sheep were to be seen. This lamb had been abandoned, and before I could think further, I had tied up the dog and leapt over the first wire fence and the second barbed wire fence, picked up the cold, bedraggled lamb and placed him inside my coat. I thought he was dying and maybe even dead already. But then I heard the faintest of bleats from inside my coat. I ran to the local farmhouse and banged urgently on the door.

"I have a lamb who is dying," I cried to the farmer. His big hands reached out, "Give him to me, I will give him a bottle, put him by the fire and have him back in the fields with his brothers and sisters in no time." The image of those big, safe, rugged hands has stayed with me ever since. Relief and joy welled up inside me, "I've rescued a lamb!"

As I walked back to the Grange, I was overcome as I felt God speaking into my heart. "There are many of my lambs out there in the fields, bleeding and dying, with no one to rescue them. Will you go and find them and bring them to me?" I experienced the pain on His heart of what was lost to Him, and in that moment of great rejoicing in rescuing a lamb, my response was, "Yes, Lord, if you help me, I will bring them to You." This was a defining moment for me. On that day I received the motivation to keep on going through thick and thin over the years. As I looked down at my coat, I noticed it was torn and muddy. Then God spoke to my heart again, "It cost my Son everything to find my lambs, are you willing?" The road ahead would be costly, but also with great reward.

I have shared this story countless times and it still touches me deeply. Firstly, I know the love of God for His creation and the price the Good Shepherd goes to, in order to bring

> "
> An abandoned lamb rescued

His lambs into the safe sheepfold, where His tender loving care and principles can bring healing and joy. Secondly, I am profoundly grateful that my encounter with Father God on that day left me in no doubt that He wants to involve us as His family, in bringing those home to Him who have been lost. It is not without cost and pain, a pain that is different from the pain of injustice. It is the pain of sacrificial love which is at the core of who God is, His nature and character.

This book has been written to share the divine love of God the Father as Creator, His principles of love for His created children, and the plumb line of truth in His Word, which is intensely practical and applicable for living in a secure and healthy way day by day.

Made in His Image

> If God is creative, then so are we!

The instinctive expression of creativity is how the Creator has wired us. We are made in His image (Genesis 1.27), and God tells us in His Word that we were made good (Genesis 1:31)! If God is creative, then so are we! In fact, everything we do from being conceived onwards is creative – we are growing and becoming, exploring and adventuring, experimenting, making mistakes, living lives of discovery, finding talents, giftings, strengths and weaknesses. Each of us is unique in our expression of both who we are and who we are becoming.

As a Father with His children, God enjoys seeing our imagination at work and the outward expression of it. Throughout this book, many real-life stories illustrate just how healing being creative is. It is part of our God-given identity and it is something to be explored and embraced. *Healing Through Creativity* is not just for Sarah and others like her, but it is for everyone. The chapters that follow contain a measure of healing and life for us all.

A Resource

This book is both spiritual and practical in its application. I cannot think of anyone for whom it would not be relevant. My prayer is that it opens your eyes to see more of the nature and character of God, His principles of bringing healing to the human heart.

You may be involved in helping people who are struggling for all kinds of reasons – the disabled, the sick, the elderly, children, orphans, those caught in addictions, the homeless, the abused or the deprived. *Healing Through Creativity* is an ideal resource for groups and clubs engaging in creative expression as a way to finding the love of God. Whatever our age or culture, the principles are easily adapted.

The following pages are brimming over with illustrations, practical insights and real-life stories of ways in which creativity can bring healing and restoration.

Sarah's life has been restored. Living now for close on twenty years without any drugs, she enjoys family life with her husband and children, holidaying and adventuring, and finds great joy and fulfilment in sharing the good news that Jesus heals, with others in need. Creativity was a major part of her healing journey and thousands more have since been touched in a similar way.

As our courses grew in popularity, so the stories of profound healing also grew. We found that God was touching people at a depth we could not have previously imagined. Most significantly, there was a common thread between all the stories, "I now know God loves me - I have experienced His love deep down on the inside." It is His love that transforms everything!

Therefore, if anyone is in Christ, the new creation has come: The old has gone, the new is here!

2 Corinthians 5:17

Part 1

Principles of

HEALING THROUGH CREATIVITY

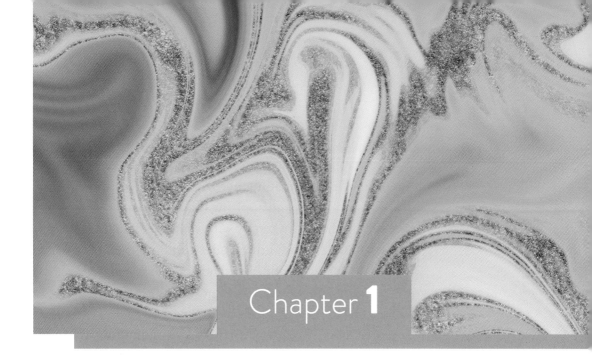

Chapter 1

DIRTY SHELLS – A VISION IS BORN!

Dirty shells, a few paint pots, some glitter and sequins. What can this have to do with healing and setting someone free from bondage? It was one of those days. It began as a very normal and routine day behind the scenes of our healing work at Ellel Grange, but what God did on that day changed everything! We would never be the same again.

What God did that day changed everything!

Sarah, the lady we were helping, had severe problems and she had bravely faced the challenges of implementing the principles of healing we had regularly laid before her. The ministry team had spent long hours over days and months helping her in her battle to take in Biblical truth, and this day was no different.

Sarah was, we thought, the perfect counselee! She would spend much time reading her Bible and follow it diligently learning scriptures and applying them. It seemed Sarah never argued and fitted in exactly with what we thought was right for her to do. But we didn't understand just how passive she really was, having deeply buried her emotions and personhood to the point that she did not know she had them!

We were about to embark on yet another session of looking at problems and difficulties, outlining the solutions and praying again into a host of issues, feeling that she was responding well to our injunction to the deeper spiritual life, when suddenly from out of nowhere an eruption took place and she screamed out, "I AM NOT A MINISTRY MACHINE!"

I am not a ministry machine!

This sudden declaration with its accompanying thump on the floor rendered us silent. I sat back stunned that this quiet, submissive person was reacting in such a strong way! Far from feeling this was unacceptable behaviour, however, I was filled instead with conviction. What on earth had we done? What was it that God was trying to show us, and what was it that this lady needed most of all?

Thankfully, the answer was swift! She needed relationship. She was a human being with human needs and not a machine to be filled with spiritual truth. God was bringing Sarah's deepest need to the surface. She needed God with skin on. She needed to know she was a person with feelings and needs. She had been robbed of her childhood, having been dictated to and forced against her will into a life of abuse and cruelty.

All she had known was existence, day by day fighting for survival, living on the edge of her wits. The very idea of spontaneous responses, such as reacting in fear, anger or pleasure was as foreign to her as it would be for a normal person to become a zombie devoid of colour, choice, negative and positive feelings.

It was a sobering time as we let go of all our preconceived ideas on how we thought God should bring healing, and allowed Him to guide and lead us into what would become a journey of grace, which would eventually flow out and bring healing to thousands of people.

The bag of battered and dirty shells was the starting place for our attempt to do something together that wasn't focussed on the overtly spiritual: to just 'be' and have some fun. Sarah looked on as we soon forgot the hardships and struggles, gleefully plastering the shells with red, pink, orange, purple and just about every colour of the rainbow, not to mention adorning them with sequins and glitter. Could something so ugly, barnacled and dirty be beautified? Our shells, painted individually by at least five of us on the team, shouted for themselves. They looked just fantastic!

> Could something so ugly, barnacled and dirty be beautified?

We sat back with satisfaction and admired them. To begin with, Sarah just stared, but then came a smile and then chuckling laughter bubbled up from deep inside her soul. For someone who had lived their life with numerous tight controls, this was the beginning of a miracle. Hitherto, she had only laughed when others had laughed. She had never known or expressed her own personhood spontaneously and freely. Her life was based on pleasing those around her and responding accordingly.

For this brief period, Sarah was released from the strain and stresses which were part of her everyday life. God had shown in a real and practical way, His love for her. He had shown her His desire for companionship and relationship and how He wanted to bring life to her with all its colour and fullness. As she dared to join in, she felt His love deep on the inside releasing her laughter and spontaneity. This was something that had been far beyond her reach. Her real identity and self had been lost on the altar of abuse, and surviving was her way of living.

God had so much to show us, and Sarah too, as our eyes were opened to see something more profound than we could envisage at that present time.

I confess that I had always seen Bible reading, praying, repenting, churchgoing etc as my spiritual life. My strong evangelical background had taught me to view life in separations. One area was my spiritual life, and the other area was my secular and human life. It has taken a journey with God to show me differently, and to learn how wrong I could be and how big God really is!

Our overtly spiritual times of reading God's living Word, the Bible, and talking to Him in direct prayer are precious and essential and, of course, it is vital to live out these truths. However, I was discovering that God wants us to find Him, and His love relationship with us, in every facet of life. When we walk out of church or are not reading our Bibles, praying etc, God does not walk away, nor do we become non-spiritual beings.

> "
> Her real identity and self had been lost on the altar of abuse

The dirty shells were more than a perfect example of how God can use anything to bring about His purposes. The fun of beautifying the shells brought home to Sarah more about God and His love on that day than anything else we could have done or shared. She entered into relationship! The very thing she was terrified of, without ever being able to articulate it, was relationship. Any relationship was threatening – relationship with herself, relationship with others and relationship with God. Up until that moment every response had been tightly controlled and guarded. Now here we were, laughing spontaneously, and with this came bonding and the beginnings of trust.

A new day had dawned for us all, a glorious day, opening up a vista of keys and insights. The Creator Himself had met with us and we sensed a vision had been born. A journey had begun, not just for Sarah, for this journey would profoundly change us too. This was a life-giving key for everyone!

If God could break through and show His love in such a revelatory way, through a bunch of dirty and barnacled, useless, old shells for Sarah, who was so desperately broken, surely He wanted to do the same for many more. The very fact that useless, dead and dirty shells could be beautified and come to life, shrieked of God's powerful redemption.

It wasn't long before we were encouraged to launch out and hold a four-day course on *Healing Through Creativity*. Ellel Grange, established and respected for its Biblical teaching and training, was about to undergo a profound shake up!

> " Up until that moment every response had been tightly controlled and guarded. Now here we were, laughing spontaneously ...

Celebration

Sarah began to be radically restored through the principles God was showing us with the dirty shells. When that spontaneous laughter bubbled up, it was something that went beyond her complex network of fears and control. Emerging from deep within were her own personhood and natural responses.

So began a joyous journey in self-expression. This was wonderful to behold since Sarah had been an empty shell herself when she first came for help from the psychiatric hospital. At that time nothing could convince her that life was worth living. She would try to stay alive if that was what God wanted, but inside death was hovering and working its destruction.

We began to celebrate the gift of life and relationship. Laughter, chatter and viewpoints were shared. A powerful connection to a buried place deep within had taken place. Sarah expressed it simply yet profoundly, "You've found me."

> Sarah had been an empty shell

Our Father's House!

I was beginning to sense that God was, indeed, taking me and the team beyond our ways of thinking and into something that was exciting, but also very scary. How would Ellel Grange look if it became what it needed to become, so that God could do the work He wanted to do in people's lives? We asked ourselves the question: could Ellel Grange be God's home where His children could come and be family; each room an expression of lifegiving creativity, where the joy of being His child could be experienced?

A nurturing home has a mother and father, aunts, cousins, grandparents, the very young, the very old, the teenagers and everything between. A home has a heart where Mum and Dad bring fun, laughter, chatter, problem-solving, healthy discipline and lifegiving relationship to the family. The family house bears the character and resemblance of the family. The garden, the kitchen, the bedrooms, the lounge and the outhouses are all expressions of how the family live.

God was showing us that He is no different. He wants His home to be where His children can truly receive His love and put their roots down into the soil of security which comes from His Fatherhood.

Ellel Grange was well suited for the job. It has a large lounge with comfortable armchairs, a large, welcoming fireplace and beautiful garden views from the windows. The dining room would be perfect, not institutional but crafted in a warm and intimate way. What was once the 'withdrawing room' (a very large lounge), again with its marble fireplace, had become the meeting room with almost a whole wall full of large windows overlooking an expanse of beautiful lawns, magnificent trees and carefully tended grounds. The backdrop to this room is the Trough of Bowland Hills – a living masterpiece and a delight to the eyes, especially when the sun sparkles, reflecting the shapes, colours and shadows in the grounds.

The previous owners had installed an indoor, heated swimming pool. This, along with the snooker table, was already providing pleasure for our guests, but little did we know what a key part they would play as vehicles for God's healing. There were simple pleasures such as the hallway with its large fireplace and thick leather armchairs placed invitingly around it, situated at the foot of a wide Victorian staircase; this was a beloved focal point for endless greetings and farewells. Deep friendships were forged in the hallway through times of sharing hearts and minds over a steaming hot chocolate at bedtime or coffee and tea during the day.

Ideas Began to Flow

Outside our backdoor and across the pretty courtyard are two large stone workshops. A married couple on our team were exactly the right people to provide woodwork and pottery workshops, which to this day have seen hundreds of people receive their healing.

Creative writing, walking, drawing, painting, drama, water, dance, banners, textiles, music and movement in all its forms, including a fine pair of adult swings placed in a beautiful setting within our gardens all played their part. Each had their place for God to bring his healing.

Yet, however wonderful the house was, it was the people within who gave it life, and the energy of love. Our team is carefully chosen for their hearts desiring to serve and sacrifice on behalf of others. It is this primary principle of love flowing outwards, that has brought the greatest breakthrough in healing over so many years. God's heart of welcome, love and training, expressed through the people, building and grounds, all of which bear a reflection of who He is.

We have now been running regular *Healing Through Creativity* courses for over twenty years, the vision has gone worldwide from the UK to Africa, Asia, Canada, Australia,

Eastern Europe, Israel, USA and beyond, and we have even extended these long weekends to a week-long course, which we call *Bridge from the Head to the Heart*. So many people are bound by the fact that their faith and belief in God is largely head knowledge. They have never experienced His all-sufficient and embracing love deep in their innermost being. Many are working, even striving, to somehow try and catch a sense of God's presence and His love.

God has honoured those early beginnings and used *Healing Through Creativity* to reach and heal countless lives, as He has met with people in their own unique and special way. What began with Sarah and a bag of dirty and barnacled shells has, under God's hand, led to the healing of a multitude.

The stories and fruit reports are all individually unique, yet they are identical in that God uses our intrinsic creative expression to reach the depth of who we are and enables us to know Him as Creator. It is the connection to this reality within that His healing comes and brings life and real freedom.

For most of us, our own securities and protections operate at a fairly simple and basic level. We have learnt to be independent and strong. For others, there are some blockages and damage, which produce ongoing frustration in the area of relationships, fulfilment or fruitfulness. There are some like Sarah, for whom life has dealt severe blows, and without a solid foundation physically, emotionally and spiritually, life is a great struggle with multiple layers of protective controls.

The good news is that God has more for us all than we can ever dream or hope for. He wants to redeem and transform our lives into a fruitful garden, full of life and health. Whatever our situation, it is not beyond God's reach and power to change.

As ideas turned to reality, with Ellel Grange providing the perfect place, the day that had begun as a very ordinary day turned out to be more extraordinary than we could ever have imagined.

"

It is in this connection to the reality within that His healing comes

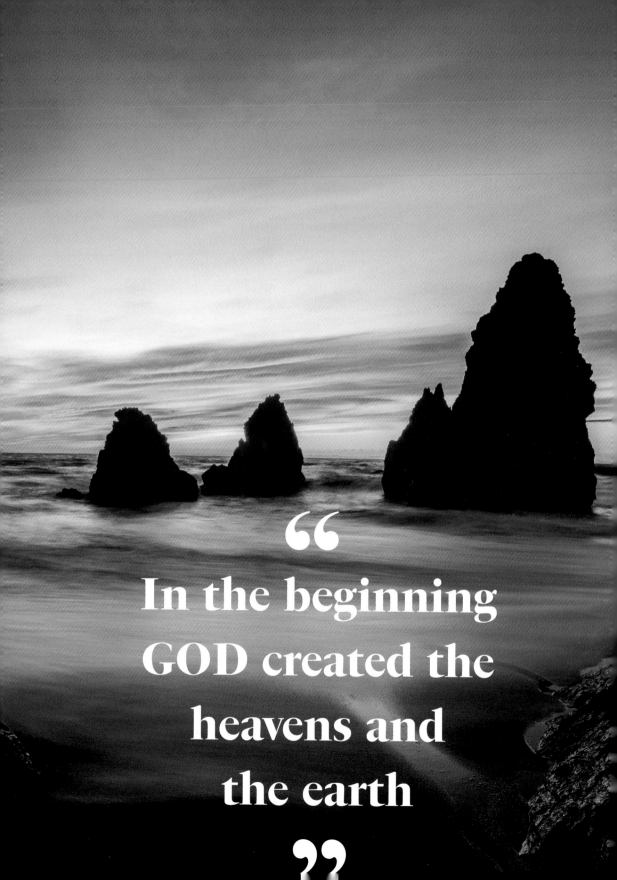

Chapter 2

MADE IN HIS IMAGE

Creator God's Master Plan

'To create' is to bring into being or form out of nothing by force of imagination. Genesis 1:1-2 says, 'In the beginning GOD created the heavens and the earth. Now the earth was formless and empty, darkness was over the surface of the deep.'

God had brought the universe into existence out of absolute non-existence and was now about to make the earth as we know it.

Reading the story of Creation, we stand amazed at God's wondrous creativity, the apparently limitless scope of His imagination as He designed and formed the Earth and everything on it – night and day, land and sea, the detail of every living thing – all kinds of plants and trees, flowers and birds, fish and animals – with multitudes of colours, and shades, shapes, sizes and textures.

> Then God said, "Let us make mankind in our image, in our likeness, so that they may rule over the fish in the sea and the birds in the sky, over the livestock and all the wild animals, and over all the creatures that move along the ground." So, God created mankind in His own image, in the image of God He created them; male and female he created them. God blessed them and said to them, "Be fruitful and increase in number, fill the earth and subdue it. Rule over the fish in the sea and the birds in the sky and over every living creature that moves on the ground."
>
> Then God said, "I give you every seed-bearing plant on the face of the whole earth and every tree that has fruit with seed in it. They will be yours for food. And to all the beasts of the earth and all the birds in the sky and all the creatures that move along the ground—everything that has the breath of life in it—I give every green plant for food." And it was so.
>
> God saw all that he had made, and it was very good. And there was evening, and there was morning – the sixth day.
>
> (GENESIS 1:26-31)

"So God created mankind in His own image"

We can see clearly from this Scriptural account that, when God looked at what He had made, He saw it was very good. One of the first and most vital principles we will need to absorb is that when God made us, without exception we were made good. He did not look at any of us and declare that we were 'bad', 'wrong', 'rubbish' or 'a mistake'.

Everything God created, He made well.

"
we stand amazed
at God's wondrous
creativity
"

For you created my inmost being; you knit me together in my mother's womb. I praise you because I am fearfully and wonderfully made; your works are wonderful, I know that full well. My frame was not hidden from you when I was made in the secret place, when I was woven together in the depths of the earth. Your eyes saw my unformed body.

(PSALM 139:13-16)

Made to Shine!

> We are designed to be creative

Creator God knows us, He made us, and He knows the beauty He placed inside every human being. We are designed to be creative, a natural reflection of who He is as our Creator.

We should never underestimate the beauty which God has placed in every one of us and the value He gives us.

Made to shine!

We are designed for relationship – as three-dimensional beings, we are three in one!

The Godhead is also Three-in-One, made up of Father, Son and Holy Spirit. Each relates to the other to bring about God's Master Plan. In harmony together, none vie for position or are in competition with the other. Their relationship is one of mutual joy and benefit.

There is a triune dimension to each of us in that we are made with a body, soul and spirit (1 Thessalonians 5:23). It is obvious that we all have a body as we can see the physical aspects of who we are. We can look at our bodies and agree that they are indescribable in their complexity and the way in which they work to keep us healthy and alive.

However, we are not just a body! We have a soul within us which contains our minds and the way we think. The soul also contains our will and the decisions we take. Then, within the soul, we have emotions with which we feel and express ourselves.

Yet, we are not just body and soul. For when God created us in His image, He also gave us spirit. 'God is spirit and his worshipers must worship him in Spirit and in truth' (John 4:24). Each of us has a human spirit, which contains our core identity with its need to worship, create and express who we are through intuition, spirituality, sexuality, conscience, gifting and personality. Our human spirit is designed by God to be the source and giver of life (energy) to the soul and body.

At the moment of our conception (whatever the circumstances) our body and soul were not developed but our human spirit was very much alive, making intuitive sense of life surrounding us. We were designed to be received by our

> We were designed to be received by our parents as a gift

parents as a gift, but for all kinds of reasons, this may not always have been the case. In Sarah's story, it was heart breaking to hear her tell of how her mother told her, "I curse the day you were born." This was an opposite truth to God's truth, but one which entered Sarah's human spirit, and she lived out her life believing she was born 'bad'.

God's plan for our human spirit, soul and body is to be at peace with ourselves and with Him. Then we are at peace with others also. We know, however, that through varying life circumstances, instead of peace, conflict and internal pressure have come.

We will look further at these aspects of being made in His image and our need of restoration and healing as we journey on. Sufficient to say, for the time being, that God has a restoration plan for the crushing of the human spirit.

The LORD is close to the brokenhearted and saves those who are crushed in spirit. (PSALM 34:18)

Why am I Here?

The cry of the human heart is, "Why am I here?" It truly is beyond comprehension that God made us for relationship. God Almighty, who made the heavens and the earth, made you and me for relationship. He didn't need us, but He wanted a relationship born out of free will with those He created. Everything within humanity is wired for relationship. Firstly, there is relationship within ourselves – our spirit, soul and body. Then there is relationship with others – we are not designed to be alone and God set us in families. Lastly, and most vital, is our relationship with God, our Maker, the One from whom we receive life and meaning.

Our human spirit was designed by God to reach out in trust and to be anchored and secure, so that our whole being, spirit, soul and body, could grow and develop strongly. Parental love and acceptance are God's design, setting the intended foundation for a trust in who He is as a good and loving Heavenly Father.

We are living in an age where human rationalism and knowledge have overtaken childlike trust and faith. People, particularly in our western nations, want to worship something more tangible than a God they cannot see. It makes sense to the intelligent mind that creation is simply a matter of evolution.

Yet, the Bible makes it clear that in entering a relationship with God, we need to become as little children, 'Unless you change and become like little children, you will never enter the kingdom of heaven' (Matthew 18:1-5). There is need for humility, faith and simple, childlike trust for us to find Him. His creative genius can never be rationalised and worked out through human intelligence alone.

Creator God's genius as both scientist and artist, is beyond human comprehension. They go hand in hand. One leads to the other in an ever-increasing journey of exploration, invention and expression. We can only stand in awe, looking at the world around us, now easily accessed through our television screens, at the breath-taking extent of creation. The vastness, the detail, the intricacy, the power, the gentleness, the extraordinary beauty and relationship there is in every aspect of nature.

> "
> Our human spirit was designed by God to reach out in trust

An ever-increasing journey of exploration, invention and expression

Creation reflects physically here on earth the nature and character of its unseen Creator. Who can fathom the depths of God? Who can doubt by looking at the natural world and the universe beyond our reach, that He is a God of order and precision?

God is love; He did not choose to love us. That would be very scary because if He chose to love us today, He might choose not to love us tomorrow. It would be dependent on our behaviour or other aspects of our humanity that may not be acceptable to Him. Rather, His whole nature and character is love, He is utterly trustworthy and faithful. The basis for His relationship with us is that He bound Himself to us in covenantal love.

> I led them with cords of human kindness, with ties of love.
> To them I was like one who lifts a little child to the cheek,
> and I bent down to feed them.   (HOSEA 11:4)

> **God looks for our response**

God looks for our response. His invitation to come into a relationship with Him is not one of force but rather of free will. Placed within each of us is the God-given gift of free will. We will keep coming back to looking at aspects of our free will later. It is one of the most important principles of healing.

When God made us in His image, three in one (spirit, soul and body) and with the gift of free will, He intended the highest form of relationship. We would not be controlled, manipulated or dominated. Rather, the relationship with God was to be on the only basis for any authentic relationship, that of trust. We are given an invitation:

> Ask, and it will be given to you; seek and you will find;
> knock, and the door will be opened to you. For everyone

who asks receives; the one who seeks finds; and to the one who knocks, the door will be opened.   (Matthew 7:7-8)

Natural Worshippers

God has placed within all of us the need to worship and there is no one on the face of the earth who does not worship something. Worship means to bow down and trust something or someone, even if that is ourselves. We make a 'god' out of something. We desire to give our lives to whatever or whoever that may be. A 'God-shaped void or hole' demands that we do so, it needs filling and the cry needs answering, "Who am I and for what purpose do I exist?" Creator God with His truth is the only One who can fully satisfy and fill this need to worship.

Answering the heart cry, "Who am I and for what purpose do I exist?"

As we look on creation, we begin to behold Creator God's genius with worship! This is the response of worship from the psalmist David, speaking of God very intimately, when he said,

> Bless the Lord, O my soul and all that is within me, bless his holy name. Bless the Lord, O my soul, and do not forget all his benefits - who forgives all your iniquity, who heals all your diseases, who redeems your life from the Pit, who crowns you with steadfast love and mercy, who satisfies you with good as long as you live so that your youth is renewed like the eagle's.

> The Lord works vindication and justice for all who are oppressed ... The Lord is merciful and gracious, slow to anger and abounding in steadfast love. He will not always accuse, nor will He keep His anger forever. He does not

deal with us according to our sins, nor repay us according to our iniquities.

For as the heavens are high above the earth, so great is his steadfast love towards those who fear Him; as far as the east is from the west, so far he removes our transgressions from us. As a father has compassion for his children, so the Lord has compassion for those who fear Him".

(Compilation from Psalm 103 NRSV)

Then David speaks to God as Creator,

O Lord my God, you are very great. You are clothed with honour and majesty, wrapped in light as with a garment. You stretch out the heavens like a tent, you set the beams of your chambers on the waters, you make the clouds your chariot; you ride on the wings of the wind, fire and flame your ministers.

You set the earth on its foundations so that it shall never be shaken ... You cause grass to grow for the cattle and plants for people to use, to bring forth food from the earth, and wine to gladden the human heart, oil to make the face shine, and bread to strengthen the human heart ... You have made the moon to mark the seasons; the sun knows its time for setting. You make darkness, and it is night.

(Compilation from Psalm 104 NRSV)

What a valuable relationship Creator God has given and placed us in. Having a Father who knows us more than we can know ourselves, where better can we go than to the Master Craftsman when we are afraid, confused, broken and do not know which way to turn?

For the Lord is the great God, the great King above all gods. In his hand are the depths of the earth, and the

and the cry needs answering, "Who am I and for what purpose do I exist?"

mountain peaks belong to him. The sea is his, for he made it, and his hands formed the dry land. Come, let us bow down in worship, let us kneel before the LORD our Maker; for he is our GOD and we are the people of his pasture, the flock under his care. Today, if only you would hear his voice, "Do not harden your hearts".   (PSALM 95:3-8)

A Father who knows us more than we can know ourselves

Even the heavens and its host worship the Lord:

You alone are the LORD. You made the heavens, even the highest heavens, and all their starry host, the earth and all that is on it, the seas and all that is in them. You give life to everything, and the multitudes of heaven worship you.

(NEHEMIAH 9:6)

Creation itself knows and praises the Creator and how much more should we!

Let the heavens rejoice, let the earth be glad; let the sea resound, and all that is in it. Let the fields be jubilant, and everything in them; let all the trees of the forest sing for joy. Let all creation rejoice before the LORD.

(PSALM 96:11-13)

He knows each star by name, every snowflake is different, the hairs on our head are counted by Him:

He determines the number of the stars and calls them each by name. Great is our LORD and mighty in power; his understanding has no limit.   (PSALM 147:4-5)

He has a created order and truth which is utterly trustworthy:

For this is what the LORD says— he who created the heavens, he is GOD; he who fashioned and made the earth, he founded it; he did not create it to be empty, but formed it to be inhabited – he says, "I am the LORD, and there is no other. I have not spoken in secret, from somewhere in a land of darkness ... I, the LORD, speak the truth; I declare what is right."   (ISAIAH 45:18-19)

God, the Creator's promise to us:

Ah, Sovereign LORD, you have made the heavens and the earth by your great power and outstretched arm. Nothing is too hard for you.   (JEREMIAH 32:17)

God is Creator but He is also intimate and so close to us. He is our Father! We can have faith and trust in Him. We will look in the next chapter at how disaster came and how God our Father has the ultimate rescue plan.

Chapter 3

DISASTER DAY – AND RESCUE

The world that God created has become defiled. There is no question that we do not live in an ideal world and that there is no sinless perfection. We cannot look at the intention of God the Creator in making such beauty, without also looking at what happened to bring death, decay and suffering.

Adam and Eve had the perfect Father and lived in a perfect place, the garden of Eden! Yet, when God gave them permission to eat the fruit of all the trees in the garden bar one, they took matters into their own hands! "Why can't we eat the fruit of that forbidden tree?" They listened to the temptation of the serpent (Satan) who whispered to them, "Why not the fruit of that tree?" The fruit looked good, and Adam and Eve mistrusted God and disobeyed His instruction.

The story of Adam and Eve in the garden of Eden (Genesis 3) is clear. Adam and Eve listened to the serpent, co-operated with his temptation and the sin of pride brought a separation from their intimate, trusting relationship with Holy God.

Sin entered the heart of humankind with the consequence that through gaining man's co-operation and agreement, the serpent (Satan) won the right to steal the authority designed by God for us, and to use it for himself here on earth. We came under the oppression of the evil one.

No one can dispute the confusion and the mess that came as a result. Adam and Eve had the perfect Father, they did not have difficult or abusive parents, yet they mistrusted Him and chose to rebel. What a sobering message to us all, that we can never wholly blame our parents, sinful as they are, for all our problems. Nor can we place the blame on Adam and Eve, taking the prideful stance that we would never have done that!

<blockquote>" not one of us here on earth is perfect</blockquote>

It is true to say that not one of us here on earth is perfect. We are all sinners, we have pride, selfishness and rebellion in our hearts. It is a level playing field, which at the end of the day is quite releasing. We do not have to pretend! At the heart of all human rebellion is the sin of pride, doing things 'our way' rather than seeking God's way.

The Fall – The Story Continues!

When sin (pride and rebellion) entered through free will choices, it separated humankind from God and a battle began. Adam and Eve immediately felt guilt and shame which had now entered humanity. The Bible describes how they tried to hide by covering themselves with fig leaves (Genesis 3:7).

Nothing has changed today. We, in our fallen and sinful condition, struggle with guilt and shame and try to cover it and hide. Our modern-day fig leaves are human 'fix its' in an attempt to make things right.

Satan is jealous for what belongs to God the Creator and wants God's place. The Bible warns that he comes as the father of lies, a deceiver, a murderer and the truth is not in him (John 8:44).

'For sin, seizing the opportunity afforded by the commandment, deceived me, and through the commandment put me to death' (Romans 7:11). To put it in a nutshell, Adam and Eve did things 'their way', and to this day the ultimate sin for us all is that in our pride, we choose to do things 'our way', separated from relationship with Creator God. We are valued and precious to God, but we often forget we are the created and He is the Creator.

> we often forget we are the created and He is the Creator

> "For my thoughts are not your thoughts, neither are your ways my ways," declares the LORD. "As the heavens are higher than the earth, so are my ways higher than your ways and my thoughts than your thoughts".
>
> (ISAIAH 55:8-9)

Through the Fall of Man, death, decay and suffering entered the world. Satan, the enemy of God and the oppressor, seeks to use our co-operation, along with stolen authority and power, to bring destruction to God's plan. The Bible describes Him as 'the god of this world' (2 Corinthians 4:4), Jesus Himself warned that the world is under the rulership of the god of this world (John 12:31). None of us should be ignorant of the fact that there is a tempter and a battle for our hearts and minds.

However, this is not a dualistic battle where God and Satan have equal power. God is still all powerful, King of Kings and Lord of Lords. He knows what is happening with His creation. Despite the mess, He has not turned His back on us. The serpent won a battle, but God does not lose the war. God has a divine plan, and this is being worked out in our world today.

The Coming of Jesus

The miracle of the incarnation is that Jesus (God Himself) came down into the mess! He came with one simple objective: to save us!

> Jesus (God Himself) came down into the mess

If we were God, would we have chosen to be born to a virgin, in a bare stable hidden from sight with no fanfare? I think we would have chosen a reputation and a palace. The infinite wisdom of God chose the lowest of places to show us how He identifies with the lowest and most needy. He is not a God who is distant, unaware of our sufferings and struggles. He allowed Himself to live on earth in a place of struggle, conflict, danger and suffering.

Jesus came to rescue us and to find us. We are all lost without our intended relationship with Father God. Jesus boldly stated, "'If you have seen me, you have seen the Father'" (John 14:9). He also said, "'I and the Father are one'" (John 10:30).

I thank God that we did not have to climb out of our mess to reach Him. We do not have to be 'good enough' or 'clean enough', but the message of the coming of Jesus is that He came to save us and lift us up out of the mess.

What an incredibly bold and audacious statement Jesus made when He said, "'I am the way and the truth and the life. No one comes to the Father except through me!'" (John 14:6). Why was this? It had to be clear that through Jesus in His humanity, God Himself had come to the earth and to the people He created, to open the way for us to be restored in intimate relationship with our Father.

What a price Jesus paid and what a gift He offers us!

Good News Day

Jesus (God's Son) overcame Satan's power on our behalf and offers us a restored relationship with Father God. How extraordinary that Jesus chose to die. He willingly gave His life over to death, so we might receive life. God the Creator sent a part of Himself, in His Son Jesus, to show us what He is like. In laying down His life at Calvary and allowing the soldiers to crucify Him with all the dishonour, rejection and suffering that went along with it, God was showing us the depths and lengths His love would go to rescue us and restore us back to Himself.

A covenant was made with man that day, which can never be revoked or broken. Jesus chose to shed His blood and pay the penalty for our guilt and shame. At that moment of His death on Calvary's cross, there was an almighty war in the heavenly places. Satan knew that his ultimate day of defeat had taken place. Jesus declared, "It is finished", as He placed Himself into His Father's hands and gave up His spirit (John 19:30).

What a genius of Creator God to leave the world in the same way as He came, identifying with our humanity. As the sinless Son of God, He paid the ultimate price for our sin! There was no fanfare. In fact, Jesus walked simply throughout His time on earth, keeping away from man's glory and adulation. He knew that was Satan's temptation. Satan tempted Jesus with all this world's riches, if only He would bow down and worship him. Jesus recognised and knew Satan. If Jesus

> " A covenant made with man which can never be revoked or broken

had bowed to just one of Satan's schemes, all would have been lost because Satan would then have had authority over Jesus, in the same way as Satan gained an authority over us at the beginning of time.

The Invitation

Jesus never bowed the knee to Satan. His motivation of love kept Him walking towards the cross. The invitation is simply to own our sinfulness in true repentance, thanking Jesus for paying the price through shedding His blood on Calvary on our behalf and to receive as a gift His forgiveness and embrace.

> Yet to all who did receive him, to those who believed in his name, he gave the right to become children of God.
>
> (JOHN 1:12)

Life from the Dead

The Creator's plan did not leave Jesus in death, buried in a tomb with all the finality of what death here on earth seems.

Only Creator God who made the earth and all that is in it, could bring about the miracle of resurrection! He alone is outside of earth's limits.

Father God looking at the suffering of His Son, the price He paid in coming to earth, poured out His power and on the third day Jesus rose to life! Not only had Jesus made a way for us to come back into a restored relationship with Father God, but He gave us eternal life. Death had been defeated, eternity had opened, and all who received Him and believed in Him could receive resurrection life.

> For God so loved the world that he gave his one and only Son, that whoever believes in him shall not perish but have eternal life. (JOHN 3:16)

> Jesus said … "I am the resurrection and the life. The one who believes in me will live, even though they die". (JOHN 11:25)

Death No Longer Our Inheritance

Hell was designed by God for evil, the devil and all His angels (Matthew 25:41). Creator God sent Jesus to rescue us from the power of death and hell. Satan's plan is to bring death and hell, and to reign over and control all that God created, including us.

Disaster Day turned to Victory

As we look at creativity and how it cannot be separated from the Creator, we can see that in all creation and creativity there is power! To an extent, power is in each of us, the power to do good or evil. Satan has limited power here on earth, having stolen both authority and power to influence and tempt us into death and destruction. God the Creator holds the key to all power. 'Jesus came to them and said, "All authority in heaven and on earth has been given to me"' (Matthew 28:18).

Power from on High

After Jesus rose from the dead, in His resurrection body He returned to the disciples and spoke to the them about going back to His Father and leaving His Holy Spirit with them. In doing this, He would never leave them or forsake them. His Holy Spirit would fill them and empower them. This was His gift to us if we choose to receive it.

A Crushed Spirit

When Sarah came to the Centre, it had never entered her mind that her life was being contended for by anyone else but herself. She was a Christian and, from her perspective at that time, had just not lived up to the mark. She was not good enough! Nobody could convince her otherwise as she adamantly described her life as being like a stick of rock (candy) with the word 'bad' inscribed all the way through.

Those of us around Sarah, her friends and her family could see the lovely person she was, even in her brokenness. It was heart-breaking to watch her desire and attempt to self-de-struct. We shared with Sarah truths from the Bible about God's enemy, and that his plan was to steal her life, get her to agree with him that she was rubbish, bad and deserved to die. As we did so, something deep within Sarah reached out and listened.

This was beyond her rationale. Sarah was and is a very intel-ligent lady, her intelligence had worked well for her condition and belief all her life, and the prevailing conclusion that, "I am bad" was unshakeably solid in her thinking. Yet, God's truth was penetrating deep within her spirit, that part of Sarah which had been crushed out of recognition, her original God-made identity.

Sarah was in a deep pit of pain and struggle. Firstly, there was nothing in her that believed she deserved a gift, and anything she received would have to be earned. Abuse made certain that nothing was freely received or freely given. The lifetime of belief that she had deserved the abuse as a punishment for being bad, made it impossible for her to accept a gift. Even though Sarah was a Christian, in fact she had been the secretary at her local church, the graveclothes of religion clung tightly to her. She desperately wanted to pay the price herself for what she perceived as her 'badness'.

What good news it is that we do not have to climb out of our mess and sin and make ourselves good enough. We do not have to appease God our Father. We do not have to buy into religious practice (legalism). The invitation from Jesus is simply to own our sin, receive His forgiveness and turn, asking Him to enter our life by His Holy Spirit, to cleanse, change and renew us.

How liberating it was for Sarah on the day she accepted the invitation to paint the dirty shells and begin to adorn them with colours. No longer was she being given rules, expectations or plans for God's healing, but He was imparting His gift to her right there in ordinary life experience! She was receiving! Nothing depended on her, except to receive and enter in. Life for Sarah was turning from black and white to glorious colour!

The graveclothes of religion gave way to life

However, after a little while a new battle emerged as contention raged inside her. Now frustrated with the interlude in her ministry, she said, "I need to get on with my healing now, this is a waste of time."

Sarah was angry. In truth, the enemy who had held her in

> "
> Sarah was in a deep pit of pain and struggle.

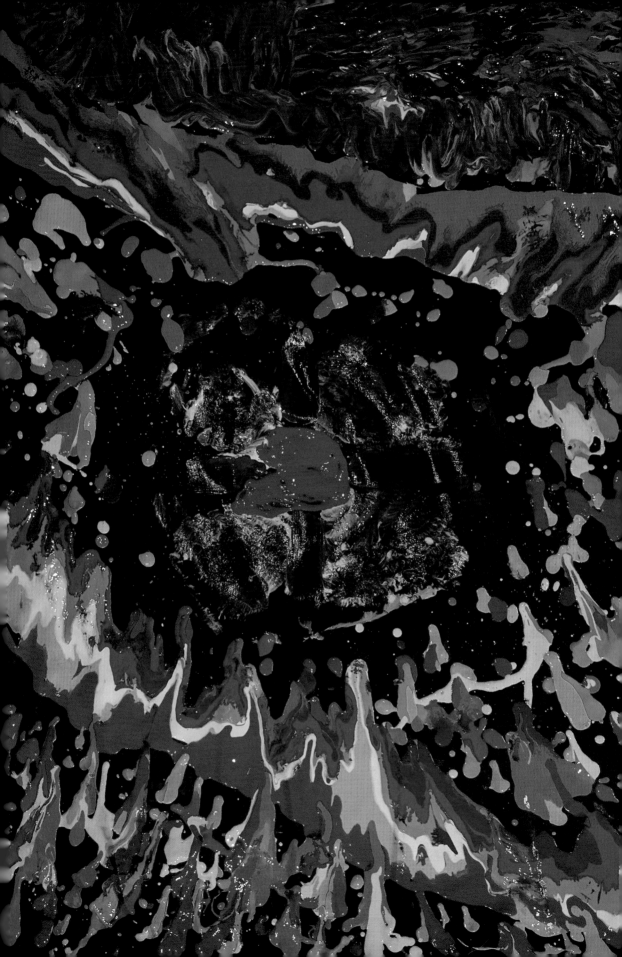

captivity through abuse, was angry too. Satan did not want her to be free and he was doing well in tempting her to shut it all down. Yet, the Holy Spirit of God continued to be at work and, as we persevered, a breakthrough came. Something precious was awoken in Sarah, the gift of life – her own responses, her own choices, something spontaneous. As she received freely, the bonding and joy was tangible. You could only describe it as life from the dead!

As Sarah began to engage in a battle for her own identity and recognise the contention that was coming from the enemy of God, it lifted the lid of despair where she had been trapped with no hope. A new confidence and trust in God's power to deliver and break invisible chains of bondage grew. The struggle to break through, which came from the simplicity of transforming dirty shells into something beautiful, was God's master plan in setting Sarah free! God broke through in Sarah's life, setting her free from Satan's plan to keep her beauty in prison.

His life within us gives us power over sin, sets us free and brings us peace. From this foundational assurance, we can begin to look further and see more of God the Creator's principles to bring healing and life.

> "
> Sarah began to engage in a battle for her own identity

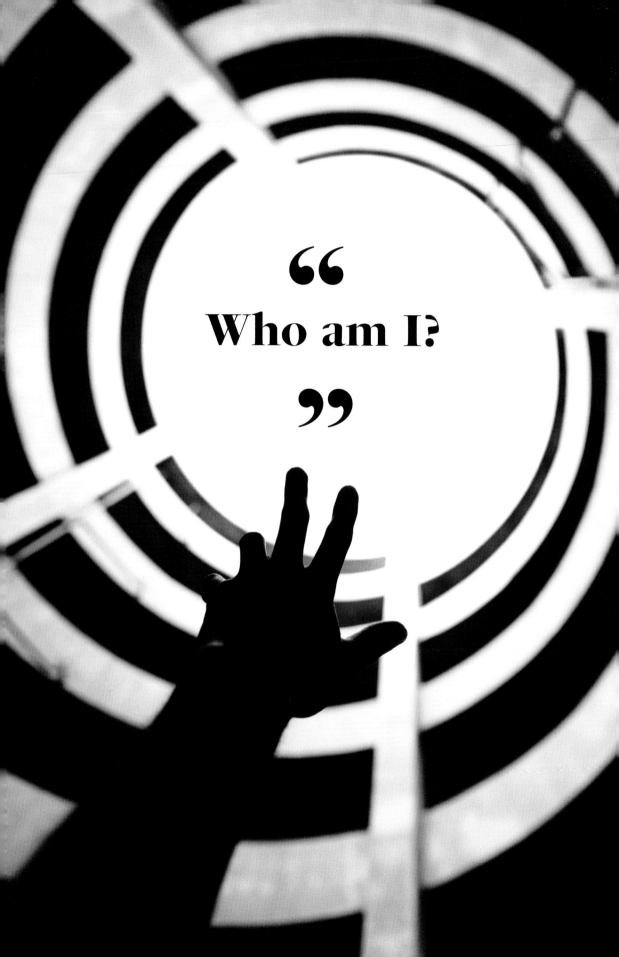

Chapter 4

ROUND PEGS IN ROUND HOLES

Identity

One of the common threads running through our work, is the basic human question, "Who am I?" and "For what purpose do I exist?" Sarah had not wanted to exist; on the inside she was full of pain. Her psychiatrist had explained to me that her life was a bit like a piece of wallpaper with no wall behind to hold it up, and no hope of ever being released from psychiatric care. She was destined for a life on the highest dosage of drugs and had been given a lifetime disability allowance. But, for Sarah, even the drugs had come to the end of their capacity to keep her alive. ECT (Electroconvulsive Therapy) treatment was to be the psychiatrist's last resort. She and her husband were distraught and hopeless.

> "
> For what
> purpose do I
> exist?

Sarah arrived at Ellel Grange accompanied by the Vicar's wife as her carer. We were told she was a danger to herself and almost anything could trigger her desire to die. I remember her bowed head and shuffling feet, she was painfully thin and pale – a picture of walking death. Yet, from my experience over many years of helping people with a background of abuse, I knew that the tender love of God wanted to reach her. I had complete faith that underneath all the sin afflicted on her, and all the pain and injustice she had suffered, God could heal.

Humans not God, Angels or Robots

I was teaching on one of our courses on the difference between sins and wounds and the necessity of identifying each, so that they can be brought to God for cleansing and healing. A gentleman put up his hand and asked, "If I give all this to God, what is it that I get to keep? Who am I?" Laughter resounded around the room! "What a good question," I thought!

I tried asking the question then, "Who do you think you are?" I received 'spiritual' answers, when I really wanted to hear answers, such as, "I am David", "I am a musician", "Fish and chips is my favourite meal", "I enjoy walking" etc. The point being, that we are 'human beings', not just 'spiritual beings'. As human beings we have personalities, desires, opinions and choices. These qualities are what God gave as a core value for healthy relationships and to make life rich.

When God created human beings, He described His work as very good! (Genesis 1:31). We were made very good, and as such we are valuable. Whatever the circumstances or vehicle of our conception, God designed each of us uniquely as a gift. When the sperm and the egg

76

came together, His creative genius breathed His life into us and we lived. If God removed His breath (loving Spirit) from the world today, no one would remain alive. It is 'in him we live and move and have our being" (Acts 17:28), 'In him, all things hold together' (Colossians 1:17).

Parable of the Runner Beans

My husband Peter is a visionary! Wherever we are or whatever we are doing, ideas come flooding into his thoughts. One day whilst out grocery shopping, Peter placed a few packets of vegetable seeds in our basket. I exclaimed, "What are these for?" "Oh," said Peter, "I just love runner beans!" I could see that the picture on the packet of fully-grown runner beans had caught his imagination, and that in his mind they were already on the plate, waiting to be eaten!

However, I was aware of the journey that would have to be travelled before these runner beans could reach Peter's mouth and taste buds! Who was going to plant them in seed pots, water them, then dig a trench for them, put up bean poles for them to climb up, and not least, who was going to pick them and freeze them? Peter, undeterred by my doubts, got home and with great joy took the first step and planted the little seeds out. What potential and destiny those seeds had, but there was a long way to go before it was fulfilled!

Many months passed, during which various friends had to be enlisted to help water the seeds, a gardener had to be found to dig the trench and put the poles up. Eventually, the flowers came out and the beans began to form. We still had some more travelling to do, for the beans needed help to overcome the onslaught of bugs, slugs, rabbits and dry weather. Even more people were enlisted to help!

Finally, the beans were harvested (by yet another friend!) who kindly prepared them and put them in our freezer. Then came the great day and we were at home to see the vision fulfilled. The beans were tasted and eaten. They were absolutely delicious! The journey from conception to their final destination on our plates had been long, arduous and costly, but it was worth it.

At our conception, God sees us and all the potential that lies in the little embryo. He sees our journey and destiny, and in His heart is great excitement and joy. He knows there will be struggles, hardships, pitfalls and suffering along the way, and it is His intention to be alongside watching over and helping us every step of the way.

God's intention is to be alongside every step of the way

Our Inner Beauty

We are all created with an inner beauty. We have talents, gifts, creativity, personality, developing character, strengths and weaknesses, all of which contribute to making us who we are. We are designed as round pegs for round holes. Creator God does not give the gift of an immense brain for it to be unused and unfulfilled. God does not give someone the gift of sensitivity, caring and loving for it to be laid dormant.

In creation no two snowflakes are ever the same, neither are two blades of grass. And so it is with us; every person's fingerprint is different, we are made with our own unique identity from which comes our own purpose and destiny (fruitful living). As human beings, we each have a God-given, human, legitimate need to be known and to be secure in our own sense of personal worth and value.

A God-given, human, legitimate need to be known and valued

As we have seen, we live in a fallen and imperfect world, where the consequences of man's sin (evidenced everywhere) is borne by us all. We also live with God's enemy, Satan, as the god of this world.

Yet the darkness cannot overcome the light. Evil cannot, ultimately, triumph over good. Love will never fail. Truth will always stand. For the poor, the marginalised, the disabled, the broken, the destitute – Jesus brings good news.

It was never Gods intention to land us in a sea of confusion to somehow make sense of life alone. We are created with a God-shaped hole for Him as our Father to fill. He is meant to be our Rock and our Guide, and He intended us to live in family and relationship here on earth.

> "
> For the marginalised, the disabled, the broken, the destitute – Jesus brings good news

GOD is our refuge and strength, an ever-present present help in trouble. (PSALM 46:1)

Truly he is my rock and my salvation; he is my fortress ...
Trust in him at all times, you people; pour out your hearts
to him, for GOD is our refuge.   (PSALM 62:2, 8)

The Triumph of Love

When Sarah came for help, she eventually managed to tell
us that Her mother had tried to abort her in the womb, and
later in her life told her, "I curse the day you were born." I
have prayed with many such people whose early existence
was hardly one of loving welcome or being received as a gift.
Maybe they were nowhere near such extreme circumstances
as this, but for many their conception was, at best a mistake
or in rejection and, for some, through the evil of rape.

"
We need
to know
how God
made us

Our human spirit is designed by God to be the source of
energy (love), the life giver to the soul. The soul is designed
to reflect the inner workings of the spirit. If we are going to
understand anything of how God heals through creativity, we
need to know how God made us.

As a team we opened His Word and prayed a very simple
prayer, "God, you made this person, you know them, please
help us find the true, God-created person on the inside, we
only want Your truth and Your way to the truth." God is
faithful. He has given understanding and keys from His Word,
which have set those in the worst of circumstances free from
the bondage they have been in.

"I am just bad," cried Sarah, "I don't deserve to live." This was
not a momentary thought or emotion or a passing phase of life,
this was her rock-solid reality. I have already shared that Sarah
came from a background of severe abuse and just wanted to
die. For her, the truths of Scripture, that speak of her as being
valuable, precious and a gift, were just about as far removed
from her beliefs as the east is from the west. To her they bore
no relevance. She believed with every fibre of her being that
she was bad. Shame and guilt were at the core of her identity.

And it was with that belief at the core of her being that Sarah had tried to be good! On the outside, and to everyone else, she was perfect! I thought we had the most perfectly co-operative counselee, but I could not see the raging torrent on the inside which, eventually, she could not hold back. The outside wall of defence, that had been held in place by a huge amount of effort and pretence, caved in. It took the highest possible dosage of psychiatric drugs to try to control the inside agenda, but even they were not enough.

In the face of this reality, would God's Word hold true, that in her conception she was made good and not bad? We began feeding into her human spirit this truth and reflecting to her something of how God made her and how He wanted to restore her. I love the word 'restoration'! My husband received the vision for what has become Ellel Ministries, through restoring an old Alvis Sports car which had been completely wrecked. There is something in us all which enjoys finding buried treasure, panning for gold, seeing something tarnished become what it was meant to be. Even as Sarah was living in her grave clothes of death, I could see that underneath there was a pearl to be found. And in time, death did give way to life!

> In time death did give way to life

God Does Not Make Mistakes!

God did not make a mistake when He made us. We are not born bad or wrong. At our conception, time in the womb, birth or ongoing life, we may have received an alternative truth into our hearts that, somehow, we are wrong, a mistake or even bad. I have heard countless people effectively tell me that somehow God got it all wrong when He made them. Everyone else is fine but they are not. However, the truth is that we are ALL valuable, 'fearfully and wonderfully made' (Psalm 139:14). But sin has overlaid the person God made, and each of us has a carnal nature as a result.

Measured to the Plumb line!

Does that mean that we are perfect and unflawed, sinless and made for sainthood? No, because this side of eternity that is impossible! We are all sinners (have pride and rebellion in our hearts, believing we know best, going our own way etc) and if we do not believe that, then we are deceiving ourselves! (1 John 1:8). The truth is clear in Psalm 51:5, that every human being is conceived with inherited sin nature, 'Surely I was sinful at birth, sinful from the time my mother conceived me.' This side of eternity, it is not possible to live in sinless perfection, but the good news is that there is a remedy!

Understanding Grave Clothes!

It is very freeing to understand that we are not alone in our battle with our sin. It is a level playing field for all of us and there is only one solution for even the worst of sin, which is in humble confession to the One who has paid the price to wipe our slate clean. We cannot wipe our own slate clean.

Through the shells Sarah was learning that the dirt and barnacles on the outside could be changed from something ugly into something of beauty. As we gently washed and wiped them clean, the shells revealed a silky inner core which was beautiful to see and touch. They were an excellent illustration of how God viewed Sarah. He saw the guilt and shame which had been placed on her by those who had so wrongly abused her.

God also saw her own responses, some of which were understandable but nevertheless, sinful ones with hatred, revenge and bitterness festering around her wounds. He understood her pain but wanted her to understand that she could not clean herself. He would come and bring 'beauty for ashes' (Isaiah 61:1-3).

As the team had fun painting the outer shells in multicoloured tones and a generous dose of glitter for good measure, God was teaching Sarah in a very tangible way that He would remove her grave clothes and exchange them for life.

Spiritual Gardening

Peter and I have a lovely garden, but we have not been able to be good gardeners! Through our many travels teaching and ministering widely over the years, our garden became very neglected. I remember looking one day and seeing how a weed, which we call bindweed in the UK, had tightly wrapped itself around our plants, bushes and shrubs. It was well out of control and had managed to climb high and crush the life out of the hardiest of specimens. A gardener friend told us that this particular weed was very prevalent, it was tenacious, and it was impossible to kill off without digging deep and treating the soil bed with weed killer and new soil.

I saw how our garden was mirroring human nature. We are beautiful plants with a destiny to blossom and grow healthily as our needs are met by God. Yet attached to us are the results of that sinful nature which wants to trip us up, beset us in so many ways and if given full birth, would bring death and destruction to our identity, our eventual fruitfulness and even to life itself. Left undetected and undealt with, we could never blossom and reach our potential.

We all need to be vigilant and to recognise the spiritual sin weeds in our lives, that want to be given identity and life. If they could, they would work their way of destruction and tangle themselves tightly around us until we could hardly breathe or know who we truly are.

Thankfully, we have a Divine Weed Killer and a Divine Fertiliser to put into our soil! Learning how not to feed the weeds and kill off the plants in our lives, is a huge step forward in knowing our true identity and who we are.

Being at peace with ourselves, at peace with others and, most importantly, at peace with God is true healing. From this place of rest, we will bloom where we are planted, and our true creativity can really flow out through all we are and do.

Time for the Divine Weed Killer

Be not ignorant of Satan's devices, the Scripture tells us (2 Corinthians 2:11). God's enemy seeks to impart torment into our wounded areas, telling us how bad we are, how guilty we are, how much we fail and will never be free, never be loved and how to turn on ourselves in self-hatred. He would try and tempt and deceive us to give in to the bindweed of sin and use our ungodly responses to increase hurt and pain.

Satan is described as 'the accuser', and with his accusations comes condemnation (Revelation 12:10). Conversely, the Holy Spirit of God brings freeing conviction enabling us to rise above and conquer the tactics of the enemy. We have the remedy! Jesus has won the battle! He will come and bring forgiveness, healing and empowerment through His Holy Spirit over temptation and sin (Romans 8:13).

Sarah was daring to believe that perhaps she was not all bad. She was seeing that underneath the mess there was something precious and that there was hope for her. As we played with the shells and beautified them, it was a time of laughter and fun. Jesus was showing us that He loves to take something which is considered rubbish and redeem it.

Underneath the mess there was something precious

Later, we will look at how her gifts and talents began to surface for the first time, and that underneath was the real, hitherto unreached, person emerging. Even in her weakness, Sarah was receiving the strength to take back from the enemy what had been stolen from her – her life. She began putting her roots down into the soil of God's love and His principles for her life, and in doing so, she was taking back the ground the enemy had robbed. Divine gardening was taking place!

Sarah was coming out of passivity and hopelessness and was tentatively choosing life. The array of brightly shining shells painted with all the freedom and fun of a small child were evidence that there was new life beginning to emerge.

An Invitation to Abundant Life

Isaiah 55:1-3 & 6-7 invites us:

Come, all you who are thirsty, come to the waters; and you who have no money, come, buy and eat! Come, buy wine and milk without money and without cost. Why spend money on what is not bread, and your labor on what does not satisfy? Listen, listen to me, and eat what is good, and you will delight in the richest of fare. Give ear and come to me; listen, that you may live. I will make an everlasting covenant with you, my faithful love promised to David.

Seek the LORD while he may be found; call on him while he is near. Let the wicked forsake their ways and the unrighteous their thoughts. Let them turn to the LORD, and he will have mercy on them, and to our GOD, for he will freely pardon.

Jesus, in Revelation 3:18, says:

I counsel you to buy from me gold refined by fire, so you can become rich; and white clothes to wear, so you can cover of your shameful nakedness; and salve to put on your eyes, so you can see.

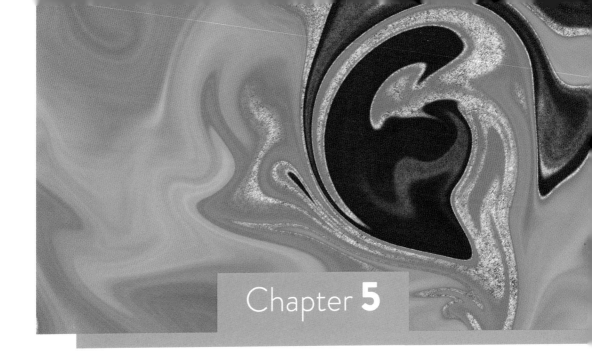

FREE WILL – GOD'S RISKY GIFT

When God created mankind, He did not create robots as machines to run the earth. God took an immense risk when He created us with the gift of free will. If I were God, I would not have taken such a risk! What would the people I created do with the free will I gave them?

Extraordinary as it may seem, God took the risk! The essence of any authentic relationship is to have its roots in free will and trust. It is to be able to freely give or freely withhold. If someone instructed you to be their friend, you would feel affronted! Our innate free will is designed to give us choice over who are our friends or not.

God has no intention of forcing us into a relationship with Him. He is who He is, and as such He invites us to respond to Him or not.

In giving each of us free will His plan was for the highest form of relationship. Free will, therefore, is a precious gift and a central part of who we are and how we express ourselves as individuals. It is part and parcel of our character and our creativity. Free will came to us as a gift at our conception. Even within the womb, the tiny embryonic human spirit has ability to choose and hold onto life. It has the capacity to feel and

know the truth of its surroundings. For example, an embryonic baby, conceived in fear, or who later in the womb experienced a fearful, hostile environment, senses those fearful situations intuitively. It is a 'knowing' which goes beyond rationale. The human spirit picks up the surrounding reality.

God planned the womb to be a safe, nurturing place for the newly fertilised, embryonic baby to grow and develop, surrounded by love and security. We are not simply physical beings. Without a welcome or protection at that vulnerable time, anxiety and insecurity can take root, at the same time as our early free will is being formed and shaped by the circumstances we experience.

A baby who is critically rejected and may have been the victim of attempted abortion, will often take on subconscious beliefs of being bad, or being a nuisance. The seeds of striving and perfectionism in order to be accepted and loved, are sown, and these often operate to override shame, guilt and anxiety later in life.

We have witnessed countless people who have experienced deep healing and come into freedom through creativity, as God has touched them right back at the time of their conception and birth. Even though their mind and brain were undeveloped at that time, the human spirit is alert and sensitive and can be affected in the very earliest days of life. For some, the spirit has become crushed and broken, which can lead to the desire to give up on life and wanting to die.

When we place our will in line with God's truth, we can receive God's best medicine – His Word – into that place of crushing: the revelation that we were never alone, and that whatever the human vehicle was for our conception, God designed us to be a gift, and He was there.

Even if we were not received that way, we remain a gift to God. We are His daughter, His son, and He knows us.

These words from Psalm 139 (overleaf) bring powerful healing to our human spirit and strengthen our core identity and, therefore, our will and motivation for living life to the full.

> " The human spirit picks up the surrounding reality.

You have searched me, LORD,
   and you know me.
You know when I sit and when I rise;
   you perceive my thoughts from afar.
You discern my going out and my lying down;
   you are familiar with all my ways.
Before a word is on my tongue
   you, LORD, know it completely.
You hem me in behind and before,
   and you lay your hand upon me.
Such knowledge is too wonderful for me,
   too lofty for me to attain.
Where can I go from your Spirit?
   Where can I flee from your presence?
If I go up to the heavens, you are there;
   if I make my bed in the depths, you are there.
If I rise on the wings of the dawn,
   if I settle on the far side of the sea,
even there your hand will guide me,
   your right hand will hold me fast.
If I say, "Surely the darkness will hide me
   and the light become night around me,"
even the darkness will not be dark to you;
   the night will shine like the day,
   for darkness is as light to you.
For you created my inmost being;
   you knit me together in my mother's womb.
I praise you because I am fearfully and wonderfully made;
   your works are wonderful,
   I know that full well.
My frame was not hidden from you

> when I was made in the secret place,
> when I was woven together in the depths of the earth.
> Your eyes saw my unformed body;
> all the days ordained for me were written in your book
> before one of them came to be.
> How precious to me are your thoughts, GOD!
> How vast is the sum of them!
> Were I to count them,
> they would outnumber the grains of sand—
> when I awake, I am still with you.
> Search me, GOD, and know my heart;
> test me and know my anxious thoughts.
> See if there is any offensive way in me,
> and lead me in the way everlasting.

Whilst praying and helping people, I have recognised that there is the need for help in understanding how the area of free will might have become damaged, either by becoming too passive or, conversely, becoming overbearingly strong. The exercising and the yielding of our will in the right way and at the right time is God's design for our health.

Expressing Free Will

Self-expression is inextricably connected to our freedom of will. Parents are well aware that a baby has a will from the word 'go' and is capable of expressing it without restraint! Children in a family are never alike, each has a personality commensurate to their particular gifting and talents, with a free will to match. Expressing will is an essential part of developing and growing. Choices come out of our will and are a bit like a piece of elastic. They can be stretched to the limits where risk and danger lurks. Alternatively, free will can

> "
> Self-expression is inextricably connected to our freedom of will.

make a person want to withdraw to a place where passivity can also become dangerous. The ability to discern our own free will is vital.

Sometimes people make a mistake in believing they do not have any will. They may feel they become automatons for what others want them to be. The concept of their own creative expression is foreign to them. But it is not possible for anyone to lose their free will. However, this aspect of God's gift to us in our human spirit can become at best lethargic and passive, and at worst crushed and buried. Creative expression is consequently stifled and needs stimulating into life.

Expressing Feelings Needs Free Will

Nobody else can feel your feelings (emotions), your pain, your joy, love, hate, anger, frustration, sadness, compassion and much more. They can empathise and understand but no one else can carry our emotions for us. They are integral to the person we are and the decisions we will take as a result.

Our free will responds to circumstances and from there our feelings flow. We can take godly self-control (Galatians 5:23), but we can also take ungodly control. We can shut down our feelings as if they do not exist, or alternatively express them inappropriately in risky, difficult and wrong places. Healthily developing children learn these things through their tantrums and their sulks! A vital lesson in life that God intends us to learn, is that we cannot always have our own way, at times our will needs to be yielded and our hard-done-by feelings relinquished.

For some, the freedom to choose, or feel

emotions as God intends, has been taken from them. Their will has been dominated by fear, manipulated by guilt or controlled to conform to another's overbearing expectation. Free will can be used to take control over emotions, sometimes to the point of completely shutting them down.

Sarah, as a young child, learnt to hide her feelings and instead to present an outward 'persona' of seeming perfection. Inside, however, was a cavern of emotions and feelings which had not just 'gone away', but which were dangerously explosive.

Sarah had never been allowed her free will to express her hatred, injustice and pain at the cruelty she had been made to endure. Instead, her free-will decisions led to her becoming very strong in her determination to keep a part of herself buried and all personal responses and reactions under extreme control. No

wonder anxiety and fears were seeping out, which eventually became full blown, uncontrollable, panic attacks with the necessary resultant compulsive behaviour to control them. The highest dosage of drugs was the only answer.

The journey ahead would need these tight controls to be yielded to God in a safe way and place. We will look later at how creativity in its broadest form is designed by God to bring an antidote and release to inner pressure.

We all, to some extent, have areas of our life where our free will has been shaped negatively through life's experiences. We have learnt behaviour or formed beliefs, which have caused our free will to be affected negatively.

Young children, loved and secure in parental protection,

need to be given the freedom to express positive and negative emotions. In formative years, a healthy child expresses themselves both negatively and positively, often much to their parent's dismay! A child will often dance from one extreme of expression to another. "I hate you, it's not fair," to, "I love you; you are the best Mummy or Daddy in the world."

Part of growing up and maturing entails the safety to make mistakes. God's plan is for us to grow and, in our growing, to learn from our mistakes. This is how we all learn. Our creativity and imagination will be thwarted if they are stifled to the point where we cannot express who we are, and how we feel, without fear. Frustration, excitement, anticipation, disappointment, sadness, joy, achievement, failure and much more are all part of the normal spectrum of expression for growing and becoming.

Who Needs Opinion?!

Some people's free will has been so dominated by another person that they hardly know who they are. When someone has inordinate power over you and tells you who you should be, what you should be feeling, thinking and choosing, it can have the effect of brainwashing, or at least, training your way of thinking so that, in some cases, access to your own opinion is, at best difficult and at worst impossible. Choices become based on what pleases someone else or what someone else wants of you.

In her growing years, Sarah had received no infrastructure to feel her likes and dislikes, let alone express an opinion. One day, at the Centre, our lunch had gone cold and we were eating cold scrambled egg! A member of the team let out a big "Ugh!" They were expressing natural distaste at something which needed heating up. Sarah looked bemused. It took this ordinary incident for us to realise that she did not have the capacity to express negative feelings or opinions. If we liked it and ate it, so would she, if we did not, nor would she. It was as simple as that for her, copying what other people did, is what made life safe, but it was not living!

Helping Brian, a man who was extremely passive, almost to the point where he was non-existent, was challenging. He was an expert in his work as an engineer but could not maintain relationships. His wife had plenty of opinion and feelings about their situation, but when asked, Brian simply said, "I do not have an opinion." No wonder his wife had become 'opinionated'; it was her way of trying to evoke a response. Any opinion was better than none.

Expressing opinion shares something of who we are, what we think and maybe how we feel too. It is often a good indicator of how well our free will is operating! Free will opinions are part of our creative flow as individuals, and it is God's intention that they should be listened to and encouraged rather than crushed. They are essential to our creativity in developing relationships. Hearing another person's opinion, whether it is the same as ours or not, is part of respect. Respect for the expression of opinion, whether it is our own or another's, releases creativity and wholeness within.

"
Expressing opinion shares something of who we are

Amanda's Story

A lovely, young, intelligent, married lady came on one of our Creativity courses. It turned out that her life was full of fears and anxieties to the point that she was extremely obsessive. We had been assuring our guests that there would be no pressure or force to 'do' anything.

Since free-will choice is so much on the heart of God, it is very much at the heart of the creativity experience, so there is complete freedom to move around from one workshop to another as much as you like. This was the trigger which made Amanda panic, "I do not know what to do," she burst out. Her face a picture of deep fear. "What if I make the wrong choice?" To Amanda, at that moment, it was a life and death decision. She needed healing for her anxiety and obsessions, and she must make the right choice, otherwise, to her, God might be angry with her or she might miss being healed.

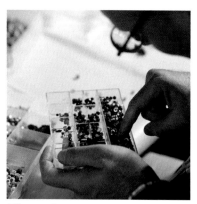

"Choosing"

Amanda's parents had, themselves, been extremely anxious people. In their desire to protect their children, they had been excessively over-protective. As a result, Amanda had no infrastructure of trust within her own personhood as an adult. She wouldn't trust her own choices, or weigh, test and measure other people's input. Instead she had capitulated to following others and copying, rather than trusting her own expression. She followed everyone else's way. Her own intelligence had been perfectly used to learn facts, figures, science etc, but her emotional growth and freedom of will was still that of a child.

Sadly, Amanda believed that God's love was conditional on her making right choices, and that in some way she would miss out if she did not get everything right. No wonder she was full of fear and anxiety. All day she wandered around unable to enter in, just in case she chose the wrong thing. My heart went out to her in her anxious state of mind, and I urged her to try something which had no right or wrong, but where she could be spontaneous and free. This was an enormous challenge. Amanda just wanted the rules. Life was easier if she had the rules, black and white with no shades of grey.

The more I spoke of relaxing and having fun, the more horrified Amanda became, and eventually, more explosive. In desperation she finally decided to put paint to paper. The colours did not matter, something had to be done, opinions or feelings had no place. I could see that Amanda was strongly in control, her decision would be made rationally, out of her head.

Bursting out with an explosion in the messy room with God

Sadly, Amanda was going through the motions of doing what she thought was the thing to do but it had no power behind it. Finally, the frustration and anger underlying her anxiety and fear surfaced and along with the black paint came an explosion of emotion. "I hate you; I hate me, I hate everyone! Why have I got to be so good all the time? I don't want to be a wife and mother. I am tired. I am tired of working and making it alright for everybody. I want to be bad. I hate my life."

We prayed quietly at her side. This was a breakthrough, the real Amanda was emerging with her real feelings. "Sorry, sorry, sorry," Amanda repeated and again, as yet more paint and negative emotion oozed out. Being with her was a privilege, as we watched the Holy Spirit bring a connection to the truth on the inside. Far from condemnation, there was affirmation of her expression. There was no need for Amanda to be apologetic for being true to herself. Jesus was healing Amanda from years of conforming and the frustration of keeping negative feelings buried.

They were coming out in a safe place where she could be real with herself, with us and most importantly, with God. He knew her struggle and her battle to please everyone. She needed to be true to herself with no pretence and constraints.

From that place of negative explosion and expression, Amanda was free to express her real self. "I don't really hate everyone," she sobbed. The tears were healing tears. Her individuality needed expression and the right place and time to do it. Amanda was breaking invisible chains, in the way she had spent a lifetime conforming passively to other people's needs for her to be what they wanted.

> "
> He knew her struggle and her battle to please everyone

Free to make mistakes

Her parents thought they were doing their best, but out of their anxiety they held Amanda into a box of their own making. They had not released her into her own free will and right developmental growth. Amanda's human spirit was crushed, along with her personality and creativity.

It had become so bad that Amanda could not even choose her own clothes as an adult with children of her own. She was still trying to make choices based on what other people decided for her. No wonder she had panicked when faced with making a workshop choice. Choice for Amanda was a dreaded thing. It's no wonder that she lived with deep seated fears and obsessions leading to such high anxiety levels that medication to help her function had become inevitable.

Amanda's story is not uncommon. Many people suffer

deep anxiety because they have never been able to express their own personhood (in a positive or negative way) through their own free will. It is as though their will has been invisibly paralysed or buried. Healing of the will is a major part of the creative healing God wants to bring.

In Conclusion

Our free will can be in need of help and healing. During our Creativity courses, people express the joy and release they have come into, through the freedom to choose, to have their own opinion, to make mistakes, to express themselves without fear, to allow negative and even explosive emotion to emerge in safety. Often there is an immature place within, which has become locked away or stuck, and needs permission to be

THIS IS ME   **THIS IS FUN**   **THIS IS MY PAIN**

> The key for release and healing is the yielding of our will

expressed. The consequently suppressed free will becomes a personal blockage to healing and the answer lies in giving permission to yourself.

The key for release and healing is the yielding of our will, firstly to God, who through His Holy Spirit will bring truth. This will then bring connection to the place within, which needs expression, in order to grow and develop in the joy of self-discovery. This is God's intention for His children.

It is for freedom that Christ has set us free

(GALATIANS 5:1)

You will know the truth, and the truth will set you free

(JOHN 8:32)

Chapter 6

SPACE, TIME AND LIMITS

In Him We live and Move and Have Our Being

In one of Paul's most expressive sermons, he spoke to religious and pagan unbelievers:

> I see that in every way you are very religious. For as I walked around and looked carefully at your objects of worship, I even found an altar with this inscription: TO AN UNKNOWN GOD. So you are ignorant of the very thing you worship—and this is what I am going to proclaim to you.
>
> The God who made the world and everything in it is the Lord of heaven and earth and does not live in temples built by human hands. And he is not served by human hands, as if

he needed anything. Rather, he himself gives everyone life and breath and everything else. From one man he made all the nations, that they should inhabit the whole earth; and he marked out their appointed times in history and the boundaries of their lands. God did this so that they would seek him and perhaps reach out for him and find him, though he is not far from any one of us. 'For in him we live and move and have our being.'

(ACTS 17:22-28)

> All of God's creation is held together by Him

All of God's creation is held together by Him. Nothing any of us can experience is outside of Him. He knows all things and He is bigger than everything He created. It is this reality that God put into His Word and which He taught to all the people through the Apostle Paul. Every breath that we take, every movement we make, is made within who He is, and it is by His grace and His will that we live.

The Son is the image of the invisible God, the firstborn over all creation. For in him all things were created: things in heaven and on earth, visible and invisible, whether thrones or powers or rulers or authorities; all things have been created through him and for him. He is before all things, and in him all things hold together.

(COLOSSIANS 1:15-17)

I Need Space!

For some reason, it had never occurred to me that God not only created matter, but He created the space between matter. It was when I joined a local art class that I began to learn the criticality of space. Space brings perspective and life to a painting, and I needed to create space in order to make my painting live.

Space brings light and movement. If everything is crammed together, there is no room for the freedom to grow.

For free will to be healthy, we need to be able to move and be spontaneous. We need space to move into. It is in the hidden and subconscious areas of our human spirit that there can be hidden controls which hold us back.

Space to move and fly

After a while of enjoying playing with the shells, Sarah told us in no uncertain terms that this was enough now! "I've done that," she said, and, "Now let's get on with my healing." As I mentioned in a previous chapter, Sarah was frustrated and reacting to the seemingly waste of time. Subconsciously she hated the gaps and wanted to crowd out the space created from 'just being.' It was obvious that she saw playing as a waste of time.

*She thought playing was a waste of time,
instead it was healing*

We were busy enjoying this aspect of her healing journey and were at pains to explain that we all need times to 'be' and not having to 'do' anything. But the exasperation on Sarah's face was clear. "Well," she said, "how do I 'do' being? I need a plan." We all chuckled as we saw the point of what she was trying to say.

Sarah's every move was highly controlled. She looked on painting the shells as a job to be completed rather than a time of spontaneous fun. For the team it was a relief to be away from the pressures and was pure relaxation. We got carried away, almost forgetting why we were there and that time was passing.

But God was showing us what He was teaching Sarah. Space and time were doing their work of healing, as they brought spontaneity into her life. Whilst her frustration and struggle was evident, at a deeper level the tight controls were beginning to lose their grip.

As human beings we can become so busy with the 'doing' of life that subconsciously the 'being' part of who we are has disappeared. We live in an increasingly stressful world with its expectations and pressures, and not least whilst having to handle difficult and painful circumstances. Where does all the pain go? It does not simply disappear. We need time to 'be', to process feelings and thoughts, and see how negative beliefs and controls can create their own hidden cycle of problems if we have no time to listen.

It is in giving space and time for ourselves, and allowing God to touch our personhood, that much healing lies. This is a God-created principle, designed by Him for our good.

At first, Sarah was too terrified to do this, since time and space to be with herself, meant she would have to face her inner struggle of pain, fear and anger. At all costs she would frantically avoid this. Her way of crowding out space was to constantly make lists. Even lists of lists! And to check and double check, in a compulsion to keep control of the internal agenda. However, it was in eventually allowing spontaneity to come into her life that freedom came. The shells were just the beginning.

I have found that many people's problems lie in the fact that they find all kinds of ways to keep themselves busy, without realising there is something subconsciously at work within which is driving them.

> "...time and space to be with herself, meant she would have to face her inner struggle

We all need space to be ourselves. The environment we live in is often far too overcrowded, and not least in these days where mobile phones, social media and television take up a great deal of preoccupation. Space to feel our own feelings, hear our own thoughts, form our own opinions and to touch our own personhood is a God-given value. That is not to say we are to become self-absorbed, but to gain a healthy and balanced perspective of our own needs, value who God made us to be, and it is from this 'personal space' we can find the energy and motivation to give to others.

Spontaneity and Movement

All children need the space, time and a place to exercise their creativity, express their imagination, be in a world of their own and, in turn, express this part of just 'being' with their playmates too. The freedom to run and play, adventure and explore are all components Creator God made for developing a healthy and fulfilled life. As adults, we do not grow out of these needs although the expression of them obviously changes, as does the time to do so.

Space to move and be

Play and imagine

Spontaneity – it's out of control!

Sarah, as an adult, intelligent lady with responsibilities at home with her husband and children, was not looking at 'play' being anything to do with her need! But the shells became the catalyst for a much wider understanding of the need of spontaneity, movement and play.

Since the day God spoke so dramatically about Sarah just needing 'relationship', we turned our thoughts to potential ways we might facilitate this. Ellel Grange is near the coast, and on a particularly nice day we decided to have an outing. Sarah was not that impressed but duly went along with our ideas.

We thought it would just 'do her good', to be out. What happened when we got to the sea was not in our planning! Sarah, who had come so empty and devoid of self-expression suddenly took off! She ran away! My friend and co-worker, Anna, and I watched in horror. We thought this was the great escape. This beach was, in fact, an estuary and covered in mud flats. Anna and I were not 'young chicks' and neither of us were very fit to run. Disappearing into the distance, Sarah was flailing her arms around. Anna and I looked at one another, the same thought going through our heads, "Maybe Sarah did need to go back into psychiatric care and the physical safety it provided!"

Our recourse as ever was prayer, "Lord Jesus, please use this time to bring your healing to Sarah, please keep her safe." As Anna and I eventually drew near we could hear Sarah shouting the words, "I am free! I am free!" The movement of her arms were like a child's, pretending to be an aeroplane.

"I am free! I am free!" – running and moving untangled inner restrictions

Oh, how much Sarah had needed the physical space to run freely and to yell at the top her voice. God's creation of the wide expanse of beach, was the vehicle where, for Sarah a most powerful healing took place, breaking down invisible controls. It was in the act of moving spontaneously and with the space to do it, that God showed us He was at work.

We have found in our *Healing Through Creativity* courses many people fear being spontaneous. It feels out of control and unsafe. Yet it is allowing this very, God-created place in each of us expression which brings release. We need space to have our own thoughts, feelings and the freedom to be spontaneous, away from the straitjacket of control.

The Clock is Ticking!

When God created the universe, He set us in space but also in time. He placed us on this earth with limitations. Time is limited: once time is spent it can never be re-spent. If we give our time to another, it is a gift. Time is valuable and when we look at our fallen world, we can see the contention over time, and the space in which to spend it.

These two God-created gifts are more valuable than diamonds! What use is life if we do not have space and along-side space the time? Time is a precious but limited resource.

The gift of technology was designed to save time. However, we know that it often works the opposite way since technology demands instant response and takes endless time to keep up with the increasing demands it dishes up. Communication has just become much more complicated and time consuming. In fact, so much so that relationships are conducted more through the technology than face to face. Quality space, time and bonding are being crowded out.

Behind this pressure is the god of this world, Satan, whose objective is to turn humans into robots. Anything God designed for good, Satan attempts to distort and bring destruction through.

In this twenty-first century, we have infrastructure to make life easy and comfortable, the washers and driers, gadgets in abundance, communication technology in so many forms: from email to a plethora of instant messaging apps and social networking platforms. However, we have been driven into an existence of keeping up with the higher demand these supposedly 'time saving' devices have placed upon us!

So many of us spend our lives in a frenzy of keeping up with the voicemail, the email, text messages, the numerous 'friends' on Facebook and the need to live in this technological world of social media. Even our enjoyment of going out to the shops is becoming thwarted by online deliveries. We are becoming increasingly more machine driven, and the core principle that Creator God designed for our wellbeing is crowded out – that of space and time for relaxed and authentic relationships.

It is not that these God-inspired inventions of our creative minds are all wrong. It is a matter of balance, and the way we can inadvertently move away from Godly principles designed for health and wellbeing, into the domain where we are stress driven. The god of this world will always attempt to push us away from God's principles.

The more we encouraged Sarah to 'just be' and to give herself the time to play, enjoy creation through walks, exploration and adventure, the more her panics eventually subsided, and fears gave way to peace.

Being and not doing was so freeing,
fears gave way to peace

No Right or Wrong

Most people do not come from an abusive background but, for one reason or another, can still be driven by perfectionism. Perfectionism is a way of appeasing an inner sense of guilt and shame, which can be rooted in painful experiences in life, or where we have taken on board that we are just not 'good enough'.

Creativity courses are a wonderful way of giving God time and space to do His healing work. Maggie came determined to achieve and was growing more and more frustrated that her attempts did not live up to her hopes. This frustration eventually boiled over as she screwed up the card she was making, threw it into the bin and vehemently declared, "It is rubbish." I carefully picked the card up from the bin and gently straightened it, while telling Maggie, "This is not rubbish and you are not rubbish, your Heavenly Father loves you." The tears welled up and fell into a pool on the table, God was touching her heart.

> This is not rubbish and you are not rubbish

Somewhere deep inside, Maggie was carrying pain of rejection. She came trying to be perfect and to prove she could do something, but God used her screwed up attempt to make a card, to bring His love and truth. He loved her in the imperfection, there was nothing she had to prove for Him, He loved her just as she was. The screwed-up piece of paper mattered to Him. Invisible chains fell away that day. There is no right or wrong to God, just the joy of the journey.

No right or wrong, just the freedom to explore and experiment

How wonderful it was to see the freedom she received from what she called the 'straitjacket of perfectionism.' Maggie passed through barriers that said, "I can never get it 'right' or 'be good enough'," into carefree self-expression. She went on to enjoy other workshops. Her joy was tangible as she told us, "I could not believe I could have so much fun." Profound restoration was taking place.

Profound restoration was taking place

Giving it a Go

For another lady called Jenny, movement was the key for her healing. The violence in her family had led to her being extremely timid and lacking in any confidence to try anything. It was as though invisible cords were binding her. As the weekend unfolded, Jenny watched the dance workshop and something inside her was stirred, "I feel I want to dance, but I am terrified." We asked Jesus to help her and encouraged her to give it a try.

Jenny's story told how she felt the Holy Spirit helping her to move her legs, arms and whole body in dance. As she did so she felt an unravelling of many years of torment. God was healing her right there on the dance floor. "As I danced with the banners, I felt the Holy Spirit wrap Himself around me, I was dancing with Jesus and I felt His love come deep inside. I felt so safe and free."

When we give God space and time, He can move by His Spirit to do marvellous things setting us free from unseen bondages, often buried beyond our own ability to reach.

> I was dancing with Jesus and I felt His love come deep inside

Limits

We ignore limits and boundaries at our cost. Our own unique identity is expressed through our free will and the ability to move. However, we have a God-given limit as to how far we can go. God's principles for life on this earth, are bound by a limit on energy, time and resource.

Recognising and learning to live within the Creator's limits of our physical life here on earth will bring health and healing. I have lost count of the number of people who have told me how precious the gift of time to 'just be' is. God wants to touch the place of our God-given creativity to bring His antidote to the pressures of life. Each person is built differently, and we all have different needs according to how God has made us.

Recognising our limitations is a healthy principle to exercise.

Sarah would go beyond her personal limits to achieve what she felt was necessary. The list never did come to an end. There was never any sense of fulfilment, it was always a case of trying harder tomorrow. We could see the exhaustion and pressure within. God was showing us that Sarah needed His 'rest'.

To rest and just be

Many people come to our centres with a similar problem. Life has dished out some heavy responsibilities, and although the underlying cause is not the same as Sarah's, the issue of limits certainly is the same, and for many this has culminated in anxiety issues, addictions and relationship struggles. We all need the gift of space and time, which is God's antidote to stress and pressure, recognising our limitations.

It was a new day dawning for Sarah as she began to listen to her human needs. Hitherto the drive to shut out anything of her own personhood had gripped her life to the extent she never allowed herself to have a need, let alone feel one or express it.

God was showing Sarah His way of receiving who He is. As she entered into playing and having fun, self-imposed walls began to lose their grip and gave way to her being able to rest and just 'be.'

> playing and having fun, self-imposed walls began to lose their grip

112

Chapter 7

BEAUTY FOR ASHES

It was going to be a difficult day. We could all sense it as we arrived to spend time with Sarah. She had withdrawn into her own shell, uncommunicative and desperate. Even our opening prayer and worship time did not unlock the door to the chasm of pain and injustice swirling around within her. We sat in silent prayer, knowing words alone could not jolt her out of the depth of her situation. In fact, instinctively we knew that words would make it worse. It is so easy to dish out human platitudes in the face of unimaginable suffering. Thankfully we held back from doing so.

Time passed and with it came the eventual answer. "What have I got to give anybody? My life is just pain and what can I give to God?" The enormity of the suffering had taken away Sarah's ability to see or believe she had anything to offer. "I am just pain," she said, "and all I can offer to God is pain. You have all you are giving to me, to offer to God, but what do I have?"

There was a tremendous sense of the presence of the Lord in the room. We knew He was very close. The anointing of the Holy Spirit fell, and I found myself saying, "Sarah, you are giving the most precious thing possible in all the world to Him. You are giving Him your pain, this is exactly why Jesus came." Sarah believed that her pain was ugly and bad, but God did not. I continued, "The Lord Jesus gave His life and died for this very reason, for your pain, your suffering, your injustice. He came into the mess of the world to bring His redemption to what has been lost."

The silence continued and eventually Sarah uttered, "How can that be?" I knew that there is nothing more sacrificial to God than that which costs us the most. The abuse Sarah had undergone had cost her everything. We had often encouraged her to give her pain to God, and her reply was profound, "It cost me everything, I cannot just give it away." Our answer needed to be from Him. "Jesus feels, carries and knows your pain. His suffering meets your suffering, Sarah. He does not wipe it away, but He validates it."

At this point a deep connection was made between Sarah and Jesus, and one which brought about a move of God in her life in a deeply personal way. The pain Sarah had borne mingled with the pain of Jesus, and she knew at that moment more than in any other way, that her pain was precious to Him and He wanted to bring her something more than a quick fix, it was His redemption.

> "
> The abuse
> Sarah had
> undergone
> had cost her
> everything

Redemption in a Surprising Way

Understanding the principle of time to just 'be', we were spending more of it in the creative fun, which paints, stickers, glue and all manner of cardmaking bits and pieces bring.

Sarah wanted to make a card to thank the team and people who were praying for her, and not least, her family. Still quite a perfectionist at this point, she spent a long time making the most beautiful of cards. We were all enjoying the freedom after quite a tense time and had our drinks on the floor alongside the activity. Then, suddenly, Sarah accidentally knocked over her drink and it spilled over her card.

I looked up to see Sarah's panic mixed with anger. We did our best to reassure her, but without us realising it, God was using this incident to bring a lasting and profound healing. Right on the precipice of the familiar valley of bitter self-recrimination, gazing down and ready to take another leap into it, God in His mercy, brought revelation to her heart that He was disappointed and sad too, not for the sake of the card that was ruined, but because she had put so much of herself into it. We looked on, as her intense self-hatred melted, displaced by unexpected peace as she received the precious truth that He cared that much about her.

We looked on, as her intense self-hatred melted

Later when the card had dried out, she cut away the part that had been damaged, and remounted it on a new background. She was surprised to find that it looked much better than the original, and again God used this to speak to her about His work of redemption: that when He restores, He multiplies and gives back even more than was lost in the beginning.

On another occasion, Sarah again wanted to make a card and was looking around for something to use. She spotted an empty chocolate box in the bin with a picture of a rose on it. She decided to cut it out and mount it on a nice background. As she plucked the scrunched-up box from the bin and carefully cut out the rose, God powerfully reminded her of how she had felt like a piece of rubbish in the bin when she was in the psychiatric hospital. But He had seen her, not as rubbish but as a beautiful rose, and He had rescued her, and was stripping away the dross, and restoring and healing her, so that she would ultimately be able to live her life, giving glory back to Him.

Rubbish taken from the bin and made beautiful spoke volumes

Today she often speaks about the fragrance of a rose, and marvels that she has the privilege of bringing the fragrance of Jesus to others who need Him (2 Corinthians 2:15).

God brings redemption into our lives in many ways, even to the most painful of losses. We can all pray, "Lord Jesus, how do you want to redeem this or that situation?"

> All I had to offer Him was brokenness and strife,
> But He made something beautiful of my life.
>
> BILL GAITHER: SOMETHING BEAUTIFUL

Art Commission Lost

A man called John attended one of our modular schools, and he now regularly shares his story with those who come on our creativity courses. John is an artist, and he is highly talented and skilled. In fact, his paintings are displayed in galleries throughout the world and he himself lectured at a prestigious School of Art in London. He came on the modular school as a fairly new Christian, hungry for all that he could learn.

But John did everything he could to avoid the *Healing Through Creativity* element of the school. At the time, we had no idea why he broke out in sweats on arrival. He had not told anyone of his past and, in fact, was busy trying to hide everything to do with his life as an artist before he became a Christian, it was just too painful.

Many people struggle to have any connection to doing creativity, preferring to simply hear the teaching and respond privately. So, John was not alone in his wandering around the building looking but not participating. One of our team members became aware of his struggle. "John, what would you like to do?" she asked. Out of John's mouth came the single word, "Draw." As he tells the story, he explains how he wished he could have put those words back into his mouth. Drawing was the last thing he wanted to do! However, our team member had already left to find a pencil, board and paper!

John wanted to find an isolated spot so, although it was the coldest of November days, he sat outside on a seat looking up at our building and he began to draw. In fact, he drew all day, evening and the next day! When our team member eventually caught up with him, she asked to see what he had been doing and was astounded to see the result! John had drawn the most skilled and stunning picture of Ellel Grange. "John, this is fantastic!" our team member said, and ran off to find some of the leaders to come and see it.

John's picture of Ellel Grange

Little did we know that John's heart was full of doubts and fears. Twenty years previously, he had undergone a severe relationship breakdown. He was working on a commission for Christie's Contemporary Art in London, and the lady he was living with became highly critical of both him and his work. One day, in a jealous rage, she punished him by tearing up his carefully crafted work declaring it to be rubbish that no one would want to buy. Something broke in John that day and he had never touched a pencil or painting brush since! He had taken on the belief that he was rubbish. The reality was that his identity was broken.

However, God knew, and He had a plan! There on the creativity course, the Holy Spirit had been powerfully at work. As John picked up the pencil and started drawing, God was restoring him. "John, this is fabulous work!", "John, where did you learn to draw?", "John, how did you do this?" The gasps of those who saw John's work were truly spontaneous. Little did we know it at the time, but God was using them to heal and pour back into John the deepest possible healing. The gifting God had given John was deeply buried under the ashes of pain. Indeed, God had found the John He made! The joy on John's face said it all.

John has gone on to draw and paint with great skill since then and to teach others how to do it too. He is full of thanksgiving and overwhelming gratitude to God for finding him after twenty years of loss, and regularly tells his story of God's powerful redemption, his broken life from the past restored.

Liberated!

Then there was James, another lovely man who came on one of our courses. He was sitting at a table alongside others who were busily cutting out pictures and words from magazines to make collages, depicting something of their own identity. James suffered with severe dyslexia and was unable to write very much at all without great difficulty. He sat paralysed in front of his blank sheet of paper.

A team member came alongside him and prayed, "Lord, please show James what you are touching." God brought to his remembrance the humiliation he had suffered as an eleven-year-old boy, when he sat the 'eleven-plus' exam, which all children in the UK had to take in those days, to determine which academic level of secondary school they would go to. James had sat in that exam, paralysed with fear unable to write even his name at the top of the page.

Our team member asked him, "What would you *like* to put on the paper?" A smile lit up his face as he grabbed a pair of scissors and a magazine from the pile and began excitedly cutting out lots of pictures and sticking them on. Then, without any hesitation, he suddenly flipped the page over and wrote the word, 'Liberated' on the back in big letters and with perfect spelling, without any difficulty at all!

> he had never been able to feel his own emotions, or relate with others

He later testified that he had never been able to feel his own emotions, or relate with others, but God had worked powerfully by His Holy Spirit through that moment. Not only did he write a word he could never have written before, but he told us he felt loved for the first time in his life, and even felt sad about saying 'bye-bye' to go home at the end of the course (something that was very new to him). But most of all, he couldn't wait to arrive at home and share with his wife the miracle that had occurred.

Talent Restored

Then there was another lady who, like John, had an art training background. But there was an aspect to it that had a very damaging, stifling effect on her. The years of harsh critical assessment, and of having her work thrown away if it wasn't up to the required specification, had crushed her on the inside. In the end, she totally rejected her God-given creative talent and, along with it, all the associated pain. But it wasn't just the pain of those years that she buried, but also of the years of her very dysfunctional upbringing.

The last thing she expected was that God would bring real healing to her through creativity! But she came on one of our *Bridge from the Head to the Heart* courses. At first, she couldn't understand what all the excitement was about, and she struggled to enter in.

Eventually, she dared to put paint onto the paper and, as she did so, God brought connection for her to the pain and hurt of her earlier life. She began to release to Him through the paint, deep feelings that had been so buried that she didn't have words for them.

It was a powerful encounter. She knew God had met with her right there and then, and change began to come. She felt warmth inside for the first time and, crucially, the dread of art had gone! She felt excitement bubbling up from inside that

God had reignited joy in her creative gifting. This lady is now passionate about helping others to come into true freedom through the vehicle of creativity that only God can bring.

Treasure in the Tip

We can be sure that God our Father is looking for what is lost to Him. My daughter, who teaches at one of our centres, told me her powerful true story of redemption. It concerned her young daughter who had lost her 'Cuddles', which is a ribbon edged blanket with a teddy head. Cuddles had gone missing on a trip to a gymnasium where she was watching her brother at his class. Desperate for her Cuddles, my grand-daughter was inconsolable, so my daughter had to go back to the gym to try and find it. The gym was now shut along with the whole school. Racking her brain, Lindsey realised the cleaners would be inside cleaning up.

The cleaners had thought it was rubbish and apologetically explained it was in the bin, and the bin men had been. What distress as my granddaughter learned the fate of her Cuddles. Lindsey's heart was breaking for Zoe and, in that moment, she determined to go to the rubbish tip, look for the bags and find Cuddles. On arriving at the tip, nothing stopped her – the filth, the stench, the disgusting items of rubbish. Eventually, she found a bin liner which contained Cuddles!

Cuddles needed to go through the washing machine a few times and eventually landed in Zoe's arms. Cuddles was found and welcomed back with inexpressible joy! This is a wonderful story, illustrating God's heart in redeeming us. He does not see the stench or the mess, He is intent on finding His lost child and will go to any length to find us.

We have numerous stories from people who tell us, "God found me." It seems that along life's way, for whatever reason, we can be a bit like Cuddles and become lost to ourselves or take on board a faulty view of who we truly are. We need

… a faulty view of who we truly are

to be found. God uses creativity to help people receive His redemption, the most significant healing being when He helps us to find ourselves.

"God found me!"

Bob, a seventy-six-year-old man, painted a very simple childlike picture of the sun in one corner of his piece of paper and a boy in a boat on the sea at the bottom. The man was staring at the boat with tears pouring down his cheeks. When I asked what was happening, he replied (continuing to stare at the boy in the boat), "That is the Bob I lost seventy-three years ago." The tears were healing tears, such was the joy at finding himself and connecting to that lost place inside himself.

For a variety of reasons, it is possible to lose a part of our personhood. Maybe it is the ability to choose, have an opinion, express emotion, to play, relax or to adventure. For some, it is a greater loss rather like Sarah's, whose whole life was built on how to survive, keep safe and please other people. At the other end of the scale, we can all lose something of ourselves through life's responsibilities and circumstances, which crowd out our personhood. God can use creative expression to help the embracing of parts of ourselves we have lost.

Antidote

Creative expression is God's design for the rejuvenation of the human spirit. It is an antidote to stress, bringing a release to tension. At one of our centres a bell is rung to signify lunch is

ready, ensuring a long line of people eagerly await their food. But during our creativity courses, it is hard to pull people away from what they are doing and enjoying! Experimenting, exploring, no right or wrong, learning a new way or skill, engulfed in colour, shape and form, all contribute to bringing life and food goes down the list of priorities. It is a good way of dieting!

God had no intention of creating religious robots! His plan, in giving us the whole of creation, was for us to enjoy and take care of it. We have within us gifts and talents to invent, nurture and develop the world we live in. Certainly, God is not dull, and the scope of human endeavour is always exploring and inventing something new even in small ways. A healthy heart will reach out and enjoy a taste of something different, a new recipe, game, relationship, book, planting new things, decorating a room etc. Ideas and imagination are meant to flourish and bring an antidote to the mundane.

> "
> A healthy heart will reach out and enjoy a taste of something different

Work and Rest

Work is a value set intended to bring fulfilment and produce fruitfulness not least through the earning of money. Anyone who has been made redundant knows the crushing this can bring. Work involves us using our skills and talents and a degree of giving out of who we are. Work produces value to others and in doing so we are contributing to the good of the whole. Alongside being fulfilling, it is also tiring!

For this reason, God provides His gift of rest. We do not live in the Garden of Eden as Adam and Eve did before sin entered. We live in a sinful and fallen world, and we battle with our own imperfect and sinful natures as well. God has a place of rest for all of us to find in Him and His way of bringing restoration and peace to our inner beings. It is 'tailormade' to fit each person. I found mine in rather an unusual way.

No Good at Perspective

This was the pronouncement of my art teacher in the third year of senior school. Alongside my parents telling me that art was a waste of time, no money could be earned from it, I must have firmly taken these critiques on board. The sewing class was more productive and useful, but it never gave me any fulfilment. I went on in life to do what was standard, office work. I considered myself very ordinary with no particular talent and certainly not creative.

During the development of creativity courses, I left all the creative side to others who were gifted in this area and I stuck to my role in teaching the course and bringing everything together. But a day came that would change everything for me.

It took us quite a while to acquire a potter's wheel and the lovely talented pottery lady was thrilled. She set it up in a place where many passed through and it was open for all to try. One day I was watching the guests enjoying this aspect of the course and dwelling on how God is the Divine Potter and we are the clay.

"Come on, Fiona, have a go. This is great fun," I heard a voice call out, but I passed by making some comment about doing it later in the day. The second time I passed by, the same voice came again, "Come on, Fiona, have a go." I found myself being tempted, but at the same time was aware of a huge reluctance within. The gentle pottery lady was adept at reassurance, "Don't worry. Look, everyone has made a pot, none of them have failed." I looked at the long line of pots on the counter, all different in shapes and sizes. A stronger resistance built up inside of me, I did not want to make a pot! But the pressure to join in the fun was not going away!

As I got on the stool behind the wheel, sweat began to build up and all my muscles tightened as my inside was telling me that my clay was going to fly off the wheel through the window on the other side of the room. I would be the failure! By this time, everyone was encouraging me on and the more they did so, the more I reacted inside and wanted to run away!

I was determined that this piece of clay was going to stay on that wheel! It was as if my life depended on it. Silly, this was just a bit of clay, and what did it matter if it came off? But, to me at that time, the clay had to stay on, and as the wheel turned, I gripped the clay with all the strength I could muster. The time came when the potter said, "Now start bringing the clay upwards," showing me how to hold it. My muscles tightened up even more, when suddenly a hole appeared and my finger went clean through the clay. My instinct was to slam the whole thing down again, and with every bit of strength keep that clay on the wheel!

Another few spins, a bit of a dent in the middle, and phew, eventually the lady slowed the wheel down. What a relief! "There you are," said the kind lady, "you have made a pot!" as she placed it with the others on the windowsill.

There was nobody more relieved or exhausted as me when I got off that wheel. At least the clay had not whizzed off and gone through the window like my worst fears had told me. I felt no elation towards the pot I had made, other than that the clay was in one piece on the shelf! What was all that about? Well, I had given it a go at least!

I had absolutely no idea what God was doing that day. I had no prior plan or thought about it. To me, I was just drawn into 'having a go' with the new pottery wheel. However, without my realising it, God had been at work.

It was some time after this course, but definitely linked to that event, that something began to emerge from within me. It was a desire to paint. Coincidentally, a new class opened in our town, *Painting for Beginners and Improvers*. An unexpected deep desire came up from within to join, which I did. Since then I have been loving playing with the colours, watching the water make amazing designs and patterns on the paper, learning the techniques with the brushes and the fun of the journey in painting a picture. This was me! It is now nine years on from that initial breakthrough moment of attending my first class and I am as hooked as ever!

Drawing and painting have opened a new world for me of finding time to just 'be,' to have rest and to meet new friends. The day on the pottery wheel was a day that something of the battle with fear to just 'have a go' was broken. A fear of failure I did not know was there, was released. I am so grateful to God and want to encourage anyone with these kinds of fears and inhibitions to dare to move out of your comfort zone and perhaps hitherto pronouncements on yourself, that you are 'not that type' or 'cannot do that' or 'won't go anything near this', and allow God to use new ventures to break inner controls you don't even know are there.

I had been struggling with having the right attitude towards all the responsibilities I was carrying. I was becoming irritable with people. I was also spending a great deal of time in other people's problems. God knew I needed an antidote, something to bring balance and fresh life to me. It is at these times of entering into creative activities that we are being refilled, re-energised and renewed in our ability to give out sacrificially to others. It is a redemptive gift which keeps giving.

"

A redemptive gift which keeps giving

Surprises!

My husband Peter, as a leader and a visionary, has always carried a great deal of responsibilities together with the problems that inevitably accompany them. It seemed to me that there was a never-ending mountain of issues to tackle, and as I watched him working late into the night, my heart ached.

I found myself praying, "Lord, what is it that Peter can have? Something just for him that would be a blessing and bring joy to him in his life?" I was falling fast asleep in bed when into my thinking came a clear thought, 'a black Labrador!' I quickly determined that this was impossible, so when I joked with the team at work the following day about the funny thought I had received, I fully expected them to laugh and agree it was impossible.

We travelled quite a lot and had serious responsibilities. Yet, here I was receiving a resounding affirmation to the whole idea! In fact, one of the group immediately did some research and came back with the outcome: there was a litter of black Labrador puppies not far away, we could go and see them! Peter's birthday was coming up and I thought, after the initial surprise, his common sense would override any wrong decision and put the idea to bed. It was going to be a fun visit whereby Peter would have a surprise, he would go not knowing where he was going and with a tea towel over his head, until we were ready to show him the surprise litter! I grew increasingly nervous as the time came and was more amazed that Peter was willing to take part in this escapade not knowing the end result.

The Day Came!

Peter looked at me in incredulity. The look said it all, "Do you mean it? Are you crazy? What's all this about?" I waited while he moved towards the litter and eventually picked up a pup. His face lit up; he had fallen in love! Harris came home to our house a couple of weeks later. And Harris had his way of keeping Peter absorbed in fun rather than work. God knew best what Peter needed!

I watched as, of an evening, Peter would come through the door, drop his brief case and be on the floor playing with Harris! Harris became his lifelong pal. Walking, playing, training, tactile stroking and not least meeting new people opened up a whole new world of joy. Our black Labrador Harris was one of God's gifts and surprises as he brought a new dimension to enrich our life.

Harris lived out his life in grand style with many friends helping out, and now we have Barney, another black Labrador who continues to bring all the life and fun to us that Harris began. We have a wonderful Father God who knows each of us and what we need. His plans are good as He redeems things which are lost to us.

More than a Brain

One poignant story came from a man we will call Arthur. When Arthur came on our creativity course, he was extremely depressed and expressed real despair at always having had to do what his parents or teachers wanted him to do. He had a fine intellect and brain and told us that he was always fast tracked in his school, university and career. However, this left a legacy of depression because there was more to who Arthur was than his intellect.

Thankfully, God does not define us by our intellect. Our intellect is a gift, but we are more than the sum of a gift, whether that is a gift of music, hospitality, motherhood or whatever. God sees the person in their entirety, and their need for variance and expression outside of gifting. It is a sad thing when a gift becomes something others just use and want from us, rather than accepting the person with the gift.

We often see the gifting within a person dominate their whole lives, and the person has somehow lost themselves as a result.

I heard a story on the news recently of an Olympic athlete. She had won gold medals for her particular sport, a tremendous achievement, but she had needed to take a year off for personal reasons. In her interview on the television, she spoke of how doing jigsaws had enabled her to find restoration. I could see how the intensity and drive to become an Olympic champion could crowd out other aspects of human need. It can be the same for any intense work we do. It is no wonder so many mental health issues arise when there is no creative release from all the pressures of life.

During the course, we encouraged Arthur to join in and do something creative. He had great difficulty in finding any reason for doing such seemingly non-essential and simplistic things. It was a completely alien concept for him. Eventually, it was the jewellery workshop that took his eye. At the end of the course, there was not a dry eye in the house as Arthur explained how he just wanted to make something for his wife and daughters. He wept as he shared how he wanted to give them something of himself to tell them he loved them. Arthur was going beyond his intellect, and his crushed human spirit was coming to life. He was bonding from deep within and not simply as an intellectual exercise. What a release!

> God was bringing a redemptive healing to his years of loss

Arthur found that by spending time choosing beads and working them together, God was bringing a redemptive healing to his years of loss — the years where he had been unable to express himself outside of his intellectual capacity. The joy and smile on his face as he showed the necklaces he had made to fellow course members said it all. God was giving back the years the locusts had eaten and bringing a wonderful expression of true and genuine love into Arthur's life and into his family.

Out of the Box

The redemptive power of God's love is always at work, and quite often takes us by surprise when we least expect it, or least can plan it. God can never be manipulated, and it is impossible for Him to manipulate us, it is not in His character. Trisha, a lady who was receiving help at our Centre for very deep and cruel abuse in her life, joined our creativity team as a volunteer. Trisha had been on one of our monthly modular weekend courses. When the time came for the *Healing Through Creativity* vision to go further afield, Trisha signed up to join us on a trip to Israel.

Running the *Healing Through Creativity* course in Israel was one of the most significant times we have had as a ministry. Many people from local fellowships joined in with great joy. We had no problem helping Jewish people to believe they are creative. Hebraic thinking, artistic gifting and natural creative expression came easily and taught us many things! It was a joy to share with Jew, Arab and Gentile believers how God wants to use creativity to heal the hearts of His children.

God is in the Business of Redeeming and Restoring His Family

Following on from the course in Israel, we had the joy of a tourist trip in Jerusalem to Hezekiah's tunnel. Everyone was excited to be going underground to traverse this amazing tunnel, which was carved out of solid rock deep beneath the surface of Jerusalem. It was built to carry water from the Gihon Spring to the Pool of Siloam, and so prevent any besieging armies from being able to benefit from the spring's abundant water supply. The tunnel is over 500 metres long and very narrow in places.

As we neared the entrance to the tunnel, I was aware that Trisha was reticent about going in and was beginning to panic. "I'm not going in there," she declared. We immediately reassured her, telling her she did not need to and if she would like, we could walk back up to the top and wait for the others. She stood still for a moment and then took a deep breath and continued into the tunnel.

Later in the day, back at the hotel, Trisha told us of an extraordinary encounter she had with Jesus whilst in the tunnel. As a child, she had been cruelly tied and put in dark, cold places with water running through. She had long buried the memories in her subconscious. In agreeing to go into Hezekiah's tunnel, her panic increased but God met her in this very place and took away the fear and panic. Her lifelong fear of tunnels and wells was brought to peace and healed.

What an amazing Redeemer God is! He took Trisha all the way to Israel. She was being obedient to Him and He poured back into her a most special and intimate healing in Israel. The radiance on Trisha's face said it all, she was overjoyed. What an encounter, and what a lesson in how God works out of the box of our thinking.

Beauty

Looking at a river, the ocean, mountains, a flower, bird or indeed any living thing, we see incredible order, detail and beauty. God speaks to us through this beauty, it is one of the main ways He communicates. You cannot go far in Scripture

without creation being used to describe His nature and character.

Every human being has the capacity to behold beauty. This to me is the evidence that God created the heavens and the earth. Otherwise what is the point of beauty, it has no purpose.

God created the highest form of beauty within humanity. Beauty is priceless and beyond description. When God revealed in Isaiah 61 that the coming of Jesus would bring 'beauty for ashes', He was declaring something extraordinary, a divine exchange.

Sarah's life, where all the pain and injustice had piled on top of her, was transformed. Sarah's beauty emerged for all to see. "I now know my Heavenly Father loves me and nothing else matters," she declared. Far from a 'religious mantra' this was the truth and evidence of a deep security and solidity. Sarah's bright and bouncy eyes and personality have remained steadfast. Thirteen years ago, Sarah made appointments with both her psychiatrist and doctor, she no longer needed her lifetime psychiatric disability pension or the drugs which came alongside. She has never needed them since, and for all who know her, she is a beautiful person full of life. Sarah gives Jesus all the glory for what only He could do.

Jesus has brought beauty for ashes for countless lives as He has done for Sarah. What a divine exchange as He transforms our pain into a garden of beauty if we allow Him.

> I will restore to you the years that the swarming locust has eaten.
>   (JOEL 2:25)

Chapter 8

FEARFULLY AND WONDERFULLY MADE – IT ALL MAKES SENSE!

We are 'fearfully and wonderfully made' (Psalm 139:14). The Bible tells us we have a spirit, a soul and a body (1 Thessalonians 5:23), and there are many references to our human spirit:

> The human spirit is the lamp of the LORD that sheds light on one's inmost being. (PROVERBS 20:27)

> But it is the spirit in a person, the breath of the Almighty, that gives them understanding. (JOB 32:8)

> The Spirit himself testifies with our spirit that we are God's children. (ROMANS 8:16)

The Spirit of GOD has made me, and the breath of the Almighty gives me life. (Job 33:4)

In teaching *Healing Through Creativity*, I recognised a need for people to understand that our Creator God made us with correlating physical and spiritual senses: the physical senses of our bodies and the spiritual senses of our human spirit, and that our creativity is expressed through both our physical and spiritual senses.

One of the most wonderful aspects of being human is our sensitivity. Where does it come from and how does it work? We are three-dimensional beings and experience life in much more than simply black and white. We see in colour, and our physical and spiritual senses respond to our environment, our circumstances and to the people we are with.

Our senses are part of how we live and breathe from the moment of our conception to the moment of our passing. Continually at work, they are like antennae constantly putting out their 'feelers' making sense of the world around us, feeding us information and giving us feelings, so that we have the means to make choices with our free will. Most crucially, our senses tell us if something is safe or if it is dangerous. This is true in both the physical and the spiritual realms.

Touch

Touching delivers to our brain a treasure-chest of information! Touch tells us if something is hot, cold, sticky, smooth, rough, prickly, powdery, wet, dry, delicate, furry, sloppy, dead or alive! It is through touch and dexterity that we make things happen, for example through music, gardening, sport, cooking, mending, hobbies and work. Touch is also a vital part of how we know and connect to our own body.

Humanly, we are wired to touch each other in appropriate ways. Human physical touch can bring comfort and kindness, it is powerful in the expression of our sexuality. God created human touching so that we can both bond with ourselves and others. God did not intend us to be alone (Genesis 2:18).

The physical realm we live in is reflective of the spiritual realm where, ultimately, we will dwell for eternity. 1 Samuel 10:26 tells us about those whose hearts 'God had touched.' In relationship with God, He can touch our spirits and we can reach out to touch Him. This is not in the physical, but rather it is an expression of the intimacy of our 'spiritual man'. We can also be aware that God has touched our spirits, which can then motivate our hearts to respond to Him.

When Jesus touches us, it changes everything – a vista, a perspective, an attitude, a situation, our circumstances. In relationship with God, His touch is expressed through His Holy Spirit bringing a powerful connection to Him and His work in our lives. We too can touch Him through our lives and our prayers.

A lady we will call Maria wrote to us following her time on the course. She felt God prompting her to do so and as a result of sharing her story, many people have been blessed by receiving encouragement and seeing how powerfully God's creativity in us brings breakthrough. This is what she told us in her letter:

> I felt to write a journal and in it I recorded what I felt God was speaking to me:
>
> "Maria, my child, my dear child, how I cherish you. You are precious to me and my heart rejoices over you. I have lit a fire in your heart, and it will consume all that is not of me.
>
> "Today my little one, is your 'splat' day, a day of healing and great rejoicing. No one can take this from you. My love will pour out as you let go. Don't inhibit yourself when you 'splat.' You are in a very hard nut which will only break open fully if you let go. Don't hang on to the inside

In relationship with God, He can touch our spirits and we can reach out to touch Him

of the shell. I will not hurt you as I crack it open. I see you laughing, and I see you crying but no longer will you hide deep in your heart the hurt and pain. That root is coming out today as I will not allow it to remain.

"I am your loving Father and I will have great joy in my heart as you 'splat' and enjoy releasing you from your hard shell. Rejoice my daughter, know me as Father."

Maria drew a picture of herself placed inside a nutshell. Outside of the shell was a very big hand coming down towards it.

The next picture was of the shell broken into many pieces with a little girl (Maria) emerging. The hand coming down was turned around in a protective way over her. Maria wrote the words on the picture: "I went 'splat' and the Lord went 'CRACK!'"

I 'splat'! I did it!!! I poured paint onto paper out on the Grange lawn and I knelt down, raised my hands high and came down 'splat' onto the paint, shouting a victory cry as I did this repeatedly with onlookers cheering, laughing and applauding. The Lord came down with His mighty hand and, 'Crack!' my shell was broken. "Yes, my dear child, your shell was broken, not just cracked open but shattered to many pieces. You will never be enclosed like that again. Trust me, trust in me. I am your ever-loving Father, you are precious to me, call me Father. Trust in your Father."

Maria went on to write to us and send us her journal pages opposite to encourage others. This is what she said in her letter.

Thank you again for your course *God's Creativity in You*. I was the one who had to 'splat', the desire started on Saturday and just grew and grew. I knew I had to 'splat' before I went home. Then on Sunday morning during my quiet time,

3.7.99 P.M.

I 'splat'! I did it!! I did it!!! I poured paint onto paper out on the Grange lawn and I knelt down, raised my hands high and came down 'splat' onto the paint, shouting a victory cry as I did this repeatedly with onlookers cheering, laughing and applauding

The Lord came down with His mighty hand and 'Crack' my shell was broken

'Yes, my dear child, your shell was broken, not just cracked open but shattered to many peices you will never be enclosed like that again, never again. Trust me, trust in me, I am your everloving Father I will never let you out of my sight you are most precious to me. Call me Father, call me Abba, call me Daddy. Trust in your Daddy.

I Went
'SPLAT!'
and
The LORD
went

'CRACK!'

the Lord spoke. I now feel prompted to send you a copy of the last pages of my journal which tell of the difference in my life since coming.

I now feel a confidence I have never had before. I saw it in others but not in me. I now find myself being pleased with my own work, even complimenting myself which is a great shock to me. In the past when people have commented how good something I have done is, I now find myself replying "Yes, isn't it" instead of picking bones with it or complaining of how difficult it was to do.

Even my housework seems to have been affected by the healing I have received. It no longer feels like a chore, but it actually excites me, and I have such plans for the décor that it is going to work out this time and not turn out a bit of a disaster.

Thank you again, you are truly hearing Abba Father as He seeks to heal His children. May God bless the work you are doing in His name.

— Maria, 1999

Sight

To be able to see is indeed a miraculous gift. The eye is the creative genius of a loving Creator God. Sight opens us up to a world of colour, shape, light, dark, movement. With our sight we can identify people and creation around us. We have the pleasure of absorbing the magnificent world – a rainbow, the stars, diamonds, seasons, exquisite flowers and sunsets; watching our children and grandchildren growing up; or enjoying a football match! The list is endless!

Sadly, our eyes can also see ugliness and evil coming from the influence of the god of this world and tempting our humanity to all manner of distortion, filth and ungodliness. Creator God, however, designed the eye to behold beauty. Beauty is the reflection here on earth of who He is. He is utterly beautiful, and we have the eyes of our spirit to discern this through His creation and in relationship with Him. The Bible is clear that God has shown Himself to us through creation and we are without excuse for not seeing and recognising that it is from Him.

> The wrath of God is being revealed from heaven against all the godlessness and wickedness of people, who suppress the truth by their wickedness, since what may be known about God is plain to them, because God has made it plain to them. For since the creation of the world God's invisible qualities—his eternal power and divine nature— have been clearly seen, being understood from what has been made, so that people are without excuse.
>
> (REVELATION 1:18)

> Open my eyes that I may see wonderful things in your law.
> (PSALM 119:18)

> But the eyes of the LORD are on those who fear him, on those whose hope is in his unfailing love.
> (PSALM 33:18)

Hearing

The sound of a thundering waterfall, waves lapping at the shore, a fire crackling, a powerful engine, the wind rustling in the trees, a musical instrument; or hearing humanity with all its clamouring chatter, laughter, and even grief, brings appreciation of life. We take sounds we hear for granted. For those whose hearing is impaired or who are deaf, this is a great loss. Remarkably, however, when one sense is lost, other senses increase in order to compensate.

Our spiritual intuition and hearing can never be lost. The hearing in our human spirit cannot be removed. Even a person who is physically unconscious can hear/sense truth in their human spirit, in the same way a baby who is in the womb without their matured physical brain, can 'hear' through spiritual sensing. A baby can hear and know whether it is welcome and wanted and, conversely, can know if the environment they are in is full of fear and hostility.

Comfort is received through hearing familiar sounds and voices. Hearing music touches and comforts us, both physically and spiritually. God's Word is His medicine for our inner beings and brings His promises to us when we hear it, not just as physical words, but through the ears of the spirit as well.

> "What no eye has seen, what no ear has heard, and what no human mind has conceived" — the things God has prepared for those who love him — these are the things God has revealed to us by his Spirit. The Spirit searches all things, even the deep things of God.
>
> (1 CORINTHIANS 2:9-10)

> My sheep listen to my voice; I know them, and they follow me. I give them eternal life, and they shall never perish; no one will snatch them out of my hand.   (JOHN 10:27-28)

> Whoever has ears, let them hear what the Spirit says to the churches. To the one who is victorious, I will give the right to eat from the tree of life, which is in the paradise of GOD.
>
> (REVELATION 2:7)

Our spiritual and physical senses contribute to who we are and how we respond to the world around us. Most of all, it is through these senses that God the Father wants to speak and relate with us. His plan is that we should hear His truth, given through His Word and through His creation. He is not distant from us, and He hears us and our heart's cry. It is through relationship with Jesus that His Holy Spirit is able to reveal things to us through our spiritual senses, which in turn bring truth and peace to us in the physical realm.

Taste

If you have ever lost your sense of taste through having a cold or for some other reason, you will know how bland and uninteresting food can be. It has lost its vital element. Taste is something that enriches life and brings enormous blessing.

We can taste if something is sweet or sour, salty or spicy, fruit or vegetable. Our taste buds tell us something about our own personhood, "Yum yum!" to cinnamon, or "Yuk!" to garlic, for example, or whatever our preferences are. Being able to taste is another of God's gifts to us. He did not need to create us with taste. Food could have been just a matter of keeping us alive with no enjoyment factor. Yet, in His kindness and goodness, He created an abundance of food source, out of which many more foods could be created with an infinite variety of taste and flavours!

It amazes me that God created a hen which could produce one of the most valuable and versatile foods on the planet – an egg. The egg makes it possible for us to enjoy so many different foods, for example, omelettes, cakes, quiches, custards or sauces. We eat eggs fried, boiled, scrambled, soft and hard, hot and cold.

The fruits of the trees, bushes and vines bring us plentiful variety. Each fruit is intricately and beautifully fashioned, not just to our taste, but to our eyes with the colour, texture and shape.

If we ever doubted that God made us for relationship, we can see in our relationship to the earth and land, how through food we are inextricably interdependent.

Nowadays we live in a world where travel to far flung places is possible and the exporting/importing of food from different cultures is free flowing. We have the privilege of tasting the culinary delights of many different nations. Cookery programmes on television are at their height of popularity, as we become intrigued by how various tastes and food sources blend together to make the most mouth-watering dishes known to man! It is astonishing to watch the creativity of the world's leading chefs and cooks. How can we not bow down and give glory to the Creator, who forged all these things through His creative genius for our enjoyment and pleasure?

God says:

> Taste and see that the LORD is good; blessed is the one who takes refuge in him.　　　　　　　　(PSALM 34:8)

> How sweet are your words to my taste, sweeter than honey to my mouth.　　　　　　　　(PSALM 119:103)

> Like newborn babies, crave pure spiritual milk, so that by it you may grow up in your salvation, now that you have tasted that the Lord is good.　　　　　　　　(1 PETER 2:2-3)

We have spiritual senses as well as physical ones. God invites us to taste Him. Taste gives us flavour, appetite and eventually fulfils our need of nourishment and strength through food. God is giving each of us the invitation to taste of Him so that He may fill up our spirit with a wealth of good things, nourish and fulfil us.

Smell

Our Labrador dog can definitely detect a myriad of doggy smells that we can't smell. But, as human beings, our own sense of smell is amazing and very sophisticated. What we smell can give us vital information that we need to know.

When our septic tank is full, we are warned by the smell of

drains! We are alerted to danger through the smell of gas or burning. Smell tells us when something is cooked or cooking. We know what is cooking by the smell. It could be freshly baked bread, a cake or a curry!

Outdoor smells tell us what is going on. It maybe newly mown grass, harvest time, the smell of the seaside or of the local farmer spreading manure!

We are designed to enjoy smell and to take it in at great depth, especially perfume. Our appetite is awoken by the things we physically smell. Our physical senses reflect something back to us of our human spirit where we have spiritual senses. Our senses are perfectly designed by God for relationship with Him and with each other.

It is interesting that when Jesus was born, the wise men brought to Him precious gifts not only of gold, but frankincense and myrrh.

> Mary took about a pint of pure nard, an expensive perfume; she poured it on Jesus' feet and wiped his feet with her hair. And the house was filled with the fragrance of the perfume.
> (JOHN 12:3)

We see from the above that a beautiful smell meant a great deal to the Lord Jesus. He created it and in bringing it back to Him, He knew by the smell, the cost and beautiful spirit of the giver.

> We are to God the pleasing aroma of Christ.
> (2 CORINTHIANS 2:15)

Creative Walking

When I was young, we sang a hymn which included the words, 'He walks with me and He talks with me, and He tells me I am His own ...' (Merle Haggard)

At the very beginning of our *Healing Through Creativity* vision, we sensed that the outdoor world would hold a big key in releasing the power of God to touch people's lives. We decided to offer people the opportunity to be taken on a creative walk, and whatever the weather (we have a lot of rain in Lancashire!) encouraged them that it would be good to experience God's creation in a tangible way, and in doing so, sense and be close to Him.

When people are oppressed and depressed, their spirit is crushed and downtrodden. Outwardly life can become an existence, a job to do and a far reach from the fullness of life Jesus told us He would bring.

> The thief comes only to steal and kill and destroy. I have come that they may have life and have it to the full.
>
> (JOHN 10:10)

On our courses we found that many had been brought up to be aware only of the responsibility life brings. It was as though their inner beings were gasping for life and breath. All manner of sicknesses, both physical and mental health issues, were crowding out the simplicity of life. But this can become easily lost on the treadmill and pain in this fallen world.

One of the symptoms of a crushed human spirit is the inability to be inspired and behold beauty, to have the freedom to express and enjoy the fullness of physical sensing, let alone spiritual sensing.

As a team helping Sarah, we were delighted with the opportunity to leave the centre and go out for a drive or a walk. Our anticipation was that this would be a break and blessing for Sarah. Although she accepted the idea, it was soon obvious that she didn't share our excitement. In time it dawned on us that she viewed it as just another 'job to be done.' It held no joy or anticipation for her.

> "
> One of the
> symptoms
> of a crushed
> human spirit
> is the inability
> to be inspired
> and behold
> beauty

Whilst out in the stunning countryside around Ellel Grange Centre with its rivers, canal, hills and moorlands, we would be full of thankful expression to the Lord for everything we saw. But Sarah would remain quiet and we were soon aware that she was completely disconnected from the place where she could appreciate such things. She would remain tense throughout. The trees, views and beauty had held no significance for her.

The creative walks on our *Healing Through Creativity* courses are extremely popular. We saw that there were many people who were struggling with life's issues and had lost themselves and their God-given ability to soak up and behold beauty and allow God the Father to speak to them through it. It seemed a dimension of their spirituality had been lost, and in its place had come a flat 'black and white' response.

If we asked, "What do you see?" the answer would come back, "A tree, a mountain, a river," or whatever the person could physically see. There was no meaning behind the words. Digging further, there would be an inability to express emotion and feeling behind the view, to appreciate the splendour, the delicacy, the strength, the colour, the smell, shape, texture etc. The only way to describe it was 'a disconnect' to something beyond fact.

So, our creative walks were designed to walk with God in His garden, and to ask Him to touch and release our spirits to 'drink in' of His creation, that He designed for us and gave to us as His created ones. We ask Him to reveal Himself through His creation: His nature and character, and He loves to do this. It is one of the primary ways God speaks to us, and when He speaks to us personally, this is healing!

With Sarah, we spent time talking between ourselves of the intricacies we saw in the birds, the insects, the flowers, and through our absorbing the magnificent views and our enjoyment of being out in God's big garden, Sarah began to heal. We did not do this for any contrived purpose, it was a natural response. At the time, we did not know it, but God was gradually touching Sarah's innate crushed creativity, and He was awakening her appetite for beauty.

Sarah's Story:

On countless occasions, we spoke with Sarah the truth about her real identity. And that through Jesus she belonged to God, that He held her in His everlasting arms and would never leave her or forsake her. But our words didn't seem to penetrate, and Sarah would continue in her striving to work at receiving her healing, which kept her in a constant state of anxiety, believing that she just wasn't doing enough and needed to try harder.

It was on one of our drives through the Lancashire countryside, as she was looking out of the car window, that God spoke to her from Scripture. He told her to 'Look at the birds of the air; they do not sow or reap or store away in barns, and yet your heavenly Father feeds them. Are you not much more valuable than they? Can any one of you by worrying add a single hour to your life?' (Matthew 6:26-27). It was a pivotal moment for Sarah, as His Word dropped right into her crushed and broken spirit, and the realisation dawned on her that she didn't really have to strive and worry anymore. She had a Heavenly Father who loved her, and tenderly watched over and cared for her, and He was working out His plan to heal and restore her.

Look at the birds of the air; they do not sow or reap or store away in barns, and yet your heavenly Father feeds them. Are you not much more valuable than they? Can you by worrying add a single hour to your life?

(MATTHEW 6:26-27)

And why do you worry about clothes? See how the flowers of the field grow. They do not labor or spin. Yet I tell you that not even Solomon in all his splendor was dressed like one of these.

(MATTHEW 6:28-29)

Are not two sparrows sold for a penny? Yet not one of them will fall to the ground outside your Father's care. And even the very hairs of your head are all numbered. So don't be afraid; you are worth more than many sparrows.

(MATTHEW 10:29-31)

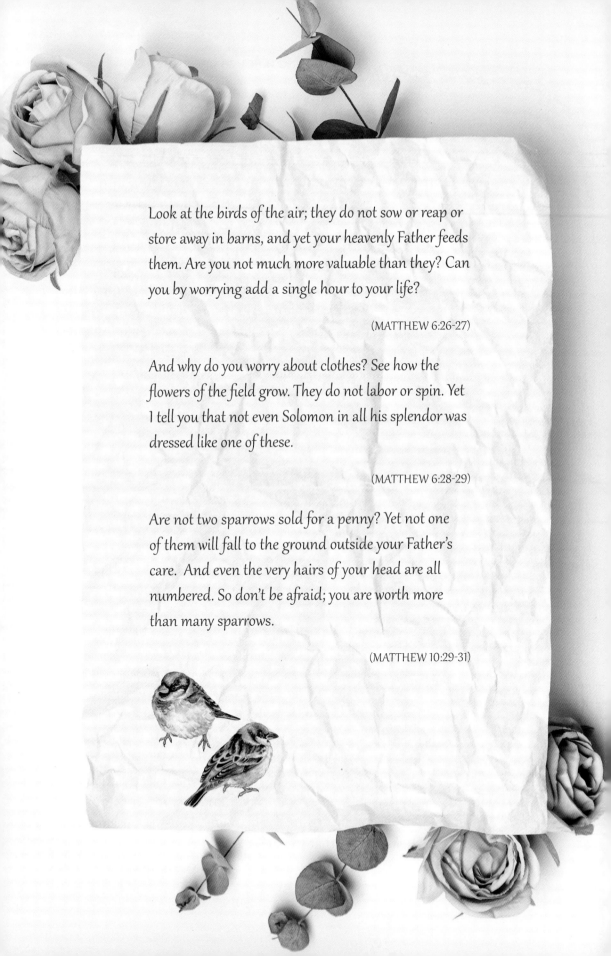

God's Garden

There is always a leader for our creative walks. The leader's enthusiasm for nature, helps others to catch it also. Some people have simply never had a parent to open their eyes and really see. They have never had the opportunity or time to walk with God the Father through His garden and see it through His eyes. When our breath is taken away by a view, we are simply mirroring back to our Heavenly Father the beauty we see in Him. How wonderful it is that as His children, we can bless His heart and have that child/father relationship with Him.

It is awe inspiring hearing some of the stories of what people have felt and heard from God in deeply personal ways on a creative walk, that has brought about healing and transformation:

I saw a tiny insect struggling to climb on a leaf. It occurred to me that that was me, my struggle to keep up with life. The thought immediately came that God made the whole tree and each leaf was designed by Him. He saw me in my struggle and would help me and provide for me. God is SO big!

A young man called Johnny went on the creative walk and, as the group were walking through the beautiful grounds at the Centre, he was wrestling in his thinking to discover and truly embrace his identity in Christ. A little boy who was there with his parents, was walking behind Johnny and asked if Johnny would lift him onto his shoulders. Johnny was a bit annoyed, but said, "Yes." As they walked together he became aware of the stark contrast between the way he made the relationship with Father God so complicated, and how this little boy just marvelled at everything, as he pointed out with excitement, "Look how big that tree is", "Look at that pretty flower" etc. It broke something in Johnny as he received deep revelation

about his own identity as a child of God in relationship with His Heavenly Father.

God's Touch

Fresh revelation of just how 'fearfully and wonderfully' God made us, how much He cares for us, watches over and provides for us, is expressed through our God-given physical and spiritual senses. Even though I have separated them out above, they are all interlinked as an integral whole within our spirit, soul and body unity.

We only need to see an ice cream sundae for our saliva to run as taste buds open up! It just takes the smell of some freshly baked bread for our appetite to really get going! We see a cosy fire and we want to draw near and feel the warmth. We look at a glorious sunset and gasp in physical and spiritual agreement. The skies open us up to see beyond ourselves. How can we not see and worship Creator God whose nature and character is imprinted so indelibly on us and all nature?

> We look at a glorious sunset and gasp in physical and spiritual agreement

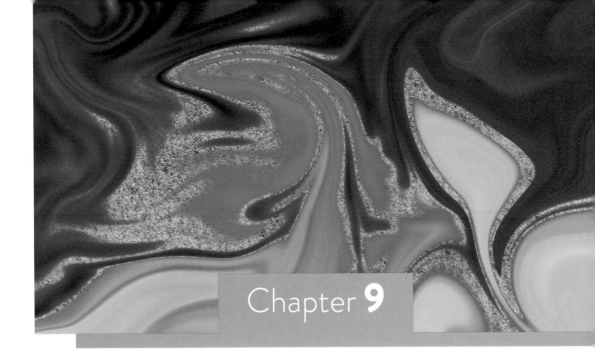

Chapter 9

CREATIVE CONNECTIONS

God (Father, Son and Holy Spirit) is inter-relational. He lives in a completely harmonious relationship with Himself, without any vying for position. All He created has protocol and order. In the last chapter we saw the principle of how He created us with interlinking senses integral to our body, soul and spirit.

In order to have a healthy balanced life for developing our creative potential, we need to be aware of how important it is to be connected to our own personhood, our bodies plus our thoughts, opinions, emotions, desires, needs and (not forgetting) our clear capacity to be sinful.

Life is full of connections! It is impossible to avoid connections, and they have everything to do with the creative people we are. We plug in the power and can instantly use a machine which sucks up dust, dirt, hair or spillage. Whoever invented that deserves a medal! We can dry and style our hair with a hairdryer; we can use cookers, dishwashers, lawn-mowers. The list is endless when it comes to the variety of mechanical and electronic devices now available, and all that electrical connection brings, in terms of light, heat and power.

The mobile phone, the computer with email and Skype, television and radio are powerful means of communication, bringing connection to the world and people around us, some of whom are far beyond our physical reach. We are instantly connected to news, with scenes of joy, or alternatively, tragedy and, even, horror.

Our homes hold powerful emotional connections to familiar objects through photographs, letters, memora-bilia, gifts received, items from a past age or a holiday we have been on. Vehicles, cars, trains, ships and aeroplanes all provide transport and connect us to new places, cultures and experiences.

Then there are, perhaps the most powerful connections of all, the connections made in relationship to those we love and trust. Conversely, there are the connections which come with difficult relationships, where there maybe mistrust and difficulty, pain and brokenness. Relational connec-tions always bring an element of surprise or shock since it is impossible to predetermine or control someone else, and how they might connect to us in either a wanted or unwanted way.

Physically, our bodies are full of connections. Our brains are connected to our thoughts. Our hearts are pumping blood around our body without which we could not live. Our joints, muscles and limbs are held in careful balance and tension, and we know it when they are not working as they should! Our physical senses translate those connections and realities to our own life and into relationships with others.

Creation is full of connections, and the consequences

of these connections bring life, or they can be destructive. For example, the sun brings lifegiving warmth to the earth, nothing can live without the sun, yet if there is too much exposure to it, or if there is no water source, it can bring death. All of life needs to be in appropriate balance. We are interconnected to the environment around us. It is not a matter of choice, we need this relationship, for example, for food to eat, water to drink and air to breathe.

It is not rocket science to deduce that connections of many kinds are vital for any source of health and wellbeing. Some we can choose, like food sources and others we cannot, such as the weather. It is good to be aware of connections and the inter-relationship we have within ourselves, with others and with the world around us. From this perspective, we can also understand more of how we are made and our human needs.

When God created us, He placed immense potential within His creation. He gave us our unique ability to grow, invent and to gain understanding with increasing levels of knowledge. Since the Garden of Eden, when Adam and Eve chose to disobey God, we have lived with all the consequences of the knowledge of good and evil that was opened up to us. With the knowledge came responsibility and danger because sin and death had now entered, and all creation was subject to it (Romans 8:20). It is impossible for us to be disconnected from our sinful nature and a fallen world. We are also warned not to be ignorant of Satan's devices and disconnected from this danger.

As human beings we are all unique individuals who contribute to the rich tapestry of life. God knows that, both individually and corporately we have the capacity to change the world for good. Yet, because of our limitations, weaknesses and fallen (sinful) nature, we also have the dangerous capacity to bring destruction. Currently, we are seeing on a wide scale the scourge of plastic waste crippling our environment and the beauty of the natural world.

> " connections of many kinds are vital for any source of health and wellbeing

My son, if you accept my words
and store up my commands within you,
turning your ear to wisdom
and applying your heart to understanding –
indeed, if you call out for insight
and cry aloud for understanding,
and if you look for it as for silver
and search for it as for hidden treasure,
then you will understand the fear of the Lord
and find the knowledge of GOD.
For the LORD gives wisdom;
from his mouth come knowledge and understanding.
He holds success in store for the upright,
he is a shield to those whose way of life is blameless,
for he guards the course of the just
and protects the way of his faithful ones.

Then you will understand what is right and just
and fair – every good path.
For wisdom will enter your heart,
and knowledge will be pleasant to your soul.
Discretion will protect you,
and understanding will guard you.

Wisdom will save you from the ways of wicked men,
from men whose words are perverse,
who have left the straight paths
to walk in dark ways,
who delight in doing wrong
and rejoice in the perverseness of evil,
whose paths are crooked
and who are devious in their ways.

(PROVERBS 2:1-15)

Jesus said, "Your father the devil ... does not stand in
the truth, because there is no truth in him.
When he lies, he speaks according to his own nature,
for he is a liar and the father of lies"

(JOHN 8:44 NRSV)

Jesus said, "I am the way and the truth and the life.
No one comes to the Father except through me"

(JOHN 14:6)

Massive Disconnect

To lose connection to God, to our ourselves or to an understanding of the work of the enemy, leaves us vulnerable. To gain understanding is part of receiving wisdom and security. It is the enemy who tempts us away from relationship with Creator God and in turn away from being connected to our legitimate God given needs.

Bonding – a Vital Ingredient to Connection

One of God's designs for necessary connection is relational bonding. We all live with a degree of inadequacy, insecurity and inferiority. It may manifest differently, but it is part of who we are, and as such we have a legitimate human need for connection and bonding with one another. Bonding is the most powerful need of all, it is akin to hunger. We need comfort, we need protection, we need reassurance and the affirmation that relational bonding brings. God has designed us with human needs. He did not create us to be God or an angel, he made us human beings with human needs. Bonding is a strength and blessing. Bondage on the other hand, can be the opposite, a weakening and a curse, behind which lies the deception of the enemy that God warns us about in His Word.

" bonding is the most powerful need of all

Bonding

This is Me!

We are created to have a right connection and bonding to ourselves, to know ourselves. The need of restoration often arises because a person has lost self-awareness. Learning to connect to our genuine needs is part of healing. Often these have been denied and disconnected from for all kinds of reasons. As a result, it is possible that part of our true identity has been lost and crushed out of recognition.

Chop and Block!

There came a time in Sarah's journey when we needed to help her see that trying to control the way God wanted to heal her, was not right. She had become so adept at covering over her needs and disconnecting from them that she became unaware she had them. When asked how she was, she would tell us she was fine, and she was not pretending. To her, disconnected from the inner issues, she was fine. It was easy to believe her conviction. Many times, we would wonder why she needed help. However, she could be talking as an articulate, together person one minute and, as if with the flick of a switch, the next minute we would be faced with sheer panic. The extremes were extraordinary.

As Sarah became more 'connected' to her own inner pain and need, she explained to us that she had developed an inner mechanism which she called 'chop and block.' This 'chop and block' took place within her mind, and she used it to avoid being connected to pain and hurt, but in doing so she was also blocking out her identity and legitimate human need. Reconnecting to her real needs was a battle for Sarah. It was a battle with her humanity, but it was also a spiritual battle with the enemy, who feeds fear into inner emptiness and uses this to drive people to fill the need in a false way, and to bring a dose of condemnation with it.

There is no empty place. The feeling might be emptiness, but the truth is that in this place is a need for connection. Separating from yourself, albeit sometimes subconsciously, brings about a disconnect which the enemy uses to bring condemnation and fear in order to control. Fear is a controlling emotion which if it builds up, acts like a volcano on the inside with possible seething emotions ready to burst.

Consequential defence and coping mechanisms will bring about all manner of 'disconnects.' These could be anything from denying the emotions there are to diverting the feelings with false comforts which could be alcohol or drugs. The fear of ourselves, keeps the separation in place to the real issue within. When connection comes, all manner of 'disconnects' can suddenly happen as the scramble to find ways of coping takes place.

Sarah was finding that instead of fear and the treadmill of 'chopping and blocking', the connection to her inner self despite there being pain and mess, brought peace to the turmoil. In truthful connection and embrace of herself Jesus was liberating her and with it hope and trust took root.

Truth will always stand and be a means of setting us free. The enemy, on the other hand, has no truth within him and his deceit and condemnation know no bounds in tempting us to swallow the hook of his lies. His primary goal is to separate us (rather than connect us) from God the Father and fill us with false love, false worship, substitute human fixers, false guilt and fear which controls rather than bringing peace and rest.

Connection to Truth

Through a creative outlet, many find an outward expression of an inward truth and find it is a safe way to allow it to emerge and become part of who they are. In asking the Holy Spirit to guide and bring truth, it may be a painful reality which is being faced but it is felt with what we describe as 'Holy pain,' which is healing and brings relief and release. The connection is healthy and restorative. It is then that a God-given healthy grief can flow for what has been lost and God's redemption is released.

Whilst sitting with one person, I asked them what is was that they wanted most from Jesus. Her answer was simple, "I just want the truth, I want to know the truth about me." There can be no better prayer that any of us can make and it will undermine and conquer the way the enemy causes disconnection. The fear of the issue is never as big as he makes it feel and nothing is impossible for God to heal and restore.

> Ah, Sovereign LORD, you have made the heavens and the earth by your great power and outstretched arm. Nothing is too hard for you. (JEREMIAH 32:17)

We all need ordinary connections to things that have remained unacknowledged, denied, pushed out of our sphere, determinedly placed in a box, things we have been unwilling or haven't wanted to face.

It can be very helpful to ask ourselves questions, such as, "Why am I feeling this way? ... Why do I hold this view? ... Why do I believe certain things? ... Why do I react or behave in a particular way? ... Why do I always do this or that?" A healthy connection to self-awareness is the road to restoration and healing and consequent maturity.

A Good Plumb Line

In years past, I attempted to decorate my daughter's bedroom. I had chosen a wallpaper with vertical stripes. In my inexperience, it had not occurred to me that the wall was not straight, and any wallpaper I was attaching would not hang from a 'true' vertical line. By the end of my efforts, I was aghast to see that the stripes on the wall had gradually gone 'off centre' and were distinctly crooked. I learnt the hard way, that I needed a plumb line, a simple weight of lead on the end of a piece of string which when held up from the ceiling would determine a straight line for my wallpaper to be aligned to.

How true it is in the spiritual realm also, that we need a plumb line to align our lives to. To make our own determination of where that plumb line should be, will lead us 'off centre' and into deception.

We need God's plumb line as our determiner of truth, otherwise our perspective will always be skewed according to the plumb line of how we see ourselves. Without a healthy bond within ourselves, and a right valuing of who we are and who we are becoming, we will also have difficulty with healthily bonding to others.

Holy Glue!

Putting wallpaper on the walls entails aligning it to a truthful plumb line, but it also necessitates a powerful glue for bonding the wallpaper to the wall. In a human sense, bonding is a necessary connection to others. It comes when we join in a unified way, for example through sharing tears, excitement or even dread. It might also be a shared experience such as giving birth, a hobby, sport, work, family. These are all powerful and rich elements of bonding which make up life. We are poorer without them. Ephesians 4:16 (NLT) tells us: 'As each part does its own special work, it helps the other parts grow, so that the whole body is healthy and growing and full of love.'

Bonding produces trust which is essential as the basis for authentic and true relationship. God created us for love, and that need is the very first one we experience in life, whether in the womb or later. It is a powerful source of sustenance and empowerment for living and one which God designed, ultimately to be filled and completed in relationship with Him.

For some people, bonding experiences have been at best shallow and, at their worst, painful with the result that the human spirit is crushed and, along with it, the expression of life. Although there may be many loving and kind people around to be with, isolation is at work on the inside producing fruits of mistrust, loneliness, fierce independence, withdrawal and a feeling of being misunderstood. With severe absence of healthy bonding comes false bonding, whereby there is an obsessional clinging onto something external, for example extreme attachment to another person, ritualistic routines, food or a particular way of life. The list is endless.

The good news is that God is a restorer and where these key elements of life have never been imparted, received and developed, He knows what we need. *Healing Through Creativity* is a wonderful way to build into our hearts authentic principles of trust and healthy bonding.

Divine Connection

It is common for people to be reluctant and fearful of connecting to God in a personal relationship. They may feel they have no right, He is too Holy or too distant or that they just do not know Him. It is also very common for people to fear God coming close to them in case He disapproves of them, punishes or rejects them. There may be a desire for someone else to pray in the belief that their prayers will be heard.

Prayer is most effective when the heart of the person who has come for help, reaches out for that divine connection. There is nothing more powerful than the cry of a lost child to their father. Those of us praying for another can add our agreement, lead a person to the place of prayer and encourage prayer. We can pray in the truth of Scripture and help bring faith and trust, but for true healing there must also be the divine connection to God by the person themselves.

Creativity provides so many ways for us to make connection to God. Usually it is through our silent or spoken prayers, but it can also come through journaling, writing of poems, singing, listening, silence, playing an instrument, reading, playing, creating something, and the list goes on ...

So often God uses the ordinary things in life to do the extraordinary. I love the way the barnacled shells brought such a powerful connection for Sarah. Now, on our courses, we are finding that there are a thousand and one things that God can use to bring about His divine connection!

In my previous book *Intercession and Healing: Breaking Through with God* (Sovereign World, 2008) I shared my passion about prayer which opens up the way for God to do what only He can do. The work of prayer brings Heaven down to Earth, and without it we are groping in the dark. It took me a while to comprehend how God also wanted to use creative elements to bring about His purposes. I wondered if I was going off track! Yet, the intercession and prayer at the forefront of all we did on *Healing Through Creativity* courses, was bringing in a harvest of solid fruit for God which was undeniable.

Ordinary Blockages

We all have hidden blockages of one kind or another and need the work of the Holy Spirit to bring about a connection with reality and our eventual release from the blockage. God sees what we don't. I have already shared my own story in this regard, about the release He brought through my potter's wheel experience.

I am so thankful to God that He knows what we need, and we can trust Him to bring connection to these needs. We will see, through the Illustrations and Stories in part 2, chapter 6, many examples of how this can take place through God's own vehicle for life – creativity!

FUN, PLAY AND IMAGINATION

Fun, play and imagination are at the heart of God's design to bring life. One of the first things a baby learns is to smile and chuckle. Playing with imagination follows on pretty swiftly as anything to hand becomes fun.

Laughter is one of God's best medicines! God created humour (Proverbs 17:22). We all need laughter as well as tears to be healthy. These are God-given emotions which form a part of who we are and how we express ourselves.

Some of us like slapstick humour, others enjoy comedy of a different kind. We all laugh at a child's funny conversation or ways. We laugh at a joke or a mishap. Laughter bonds people together in a shared experience.

For some people laughter has become trapped on the inside, it does not bubble up very easily and for others, not at all. Sarah told us that she learnt to manufacture her laughter and copy others. For her it was a miraculous day when spontaneous laughter came bubbling up from within and she experienced a powerful connection to herself.

Relating to Self

Throughout Sarah's life her predominant emotion was fear and panic. It would not be an exaggeration to say that Sarah's whole identity was lived out with the emotion of fear controlling every move. Now at Ellel Grange, playing on the floor with glue, paint and glitter, Sarah was daring to join in something which was just 'fun'. It had no right or wrong. This new experience of relaxation brought wonderful release.

Rather than fear controlling life, here was something designed to be enjoyable, restful and fun! At first Sarah hated it and another emotion rose up, that of anger. "If you are doing this for my sake," she blurted, "don't bother, it's a waste of time." It was time for Sarah to let go of her very tightly held control of fear and begin to find herself. The dirty shells were perfect to begin with, and as time went on new aspects of creative expression emerged. Cross stitch, jigsaws, piano playing, sewing, writing, reading, singing, walking, gardening and adventuring to new places, all became a natural part of Sarah being Sarah!

Finding herself through the play and fun

Far from being a waste of time, Sarah was finding herself through the play and fun. She was bonding to herself, trusting herself, and most importantly, liking herself! Chains of oppression with all their pseudo life guards were falling away. The hitherto solid belief that she was bad, melted as joy and life gushed up from within.

"Chains of oppression were falling away

Jesus said, "I have come that they may have life, and have it to the full "   (JOHN 10:10)

Life is for Living

Jasmine expressed her story this way, "God has been encouraging me to be creative, releasing me to enjoy myself and have fun and through it, He has been restoring my crushed spirit. He has used the gentleness of the creativity course to get in touch with me back to the moment of conception. God taught me to have patience, to have laughter and fun, telling me I truly belong to Him and that this was a special time just for myself. It was so healing to be part of family and be able to pass through barriers and not be judged."

> " in touch with myself right back to conception

Disconnecting is common for many people

Invisible Triggers

When Sarah felt she had got something wrong she would withdraw, disappearing into a protective shell inside herself. We were all left knowing something was amiss, and it became a futile exercise trying to 'connect' back to the Sarah who had been enjoying playing until that point. It was as if an invisible switch had gone off in her head.

Much later, we realised that it was something in the present that triggered directly into her subconscious areas of pain, that caused a disconnection to the play and fun taking place. Even Sarah herself could not have explained it, so deeply buried was the real issue. As Sarah learnt to listen to herself instead of repelling herself with panic and fear, she began to connect to her own pain, which in this situation was one of being cruelly punished for the slightest mistake.

Disconnecting is common for many people and happens when a subconscious trigger takes place. The result being that an intended trust or bond with your own self becomes impaired or even impossible. This then becomes a ground for lack of confidence or even self- hatred to breed and take root. The enemy loves this spiral.

Imperfection is Healing!

One day, whilst I was having fun and attempting to make something, I expressed great exasperation and frustration. Nothing had turned out the way I wanted! Another team member began laughing at my attempt. I began laughing too, what did it really matter that it was a funny shape, the glue did not stick in the right place and the finished result was less than I had envisioned. I had enjoyed the journey, the fun, the play and the companionship along the way.

Bonding in relationship comes in many ways. Learning to laugh at your own mistakes, learning to laugh with others at your own mistakes and learning to see that playing and experimenting is not about a life of perfection, but of having the freedom and joy of experimentation and imagination. Sarah told us that watching how the team bonded, played and gave each other the safety to make mistakes was deeply healing for her.

Sometimes when we were with Sarah, we played games with her. We experimented with colours and textiles, we went on outings which we called 'adventures'. We had ditched the 'planning' and were enjoying playing and having fun. Little did we know then, that God was going to take what we were learning far wider than we could have ever imagined!

> "
> We experimented with colours and textiles

Family Evenings

As a team, we were beginning to realise that many people have not experienced the joy of family as God intended it to be. On our Creativity events, I felt it was important that 'family' should be at the heart of all we did. After all, God is our Father and we are His children!

I am so grateful for the gifting God has placed within some people, of being able to make others laugh. We have two such men on our team at Ellel Grange. I am sure they could make a living as stand-up comedians! It was not long before we discovered that God was using their gifting to bring about a wonderful healing in many people's lives.

God's gift of humour

Creative sharing evenings are a time to share a joke, tell a story, dance, sing, do a funny sketch. It is never about being

One lady from a communist background described an immense freedom when she painted and Jesus showed her He enjoyed playing with her.

a 'world talent' although we often laugh as we talk about buying prime front circle seats for the elite performance!

On one occasion Bob (the man who painted the childlike boat picture) told his story of how he approached the clay modelling workshop with great ambition and enthusiasm. As Michelangelo had 'seen the angel in the marble and carved until he set him free', Bob saw the juggler in the lump of clay and was sure he could set him free too! Bob could hardly continue his story as peals of laughter bubbled up from within, punctuating his every word as he explained that no matter how much he cut and shaped and moulded he just couldn't find the juggler!

Bob wasn't staying at the Grange for the course but had booked in at a local bed and breakfast. He told us that overnight the Lord told him, it wasn't a juggler in the clay, but a snowman! Tears of laughter rolled down his face, and the whole room couldn't help but join in, roaring with laughter with him as he went on, "So, at breakfast I asked my landlady if she had a golf ball, and she kindly gave me one!" With the broadest smile and to resounding laughter and applause, Bob held up his white-painted, clay-covered, golf ball snowman for all to see.

It is hard to describe in a book just how this man's expressions and his own inability to contain his laughter, was used by the Lord to set the whole room into belly-aching laughter. We could not stop! The release was palpable. Nothing was contrived, it was a sheer breaking forth of spontaneous, healthy laughter which brought about a bonding and joy in this 'family of God' setting. In various circumstances, this has happened numerous times and is a huge part of a God-given anointing for healing, bonding and restoration.

As a team, we could feel the darkness and oppression lifting. God was in our midst. Jesus was healing people in His way. Through fun and laughter, addictions and compulsions were losing their grip, depressions were lifting, bonding was taking place to self and to others, and vitally, with the Lord Jesus.

Whilst these were wonderful times of release, it was heartening to hear stories of how the healing had continued back home with a new ability rising up: to laugh, bond, trust and appreciate others. In essence, the Holy Spirit was at work in unique ways, releasing tension and inner blockages through something as simple as the joy of relationship.

Having fun releases pressure and tension

I have discovered the enemy wants to keep people in a straitjacket of rationale or even religion, when God is far bigger than all these and He is truly out of the box of our thinking.

A Surprise Visitor

"You are the only ministry I know which has built a bridge from the head to the heart," an American visiting speaker told me. I was quite taken aback and had anticipated that my seemingly childlike course on *Healing Through Creativity* would have been viewed as 'irrelevant' to the higher spiritual life! David, on the other hand, was urging me forward. I knew he 'got it' and intuitively understood how God was healing.

So many people tell us that they have much knowledge and understanding, especially of Christian principles, they know the truth of God's love in their heads but they long to feel it in their hearts. David had walked his own painful journey and I thank God today for his encouragement and willingness to join me in taking the vision yet further and provide a week where God's children could come and experience Him as Father.

A Bridge from the Head to the Heart

It was time to expand the course from four days to a week to encompass more of the family experiences. God was showing us that His covenantal family is His design for healing and restoration. Our intercession seeking God's presence through just being His family went up a gear. We were not to be disappointed and our faith was rewarded.

Our Scottish Centre (Blairmore House) seemed exactly the right ambiance for a week especially as it has a designated large art room with built-in sinks and cupboards galore. We include a beach outing, a games evening as well as the family sharing nights. The stories of how God uses these and the workshops which are interspersed with inspirational teaching encouraged us to keep going.

What God had done for Sarah, He is now doing for countless others. Many people have not experienced family life and safe nurture. In giving God the space and time, we can see Him move in people's hearts in unexpected healing ways.

Whether it is playing a game, sharing a talent, finding gifts which may have been lost, God wants to bring healing through the setting of family. I remember a lady who had hidden her talent for singing. She was now in her middle years but had stopped singing back in her early years. She had been ridiculed and mocked.

As a child who was blind, she had been taken around pubs and clubs to do an 'act' which eventually became incredibly painful. During our family evening, she had a desire to sing again. We all encouraged her, and none of us will forget her sweet and beautiful voice, but more than that, the joy and completeness she came into as she shared her talent for the right reason. God was using this time with His family around her to heal this crushed aspect of her identity.

The Beach

In taking our *Bridge from the Head to the Heart* theme further at our Centre in Scotland, it opened a new vista of possibilities for healing through family and creative expression. Every family likes to go on a family trip, an outing!

Excitement grew as we piled buckets and spades, flags, bats and balls, plastic containers, kites and towels into the coach and headed for the beach at Cullen in Scotland. No outing would be complete without a picnic. The joy was palpable as we set off, chattering away and eating our bag of goodies! I reflected on how kind and good our loving Heavenly Father is, and once again thanked Him for Jesus who paid such a price for our freedom.

Where would this beach trip lead to? I had no idea what God wanted to do, as a team we were just following the prompting that a family outing would be healing. Once on the beach, it was not long before socks and shoes were off, sandcastles were being built and the moat for the sea to come into was being dug! Cries of, "We need this," and, "We need that," were flying around. Everyone was urged to join in, "Come and play! Come and help!" followed by hoots of laughter as imagination ran riot. When the sea eventually lapped around the moats, the digging became more frantic. I have never seen such enthusiasm and teamwork, life depended on it!

Family fun on the beach progressed to water fights, ball games, paddles and fun in the sea. The younger ones were brave and active, the older ones enjoying being looked after and watching belongings. It was a family scene. I stopped in my tracks, looked heavenward and gave thanks to Almighty God for His amazing grace and provision of family. No one was excluded. I was overwhelmed at the joy I was sensing that it brought to His heart.

The highest joy as a parent is watching your children enter the plans and provision you have made for them. More than likely, it would involve taking your children to places you once went or to share a favourite experience, or to enjoy a gift you have given them. Nothing is different with God's heart. His heart is blessed and overjoyed to see His children entering into all He has created and planned in His love.

I was particularly touched on one of our family beach trips. Olive was an elderly lady in her nineties and had experienced abuse in her younger years. Her heart was broken, and she desperately needed healing from the Lord Jesus. Life had seemed pointless to her, depression had taken its toll on all aspects of her life. On the same course was a highly gifted and talented professional young man who also came with deep depression.

I could see that this beach trip had not been top of their list in terms of there being any expectation that it would bring healing or even hope. Yet, somehow God wove a wonderful miracle which unfolded before our eyes. We were helping Olive to make a sandcastle. Being of an older age, she had little mobility but was enjoying feeling the sand and piling it up. The depressed young man sitting close to her suddenly said, "What do you need, Olive? Can I get you something?" Olive replied that she would like some shells and feathers. The young man picked up a bucket and returned with his collection.

At this point, I took a back seat and watched God use the young man to help Olive make a lovely sandcastle. They were talking, sharing and building! To this day, I have no idea how the conversation went but I knew God was at work and a beautiful bond was taking place.

This was more than a 'head' conversation, it was the meeting of hearts. The young man's need of healing from failure and loneliness was being touched by this lovely lady who went on to tell us with joyful tears pouring down her cheeks, "This is the best day of my whole life." Olive meant she had found the child inside herself, and she was able to play and have fun without fear for the first time. There are no age restrictions to the way God heals His children.

A young woman called Jill struggled for years with the consequences of her abusive past. Desperate for healing, she came on a creativity course. Trust began to be built, she began to enter into relationship, and she caught a glimpse of

> "
> God was at work and a beautiful bond was taking place

real freedom. So, she came back on another creativity course, and another, and then progressed to coming to the week-long *Bridge from the Head* to the Heart course.

It was wonderful to see her bowed head lifted and a smile lighting up her face, and to see her emerging from deep depression. She told us that, yes, there had been tough moments and tears, but she had so enjoyed learning about herself and about Jesus and what she liked doing. With great excitement, she expressed, "I enjoyed having fun! Paddling in the stream was a real breakthrough for me. Jesus released laughter and fun in me. I giggled and laughed a lot and it took me a while to realise the laughter was coming from me. It felt like it didn't belong to me. I could hear laughter but thought it was someone else and then I realised it was me! I was actually laughing freely. I couldn't stop smiling! Healing has definitely taken place here."

Imagination Unleashed

Watching my grandchildren, I see unbridled ability to be imaginative, experimental, visionary, and above all, lost in fun and play. They have no care in the world. Their trust is implicit in their parents' ability to meet their needs, and there is certainly no restraint in asking for whatever it is they would like!

I have mused over the way these creative qualities easily become lost. With age, more and more responsibilities take over. Yet, creative qualities remain a vital part of who we are, and we all have a need to express them even if it is in a limited way and time frame in comparison with our younger years. These positive childlike elements bring life.

Play releases the imagination and brings connection to other emotions, it has no right or wrong and lacks control. Many people are fearful of play because of this. They would rather have the control, which fundamentally keeps a tight grip of everything they do. However, God designed play to

be a divine relaxant, a complete antidote to stress, fatigue, emotional overload, heaviness, despair and more. It is easy to consign play to the irrelevancies of life now we are adults.

Dare I say it, there are more people afraid of play than can be imagined. Play and spontaneity go together. When I have asked people on our courses whether they are fearful of spontaneity, at least one third put their hand up, whilst many of the others are still thinking about it! I guess we all have some reticence when it comes to being spontaneous.

If we have not learnt to play as children or been tightly controlled in play, it will lead to a restrained way of life in later years. That restrained life can have devastating and unseen consequences with hidden controls of fear in the subconscious. Sad to say, there is a huge rise in the numbers of people in need of help with sleep disorders, depression, anxiety and panic, many of whom are on prescriptive medical drugs.

We live in a world today where technology has become an addictive substitute for imaginative play. Computer games have overtaken the joy of playing out, making dens, altering the courses of streams, climbing trees, playing with natural elements and make-believe games. Most games today are geared towards an achievement, whether they are with a ball or with music or drama. Many things have been eliminated due to over protection, fear of risk taking or lack of time. These things can be understandable, but they lead to tremendous levels of insecurity within the formative development of a child. There is no substitute for an imaginary outlet in play and having fun.

During one of our courses, I was explaining how being on a child's swing can help some people to touch areas of their inner being in terms of a particular movement or memory. A lady, deeply impacted by what I was saying, came up to me later and told me she felt the Lord had prompted her to give a donation for Ellel Grange to buy some adult swings! I was delighted, and today we have a fine pair of swings in our woodland where many people go and find it relaxing to talk

> "
> There is no substitute for an imaginary outlet

to Jesus and allow Him to minister healing to them.

The swimming pool has also been greatly used in our creativity healing journey. Trisha, a lady who we had been helping with her own issues, was a lifeguard and swimming instructor. She shared with me that she would be willing to help people with fears of water. I had no idea that the pool would be such a perfect place for God to do His healing work. In fact, initially I doubted anyone would sign up for an individual swimming session, but as it happens this particular workshop is the one that is booked up at the outset!

Trisha would tell us how God used the water to speak to people of His ability to hold them afloat and embrace them in His arms in safety. People also shared how the water helped them to touch deep areas, even back to a womb experience, God used it to put trust into their lives. The radiance on their faces as they told their stories was evidence enough that God was working powerfully in the swimming pool.

Play in the swimming pool with rubber ducks, balls, rings and floats inevitably began spontaneous games. Before long, a group of people who might never have known each other were laughing and bonding with unabated glee. Listening to the rise in decibels on the way home through chatter and laughter was enough for me to know that God had been with His children and instead of pain and suffering, they had received His gift of life.

God's Family

It is all about God's design. He made us for family. He gave us the prayer to pray every day, *'Our Father in Heaven.'* Primarily, we are family as the Body of Christ. We have a Father, we are His children with brothers and sisters, all unique, and we have a purpose. Our lives count in working for the family business, but our lives count in just being His children too. Our Father made us for relationship, and it brings His heart joy to see us entering into all He has made for us.

Jesus prayed in John 17 that the world would see the love we have for one another. He prayed for us to be one. He prayed for us to be protected from the evil one, the false father.

We have discovered that as we receive His principles of love through the gift of play and fun, something good is being built in. Strengthening takes place and an inner peace comes. We all need to be human 'beings', and not human 'doings' all the time. Work is a value set given by God, but in its fallen condition has become toil. As such, we need an antidote to the pressure, and the ability to have time set aside as family together building in something of life's joy.

"
We need an antidote to the pressure

Sport

Sport is part of play. It is play with a purpose as it involves skill and practice. Some of the first things we learn as a child are to run, catch, kick a ball, ride a bike etc. When God created the earth, He did so in the shape of a ball. Even the smallest ball on the earth brings great opportunity and pleasure. Again, we see God's character coming through the things He created which He knew we, as His creative people, would be blessed by.

God designed sport to be a way of bringing fulfilment which is healing in so many ways. Most sport is exercise, and as such, healthy for the body. Teamwork is bonding, since we learn that life is not simply all about me, it has consequences for others too, and we in turn are affected by the consequences (the good, the bad and the ugly) of others. Sport, again releases emotion with feelings of anger, disappointment, frustration, excitement, desire, etc. Sport challenges attitudes, character and our way of thinking. Sport touches our human spirits in the way we believe in ourselves, our ability and talent.

To get on a surfboard and glide along the waves means you cannot think of anything else except keeping steady. In doing so, there is the necessary switch off from life's normal routines and responsibilities. It takes great concentration and effort to keep afloat, but it is also a release from daily routine and work. Some fun and play is competitive. Competition is not wrong; it raises the bar of our expectation and takes us beyond our *status quo* into furthering our attempts and improving our results. Competition can hold joy but also disappointment. Every child growing up has to learn how to lose a game as well as to win. These are elements which are part of life's rich pattern.

Stress

In a stressful world, full of challenges and suffering, God wants to bring His personal redemptive purpose, restoring something back which has been crushed in the area of fun, play and family.

Stress and pressure are closely linked and can build up for all kinds of reasons, but no one is exempt. It is worth exploring how something of fun, play and imagination can come into our lives. We all need these times of release.

The enemy of God would try and keep us on a treadmill. It is his way to bring false guilt to keep us from entering into God's principles for life and health. He can obviously also try to take us to the opposite extreme, whereby we overdo pleasing ourselves, with no sense of true guilt regarding also rightfully meeting the needs of others. It is a question of balance and order.

Seeing Sarah laugh and play today, totally free from taking the high dosages of antidepressant drugs, no longer a zombie and enjoying being a loved wife and mother convince me that God created these principles in His love for the healing of the human heart.

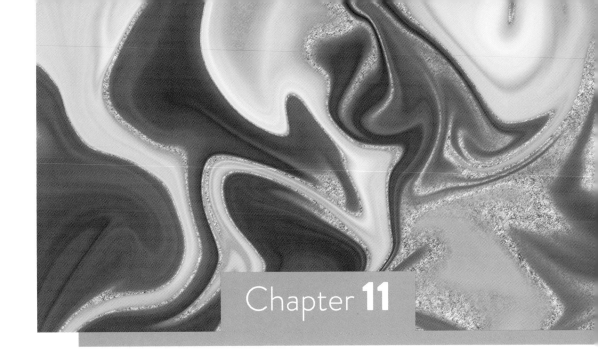

Chapter 11

WHAT A MESS!

Plenty of space, big sheets of paper and large bottles of paint in blue, red, green, black, white, yellow, purple and orange plus a shaker full of glitter for good measure – this is where it all started! We had no idea whether anyone would want to go to a place where splodging paint around on paper with no apparent relevance would be attractive. To our astonishment, this aspect of our *Healing Through Creativity* course is consistently where most breakthroughs occur. It is the most popular, but it is also for many the most scary.

We knew from our experience with Sarah that going near mess was her ultimate dread. Living life with compulsions and tight controls, even when they are subconscious, keeps any inside mess under control. God began to show us as we walked the journey to freedom with Sarah that at some point she would need to 'let go' and spontaneously allow expression to flow from her human spirit without holding back.

Obsessive compulsive disorder was how Sarah had been psychiatrically diagnosed, and she was on the extreme end of this condition. Sarah tells in her story of how making lists of lists, endlessly tidying up, regulating life, checking and re-checking again and again closed life down until she was living in a top layer of behaviour with a cavern inside hidden behind her wall of obsessions. As healing progressed, these well-established controls remained in place and it was time for them to be challenged and dismantled. This was a very difficult part of the journey for Sarah. She had learnt to rely on them, and although her rational mind knew they were no longer needed, she instinctively and habitually hung on to them.

We talked about letting out more than tears. There was the need to let go of anger, rage, injustice, hatred and the pain of abandonment and the sin that had for so long festered like pus around the wounds: jealousy, resentment, bitterness, revenge and more. "It's all too big," Sarah would explain shaking her head. No matter how much we tried to reassure her that nothing was too big for God, she needed a practical and tangible breakthrough. Saying words, agreeing with the injustice, empathy and even the Scripture alone was not enough to break down the wall protecting what was inside.

It became clear that it was crucial for Sarah to come to a place where we as a team were irrelevant, a time where she and God alone did business. I became aware that I and the team too could be a barrier and even a hindrance to what the Holy Spirit wanted to do in Sarah's life. This was time for a divine encounter and transaction. Our team interceded and trusted that the Lord knew what was best. Ironically, it was not simply a time for Sarah alone to place her ultimate trust in the Lord but us as well.

The day came when it seemed right to go outside with some huge sheets of paper and the paints. We certainly did

> " This was time for a divine encounter and transaction

not want to contrive anything but rather facilitate what God was doing. Sarah had been working hard at trying her level best to keep her inside panics under wraps but the more she tried and the more we tried to fix it with words, the worse they became. Outside we went and, then the small team alongside her retreated, leaving Sarah staring at the paper.

It was one of those occasions where either God would break through the dam of Sarah's controls, or it would be a self-controlled exercise of doing 'what was right and expected', a planned mess! What a glorious day it turned out to be, as Sarah allowed her inner self to explode onto the paper and even to spill over onto the grass beneath it. The non-verbal nature of messy expression was just what she needed, and alongside that came the deepest screams and cries imaginable. Father God knew what was trapped inside her desperately wounded human spirit and the need for this to come to Him.

A way of expressing words and feelings without being verbal

The freedom Sarah was experiencing as we walked back inside was tangible. This was a turning point which has stood the test of time. Sarah, in that moment was alone, connected to her mess and trusting this buried, tangled knot of pain, anger, injustice and sin to her heavenly Father. Through this experience Sarah shared her liberation in being free to be herself and vitally, to receive and know the presence and love of God in the deepest place of her identity. This secure and deep love has never left her to this day.

Miracle

The miracle of the Incarnation (the coming of Jesus to earth) is that God came down into the mess. He did not expect us to climb out of the mess to Him. He is there with us in the mess. This is the place we need Him the most, and His work transforms the mess and redeems it. We have experienced this on so many occasions now, where there is an outpouring of the Holy Spirit when people come to Jesus in their mess. So much so, we call this aspect of creativity, 'the anointed mess'.

Sarah, no longer needing medication, no longer fearing people, no longer desiring to hide and no longer locked in a prison of fear and panic, was living out God's miracle in her life. She once said, "Healing must be being the same on the inside as the outside." How true! Her relationship with Jesus, trusting Him and allowing Him to transform and redeem her pain and her sinfulness brought about this miracle of His grace. She was never expected by the medics to be off the highest dosages of psychiatric drugs, she had a lifetime's disability pension, and permanent care from psychiatric staff was available to her.

> God has transformed her mess

But God has transformed her mess in His grace and love, and she lives now fully at liberty. She is off all drugs, disability pension, psychiatric or indeed any other help. She has found God as Father, and in this place of her heart, she is secure and rich. Sarah has come home! Watching her like a butterfly out of a chrysalis, it is impossible not to be convicted by the truth that God is Creator, He made us, He knows us, and it is He who sets us free. His Word is practical and applicable to all situations pertaining to our lives.

Did all this make Sarah perfect, never to feel any pain again nor to be sinful in any kind of way? No, it did not, but Sarah has found the safest place to go, where sin is forgiven, and pain no longer has the power to destroy life. Jesus forgives our sin and He comforts and heals our wounds.

Get Cleaned Up!

Whether we like it or not, broadly speaking we try to hide any mess we have made. Certainly, any inner mess which causes us to feel dirty, ashamed, guilty etc, we become adept at hiding. At best, we put it in cupboards, and at worst we try to kill it off and declare it gone. The problem lies in the reality that the mess is not a separate entity to us but has become part of who we are. The hidden mess on the inside is the 'suffering me', the one who carries the pain, shame and emptiness, and which as a result, sin clings to so profoundly.

the mess is not a separate entity to us but has become part of who we are

In general, our upbringing has taught us that we must be good, and we should be clean and tidy, perhaps even to the extent that we were never allowed to be messy, make mistakes, waste time or experiment or were never given the safety to fail. Many people have lived on a treadmill of perfectionism, trying to live up to expectations, largely out of fear. Messages may have been received to "Grow up!", "Pull yourself together!", "Get your act together!" and, "BE GOOD!"

Worst still, many have been manipulated into being good with threats of what will happen if they are not. Blame and shame has been transferred like a blanket, "It's all your fault." I know of people who have lived their lives in fear of upsetting someone because they have taken on board subconsciously the consequences of their supposed bad behaviour. Instead of a freedom on the inside, controls are in place holding back any spontaneity or ability to just 'be'. There are hidden strangleholds crushing any life from emerging.

It is not an irrational belief to carry that unless we are good, we do not come up to the mark, are somehow unacceptable and, at worst, not worth loving and bad! But where do all the 'bad', 'messy' and 'negative' feelings go? Do they disappear?

> " But where do all the 'bad', 'messy' and 'negative' feelings go?

Condemnation

Sadly, in our Christian culture Scripture is often used to dish out an unhealthy dose of condemnation, which can be highly manipulative to ensure the compliance of 'being good' in the name of Jesus! We read in Romans 8:1, that 'There is now no condemnation for those who are in Christ Jesus.' The price has been paid! As we have already seen, Jesus came into the mess of this world, and the mess of our lives to redeem it. Through His sacrifice and shed blood, our true guilt, when owned and brought to Him for cleansing, is forgiven and covered.

Being condemned does not lead to sanctification and a holy life! It only serves to keep us in an ungodly fear, most likely of ourselves as well as God. In truth, it is a barrier to an open, trusting, authentic relationship. It is impossible to cleanse ourselves, make ourselves righteous and good, yet it is something that Satan tries to get us to do, as he regularly reminds us of our failures and imperfections, which keep us

on the treadmill of a 'do better', 'try harder' path of beating ourselves up.

Conviction

It is the Holy Spirit's work to bring conviction, and conviction is different to condemnation! Condemnation is the work of the accuser, Satan. Condemnation says, "Guilty! Pay a price and live out a sentence!" Conviction, on the other hand, helps us to see and recognise our sin and our need. It brings light and truth into our mess, which is releasing and not hopeless. Conviction allows and empowers change, "Oh Jesus, I see now how wrong that was, how I responded, my attitude, my acts of selfishness, my bitterness, my greed, my desire to hurt and lash out," etc. Jesus looks on us with compassion, He sees where sin is like graveclothes eating away at us and our wounds, which need His touch and healing.

Messy Release!

One person expressed it this way:

> Wow, isn't the messy room powerful! I never before experienced being able to get in touch with what was deep down inside me. I have been through years of counselling and psychotherapy, but the messy room somehow released the stuff in me. I knew it was there but this time, I was enabled to get in touch with it. It took the messy room to give me the breakthrough.

liberating mess!

In needing a breakthrough to areas that seem, at best out of reach, and at worst disconnected, the messy room provides an uncontrived place for the Holy Spirit to bring freedom. Our team are there to support and facilitate and gently stand alongside, without imposing their own agendas, thoughts or opinions, trying to interpret or in any way judge.

Having received some teaching on God's desire for us to come to Him just as we are, with all our hang ups, difficulties, doubts, fears, inner feelings and sins, people enter into a new way of relating to Him through the various creative workshops. The messy room is one of the most popular. Large bottles of paint and big pieces of paper laid out on the floor invite those courageous enough, to trust Jesus and to allow free expression to emerge.

I wasn't expecting to have such a roller coaster week as regards my inner emotions. God certainly surprised me with triggering off unexpected feelings and memories, which I know He wants me to bring to Him to deal with. It was so wonderfully liberating to be given permission to make a mess. I have had problems with perfectionism since I was a child. God has shown me He wants to heal the remaining mess.

This story is very typical of the kind of feedback we receive following our *Healing Through Creativity* courses. In His love, God wants to come into the mess of our lives and bring His peace, freedom and healing. Our problem is allowing Him into these, often fiercely guarded, areas. We have often learnt to protect and guard our hearts over many years to avoid further pain and hurt. Only our Father God, who knows us, can help us connect and find ourselves. Despite our fears, He does this in gentle and kind ways if we allow Him.

> God spoke to me on the *Healing Through Creativity* course of His love and His Father heart. For the first time I know deep down in my heart that He loves me. Before, it was only head knowledge. Before I came, I felt too scared to let Him close, too scared to let His love in because for me love hurt. But now I know God's love is safe. Painting my 'healing journey' in the messy room brought the break-through for me.

This story tells of another commonly held, deep struggle. Many have experienced deep rejection and abandonment by those who were designed by God to give them that unconditional love and acceptance. Often these were mothers and fathers - the people closest to them. For some people there has been neglect and their suffering has come about through life's general circumstances: another's inadequacy, immaturity, weakness or illness. Sometimes, the sinfulness of the human heart is the core issue, which has wreaked havoc with those who in childhood were vulnerable and in need of stability, security and safety. For yet others, cruelty has been a deliberate act. When deliberate cruelty is dished out by a natural parent on their own child, it is one of the worst forms of man's inhumanity to man.

> I was never allowed to play as a child

I was never allowed to play as a child. My father was an extremely angry man and as children we all feared his drinking. We knew he would come home and beat us. On this weekend, God touched the child in me and in the messy room He brought all the black fear and depression out. It was wonderful to release and express it. Then I felt the Holy Spirit surround me with warmth and I put red and gold glitter on top of the blackness. Daddy God has become real for me – before I would never have dared believe this could be true.

Free to be the child I was never allowed to be – so healing

The starting point is always allowing God to do what only God can do. Through His Holy Spirit, we find He is at work reaching His children, and He knows what they need. We can honestly say that the messy room is one of the most liberating experiences in ministry, since God uses it so powerfully to break down invisible barriers in people's lives, which might have taken hours of talking to reach, and even then, it could easily be an understanding of the head rather than a breakthrough to the heart.

I made a lot of mess in the messy room! I discovered I had terrible control over myself, events and people. I received wonderful release giving God my control and allowing Him to be in control. It took the messy room to do this for me.

Explosions Need to Come Out

One of the greatest fears and deceptions Satan has over us, is that what is inside must never come out. Often the belief and feeling are that what is inside is so utterly shameful, dirty, sinful and big that it will be out of control. Years have been spent in covering it up and keeping separate this part of our inner self. Yet, in truth, this is the very place which God is looking for, to bring peace and release.

God is not afraid of our anger or our negative feelings. He is big enough for all of them, even anger towards Himself. Satan, on the other hand, would want to use this hidden 'power pack' to keep a control on us, keep us on a treadmill of endeavour to keep things going on the outside. Depression, anxiety issues with addictions and compulsions, mood swings and personality problems, can all be rooted in the controls, which keep a part of ourselves buried.

When I went into the messy room, I was so angry. I was thinking about which colour to use and I chose red. The paint was thick, and I was pushing it about, trying to get this anger out, crying at the same time. I want to shout. I want all this anger out. All the things that had been done to me came flooding up. I saw what Satan had done and shouted at him. As the paint poured onto the paper, a peace and liberation filled my heart. Later I came back to the mess and poured glitter on top of it and gold paint representing the heart of God. I will never forget this. I am a child of a beautiful, magnificent, wonderful God.

Forgiveness

Keeping stocked up with red, black, white and yellow paint is a priority standard order for *Healing Through Creativity*! Black usually represents darkness, sin or pain. Red, on the other hand is used to represent personal wounds or depicts the blood of Jesus which forgives, cleanses and covers. White or yellow signifies new life coming and the work of the Holy Spirit bringing comfort, healing, fresh life and new beginnings.

A heart that is understood and a heart that is heard is a softened heart. God our Father is clear in His Word that His heart is tender and kind towards our hurts and pains.

> He heals the brokenhearted and binds up their wounds.
>
> (PSALM 147:3)

> Praise be to the God and Father of our Lord Jesus Christ, the Father of compassion and the God of all comfort, who comforts us in all our troubles.
>
> (2 CORINTHIANS 1:3-4)

'We love because He first loved us' (1 John 4:19)

When Jesus is allowed to come by His Holy Spirit and bring healing, then repentance and forgiveness are a natural consequence for the recipient. When God fills our hearts with His love, we are enabled to see sin from a new perspective. As hurt and the power of pain melt away, there is room in our hearts for the love of Jesus towards ourselves and others. We fall in love with Jesus.

It is when our hearts are guarded and hard that bitterness, malice, resentment and even revenge festers. The enemy loves that, and his expert condemnation and hatred exploits these areas to the full. Confession is always the best place to begin the journey to forgiveness. As James 5:16 reminds us, 'Therefore confess your sins to each other and pray for each other so that you may be healed. The prayer of a righteous person is powerful and effective.' In 1 John 1:9 we read: 'If we confess our sins, he is faithful and just and will forgive us our sins and purify us from all unrighteousness.'

Creative expression of mess brings a powerful connection to things inside, which often cannot be verbalised, they are deemed to be too ugly. It is as though words alone are not enough, but God knows and He leads the person with extraordinary outcome.

The language of the human spirit

Someone who had suffered abuse came for help, full of shame and guilt. They were not really thinking that doing something creative could help. This lady was too frightened to allow anyone close to her. However, she knew that there was a need to forgive her mother. With great courage, she entered the messy room not knowing what might happen and really wanting to run out. During the teaching, she had taken on board that God wanted her to let her cry from the inside come to Him.

The righteous cry out, and the LORD hears them;
he delivers them from all their troubles. (PSALM 34:17)

In the messy room, God spoke to her, telling her that He could see her mess and urging her to give it to Him. She knew she would need a great deal of paint! As the paint spurted down on the paper, she felt her heart opening and a stream of forgiveness flowing down from it onto the paper with all the hurt and pain. Jesus went on to lead this lady to the pottery room where she felt she wanted to make a large hand. She then made a broken heart in the clay and put it in the hand. God was healing wounds as she did so, and she later wrote about how she felt God holding her; despite struggles she now had a profound security that she had never experienced before.

The Release of Being Me

A young man wrote:

> I want to touch the pain, I want to put my whole hands in it. Something deep inside of myself wants to express what I have kept hidden. It is something I have locked away, something I have not even acknowledged to myself. At long last it can be realised and flow from me. I feel real for the first time in my life. It feels like I have come alive.

It is a wonderful gift to be free to be yourself, not to have to cover yourself up in any way and know you are loved. God loves us this way. His love is unconditional. God is love (1 John 4:16), He does not decide to love, because if His love was a choice, how insecure would that make us as His children? One day He would love us, and then the next day He could decide not to, depending perhaps on our performance. God is love, it is His nature and character. He cannot change. His

It is a wonderful gift to be free to be yourself

love is covenantal not contractual. It is not a case of, "If you do that, then I will do this." It is offered freely as a gift. But a gift needs to be received and tasted.

One story we heard was very profound. This lady drew a large circle with the paint. She explained that she had always kept God's love at a distance, under her control even though she had longed for it deep within her heart. During the messy painting, she kept going over the circle, round and round until at one point she realised what she was doing. She heard God's voice speaking to her as His child telling her that He wanted to come inside the circle, He would not harm or hurt her.

She pushed a dent, and eventually a break, into the circle and wanted to pour red, black, blue and green inside. She knew the colours were merging together. This was her life with all its pain, its sinfulness, the good things (like her children), and those things which were circumstances out of her control. It felt good to push the paint around with her fingers. She looked at her hands and as she did so, she felt deep compassion rise up and she knew the love of God had come into the inside of the circle. She told us this was one of the most important days of her Christian experience. God had always been on the outside but that day, He came close into her heart. Her radiance in telling the story said it all.

Dirty shells, messy paint ... what can they do? Under God's hand and in His way, the Holy Spirit releases conviction, draws people to Jesus the Healer, and through Jesus flows the heart of the Father, who calls us His child and whose family we belong to.

The messy room is simply the outward expression of an inward truth.

> See what great love the Father has lavished on us, that we should be called children of God! And that is what we are!
>
> (1 JOHN 3:1)

The messy room is simply the outward expression of an inward truth

Chapter 12

GOD'S CREATIVE FAMILY

I began this book by explaining how God had given a vision to make Ellel Grange into a home for His children. When He created human beings, He did not create them to be alone: 'Then the Lord God said, "It is not good for the man to be alone, I will make a helper suitable for him"' (Genesis 2:18). God's creative order is for family: 'For this reason I kneel before the Father, from whom every family in heaven and on earth derives its name' (Ephesians 3:14-15). It is the revelation that God is our Father and we are His children that brings the deepest peace and healing: 'Yet to all who did receive him, to those who believed in his name, he gave the right to become children of God' (John 1:12).

God designed His family to be a place where love and acceptance, righteous and just discipline and authority could mingle, and where our unique God-given personalities and gifts would freely flow, bringing the increase of fruitfulness for the good of all.

Whatever our background, culture and journey, in belonging to Jesus we are family. Together we are about our Father's business. Divisions should lose their grip since our unity cannot be determined by opinion or dogma but on the basis that we are all human, we are all sinners recognising our need of Jesus, our Saviour, who has opened up the way for us to be restored to our Father. As family, we belong together. In John chapter 17, Jesus prayed for His family to be 'one' and to have His love in our hearts so that others in the world might also believe.

None of the above means that we get to live in some kind of 'holy huddle' for the rest of our lives. The world we live in is fallen, broken and brutal. God's heart breaks for the lost and those lives that need Him, His salvation and safety. However wonderful Ellel Grange centre or any other place is, it could never be a place of permanent home or human parental care for anyone including Sarah. However, God's creative plan was to use the centre and team as an oasis, a place of respite and healing on life's journey and for His children to be passionate in taking His life to others.

> *an oasis, a place of respite and healing on life's journey*

An Exchange

As a child growing up, Sarah knew nothing of normality apart from school. She dreaded the return to what we will call her house, for it was certainly not a home. Now years later, God was bringing His redemptive plan and His heart for 'home'.

Sarah wanted a plan for her healing, she was unaware that healing would take place through being family. It is so easy for any one of us to do the same. We look for a technique, a methodology or a therapy as an answer. It is not that any of these things cannot help, especially when they include

God's principles within them, but it is not the fulness of what God offers.

> I am the Lord, who heals you.   (Exodus 15.26)

> A father to the fatherless, a defender of widows, is God in his holy dwelling. God sets the lonely in families, he leads out the prisoners with singing.   (Psalm 68 5-6)

True healing comes through entering a relationship, and through this relationship we gain brothers and sisters in the family of God, who are also part of the healing. It is learning a new way of living. I am not my own anymore, I am part of a greater picture.

Out of Isolation

At first Sarah was aloof, in her own world isolated from the rest of us. A measure of healing was being received through traditional prayer ministry but the isolation, which was the worst part of the legacy of her past, continued to eat away on the inside seemingly undoing the good we saw on the outside.

All Sarah had experienced and known growing up was isolation. God was showing us that He wanted to bring her from the outside into the middle. Following the breakthrough with the dirty shells, relationships came into a new dimension. We were now developing friendships and sharing life!

Sarah was not just a person to be ministered to. It was not that she should be any more special than any one of us on the team to be elevated either, but the Holy Spirit was showing us that He wanted her out of her 'inner isolated world' to be part of us. God wanted to embrace her as much as He wanted to embrace us. He absolutely has no favourites in His family. We are all sons and daughters, brothers and sisters.

As we chatted, played, ate together, went on outings etc,

God was forging deep bonds of trust

God was forging deep bonds of trust into Sarah without her or us realising it. Her crushed and broken spirit was returning to life. She was part of a wonderful and permanent family and this began to dissolve years of fear, isolation and survival controls. Crucially, it undermined the abusive and cruel parenting of the past, building in good memories, fresh trust, hope and new life instead.

The walls of isolation came down

God is not just taking an old house down and emptying it, He is at the same time building in the new house with its solid structures and safety. His creative design is for family to be part of this restoration work.

Family Imperfection and Flaws!

Despite all our attempts to care for Sarah and to do everything right, nothing could disguise the fact that as individuals and as a team we were all far from perfect. We could not attain to saying everything in a perfect way, avoiding tiredness, being fed up and, at times out of frustration, becoming irritable. We would try and fix things with human thinking and logic and even run out of patience despite all our best efforts. We all live in an imperfect world where circumstances change, and best efforts and intentions change with it. Sarah was learning real life. One of the most healing aspects of experiencing family was that she learnt to fit in and be normal like the rest of us!

Sarah later told us how our imperfections and the way we handled them, helped her embrace her own imperfections and allow herself to be human. God was showing us that. He knew His family was not perfect, nor could we ever be. However, we could live in love and acceptance of each other and allow Him to help us in our weakness and yes, our sinfulness.

It was impossible to attempt to achieve a high level of spirituality which, if attained, would crush and defeat being human. It was not a natural way of living. God was showing us that Sarah was subconsciously trying to change her crippling perfectionism into some kind of 'holy perfectionism' – a spiritual standard which the human heart cannot produce.

The family of God is not perfect, it has plenty of lumps and bumps! There is weakness, sin and inadequacy in all of us! Sarah was being set free by experiencing the joy of being human and not a spiritual machine! Condemnation and false guilt lost their power as forgiveness and grace flowed in the normality of life's circumstances.

Nurture

Some of our team are natural mothers and fathers. We remember a day well, when Anna, who is a lovely nurturer, both in the faith and in natural things too, made a plateful of toasted 'soldiers' (fingers of bread) to go with our boiled eggs for tea. It seemed natural for us to remember childhood delights of dipping them into the yoke of the egg, a small joy Sarah never had as a child. God took this simple act to touch Sarah's broken heart and place into it trust and joy in family. This simple action built in a happy memory for Sarah which went a long way to help nullify the ugly and negative ones.

Looking back, we had many such moments where the Holy Spirit was at work in the ordinary and creative things of life whether it was playing games, going to a café, walking the dog, picnics, birthday celebrations etc. God's family business was taking place on earth! He was showing Sarah that trusting others did not mean they had to be perfect. He was showing her safe boundaries in relationships, and that controlling and attaching was destructive to authentic relationships. As a result, compulsive bondages lost their grip. Embracing this new way of life became more attractive until it was natural for Sarah to trust. Genuine and normal family life had been built in.

When your heart is full of trust and love, you are no longer threatened by anyone, you see them as God sees them through eyes of compassion.

Loss, Bereavement and Suffering

All of us undergo loss and bereavement of one kind or another. It may be the loss of a relationship, the loss of health, the loss of a baby, loss through death or loss like Sarah of something God designed for us. It is hard to live with the loss of things that can never be, such as ability to conceive and bear a child, to be married or through the pain of divorce. The loss of our own identity is a powerful aspect of loss.

In a family setting, being able to talk about our losses and express them brings comfort and healing. Though praying as the family of God for those who have perhaps miscarried or aborted a child or who bear deep grief for someone dear, God has led us to do something physically creative and meaningful. It might be planting a rose in the garden, painting a picture or writing out words in a journal or as a poem. It is during these times, the Holy Spirit, the comforter brings release to the sting of death and He can then bring redemptive healing and purpose from our losses.

I remember one very depressed lady. She was making a card and when I drew close to her she began to sob. "I just want to tell him I love him," she kept repeating. In her hands was a rose bud, a tiny silk one out of a bag of many others. She had lost her son. "I was brought up in an orphanage and I never could tell him I loved him," she told me. I replied, "Why not do that now, you could make a card and say all the things you want to say, and we can ask Jesus to tell him the truth."

I left Shirley tentatively getting the glue to stick her rose on the paper. When I returned later to see how she was, I was staggered by not only the card she had made but the box she had covered with roses and inside the box, the sweetest message of love for her son. God knew of her deepest need to be with family to express her love, regret and pain of loss. I saw the depression in her eyes lift to eyes shining with love as she held her card and box, with others in the family of God around her sharing her memories.

Suffering is part of life and we all need each other to support and encourage us. We may have physical disabilities, personal struggles, mental health issues, sickness and disease or may be facing the end of our physical life here on earth. God uses creative expression especially in His family to bring strength, release, comfort, guidance and most importantly to undermine hopelessness and false guilt. The accuser loves isolation to keep us locked in suffering, but God has provided the best possible answer through family.

Whatever our need might be, we have seen that family creativity brings life and freedom into seemingly impossible circumstances and in unexpected ways.

> "
> Family creativity brings life and freedom

Victoria's Story

Victoria was another lady who received deep and lasting healing through the safety of God's family. She was brought up by an angry and violent alcoholic father. Whenever he was around, their mother constantly told them to "Be quiet." The children grew up in fear of arousing his temper. As a result, Victoria did not make any noise and when she did speak, it was in the lowest of tones. During the week, a desire to make noise grew in her.

We always have instruments available but not the professional kind. Rather, the instruments are for everyone – spoons, shakers, tambourines, pan lids etc. Victoria took the pan lids outside and made the loudest noise she could. She went on to share that she had been set free from years of bondage to silence and fear of noise.

Corporate Expression

Whilst understanding the healing of one person, we were being challenged by God to understand He was also healing His family alongside using His family to bring healing. We were being led to do things which contained a corporate expression.

A Project!

During the time we took the *Healing Through Creativity* course to Israel, Trisha, a lady who had experienced deep and cruel abuse in her life (see chapter 7), but was now growing in her own healing journey, made a wonderful poster of Jesus as the Good Shepherd with a crook in His hand overlooking a massive field. Trisha had prepared many hand-sized, cut-out sheep in all kinds of coloured card. She went on to ask all the people to put something of their own identity, likes or dislikes, pains or joys onto their sheep, something that was meaningful to them. It could be depicted in colours, textures, words, pictures, flowers or paint.

Wow! What a return! It was truly amazing to see around sixty sheep at the end of the day, all placed around Jesus the Good Shepherd in His sheepfold on the poster. There were bright ones, woolly ones, silky ones, bejewelled ones, flowery ones, black ones, empty ones, funny faced ones and just about every description you can think of in this sheepfold! Nobody was in any doubt that here was a visual expression of an inward truth and that we belonged to the Shepherd and He had a wonderful family with lots of personalities, journeys in life and with lumps and bumps to keep Him busy!

All depicted different things of unique individuality. Nobody knew whose sheep was whose, nor did they need to. The fact was that we were all His sheep, wonderfully unique but no different to each other in that we were all sheep and

> "
> we were all
> His sheep,
> wonderfully
> unique

we all belonged to the Shepherd, we were all in the same sheepfold and we were and are all loved!

God the Father was using Trisha's simple depiction to break down walls of hostility. At the end of the day what does it matter who is Jew, Arab or Gentile, English, Spanish, Russian or South American? Does it matter where we worship, or what denomination? To God the Father, we are simply His children, His family and He is our Father.

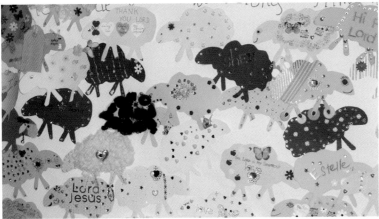

Family Songs

We call it 'worship with a difference!' Coming to God as a little child is not so easy when we are adult having had the hard knocks in life, many experiences, knowledge and ways of seeing things that an innocent child could not perceive or know. Yet Jesus explained that coming to Him as a little child was necessary to enter the blessings of His Kingdom! 'He called a little child to him, and placing the child among them. And he said: "Truly I tell you, unless you change and become like little children, you will never enter the kingdom of heaven' (Matthew 18:2-3).

A child sees through the eyes of trust and out of that trust learns to submit to their parent's authority. God requires us to trust Him. It is easy to see things through our own authority and our own perspective of the truth, which often doesn't match with God's truth. This is especially so when we need healing. Seeds of self-rejection and even self-hatred have taken root and the fruit is destructive.

Arising from when we had time with individuals in healing, where we would occasionally spend times singing children's songs, the idea arose to do so corporately. The words were particularly simple and relevant, the melody line tuneful and the actions alongside brought out a light-hearted yet deep way of receiving the love of Jesus.

Worship with a difference brought a powerful anointing which was breaking the yoke of bondage in people's lives. God the Father was touching His children through the simplicity of the children's songs and the truth they contained with words such as 'Yes, Jesus loves me' and 'I thank you Father for making me, me.'

> God was at work melting and breaking the barriers

Tears flowed as people came into powerful agreement with God's truth. Some wrestled and struggled to enter in or to do the actions simply because there was such a fight to accept the simplicity but power of truth. For some it was painful to allow them to penetrate the defences and strongholds within. For others, rationality stood in the way and for yet others, the pain of loss was just too great. Yet God was at work melting and breaking the barriers.

Fun and laughter released joy at doing the actions which in turn brought the reality of truth back into our hearts. Coming as little children and singing the children's songs together is a fantastic way for God to melt our adult stereotypes and reach deep into the core of where our hearts, at the most basic level, need Him most. Strongholds of pride, hate, self-sufficiency, independence, self-rejection and pain lose their grip during these precious corporate family of God worship times.

Working Together

Expressions of family flow during the creative workshop times. Affirmation and encouragement build one another up, "Wow, did you make that?!", "What a great choice of colour!" etc. Then by simply helping each other, "Can I hold this for you?", "I can thread that needle", "I know where there is a silver pen", there is something of the heart of God being expressed which brings healing.

These things may seem small, irrelevant or even childish, but God uses them to break down hardness of heart, to build bonding and trust and to allow love to flow. Seeking our own ends or needs to be met begins to change in the light of another person's need or struggle.

It is during these 'off guard' moments, that God seems to do a magnificent work.

We are often taken by surprise at the end of the course when people share how some of their healing came through the others on the course. Recently I heard a story from one of the workshop leaders which is a good example of how God redeems and uses family life to bring restoration.

Our jewellery workshop lady had a large plastic box divided up into small compartments. Within each compartment was a type of bead or sequin. By mistake the box was tipped over onto the floor throwing hundreds of beads in all directions. Everyone rushed to pick up the beads but of course, they were now well and truly muddled up. One of the ladies came along desiring to help to sort them out. "No, don't worry," said our workshop leader, "I will do it later when I have time." However, the lady on the course wanted to help and wanted to do this causing our workshop leader to be concerned she would miss out on her time, but she insisted on carrying out the sorting. At the end of the course, she gave a wonderfully surprising testimony of how God used the sorting out of the beads to show her how He was sorting her life; He did not miss anything and looked for any part of her life that was lost to put it back in the right place.

> " ...how God used the sorting out of the beads to show her how He was sorting her life

Sons and Daughters – not Orphans

In belonging to Jesus, we are described in the Bible as sons and daughters, co-heirs with Him. We have an inheritance waiting. All we are and do is not futile but holds an eternal dimension, which is producing fruit for the 'family business' which cannot rot or decay.

Very sadly, we meet many lovely people who are not living in the security of being a son or daughter but rather living out of an 'orphan' place with God. Someone who is orphaned has to fight for a place of belonging. Being an orphan creates jealousy of another. To be God's child is not a competition. We have this right through what Jesus has done for us and we do not have to fight for our place.

It is a wonderful privilege to see many who live their Christian life on some kind of treadmill, receive freedom. To receive an inheritance not because we deserve it or have earned it, but because of what Jesus has done for us is a priceless gift.

Am I Creative?

I never see a more animated group than when I ask, "Are you creative?" followed by, "Who likes cooking?", "Who likes gardening?", "Who likes do-it-yourself projects?", "Who likes

talking?", "Who likes writing?", "Who likes sport?" and "Who likes science?" The list could be endless. The answers come back with a good number in each category. The buzz in the room is tangible!

I go on to dig deeper to find out exactly why some people like a certain thing, and the replies are not short! "I like putting my hands in the soil and mud!"; "I love feeling the texture of the dough"; "It's the exploration of science, the logic, the finding out how things work, how they can be bettered"; "Sport takes me out of myself"; "It's the smell of cooking giving me an appetite, I like seeing a vision from a recipe come about"; "I feel I've achieved something when I plant a seed and watch over it until it blossoms, seeing something from nothing become beautiful"; "I like DIY because I put something of my imagination and myself into it"; "Walking takes me into the fresh air, I feel free and invigorated, I love seeing and feeling creation."

This is God the Father drawing us close! The painting, the gardening, science, technology, sport, walking, cooking, building etc are all things of His imagination and creation. He is the initiator of all that is good for us both individually and as a family together. We are all creative, God is Creator and we are made in His image.

A Celebration and a Festival

It looks like harvest time at the end of our creativity courses! Everyone brings their 'creations' to the front of the room where we hang the 'anointed messes' all around the walls and display the woodwork, the pottery, the glasswork, the felting, weaving, sewing, knitting, kites, collages, handmade cards, water colour paintings and more, together.

Indeed, all that has taken place, along with the half-finished pieces, the ones which did not work, the wonky ones, broken ones, the marvels and the messes! It is time for celebration and declaration! God is pleased, it brings Him joy. The rich variety and abundance shrieks that we could open a shop and start a business!

Conversely, it is a celebration Satan hates. It is life not death. He wants to bring pain, a treadmill of endeavour, hopelessness and despair. The room and the people within it speak for themselves of life from the dead returning. This is a tangible way of showing the enemy that we are not afraid of our mess and our pain and that we have a conviction that he cannot rob us of the life God has won for us through the Lord Jesus.

> we are not afraid of our mess and our pain

215

Our final celebration song with dance, banners, tambourines bring Jesus the glory. Thankful hearts usher in God's plan that we would be 'one', His family living in harmony.

Into All the World

We now have the privilege of taking the *Healing Through Creativity* vision to many different nations around the world – the principles are the same wherever you live and whatever your culture. God is not bound by borders and His family is worldwide!

> He brought me to the banqueting house, And his banner over me was love.   (SONG OF SOLOMON 2:4 NKJV)

SOME TESTIMONIES FROM THE NATIONS:

EASTERN EUROPE and RUSSIA

During the communist era, all creative expression was crushed and suppressed. Everything was in shades of grey and, indeed, sometimes still is. Pessimism, depression, hopelessness and fear defined not only individuals, but whole nations. Life's difficulties caused us to grow a hard shell around our hearts, deceiving ourselves that this would protect us. Unfortunately, it not only kept pain out, it prevented life from coming in.

We found that through creative expression, God can by-pass that hard shell and touch our heart at the core, helping us face suppressed fears and pain, restoring life, joy and hope and bringing freedom, healing and colour back into our lives.

When God breaks through, healing takes place – and there is sparkle and joy in eyes that had never experienced it before!

Roger Pook
— Former Eastern European Regional Director

We were amazed at the impact of creativity teaching. Many said, "This is the first picture I have ever painted", and when we praised their work, it brought tears of joy, as they were healed from childhood deprivation, pain and rejection. Being able to paint whatever and however they wanted was marvellously liberating and brought healing to their human spirit.

But it was the "messy painting" that brought the greatest healing. One woman splashed the paint violently on to the paper sobbing that "THIS is my drunken husband, and THIS is my divorce, and THIS is how I was treated." God touched all her painful emotions and she found wonderful healing. She then screwed up the paper, started again, and produced a beautiful delicate drawing. In every creativity session we saw how changed lives brought immeasurable blessing.

> it was the messy painting that brought the greatest healing

ASIA: Titus and Esther Soo
— *Regional Directors, Ellel East and South-East Asia*

Asia, our beloved continent, needs this teaching. Fiona Horrobin wrote the book with us in her heart! She saw the deep brokenness, dissociations and fragmentations of the human soul and spirit, hidden and forgotten in the deep recesses of people's hearts. This brokenness often affects our lives, our families and work. But we did not know what to do.

At a creativity school, Fiona powerfully brought this means of healing to Asia and for the Chinese people. Many lives were wonderfully healed. A new spiritual floodgate was opened in Asia, particularly for the Chinese people. Through creativity, the Holy Spirit has brought God's truth and love to the core-person. The person is set free from past bondages and brokenness into true freedom in Christ.

> "
> Many lives were
> wonderfully
> healed

UK: Robert Steel
—*Centre Director, Ellel Glyndley Manor, UK*

I have struggled with asthma all my life. In the creativity room, I stared at a blank sheet of paper and was encouraged to put something down that represented me. I put a black dot on the paper, then I drew a circle around the dot. I saw myself in that dot as a horrible, ugly, shrivelled, gaunt person who I didn't want to know or accept. I knew my mother had tried to hide her pregnancy and then, later, tried to get rid of me. As I stared at the paper, I felt hatred towards the dot and pushed away the child God had created. The circle represented the barrier I had placed around the core of myself. I knew that something had to change. I decided to invite Jesus into this place of my conception. It was a struggle, but once I made the decision to let Jesus in, I used my fingers to draw paint from outside the circle into the centre. Peace came over me and I knew the battle was over. Then I realized, I was different. I could breathe again! It was as if life had entered the core of my being.

That night when, I went to bed, I felt a warmth in my chest and my spirit was so alive and kept affirming who I was. The asthma has gone and I thank God for all He has done, and I give Him all the glory...He is an amazing Father who can heal all our sicknesses and diseases (Psalm 103:3-4).

AFRICA: Derek Puffett
—Regional Director, Ellel Ministries Africa

Not knowing how God would touch the innermost parts of deeply traumatised people, we introduced healing through creativity to a group of survivors of the Rwanda genocide. To our absolute surprise and delight, we witnessed God heal and transform deep inner pain and unforgiveness, bringing joy and freedom. What a gentle yet powerful tool this is in the hands of our Creator God and healer.

AUSTRALIA: Paul Ryan
—Regional Director, Ellel Australia Pacific

This book is the unique work of a pioneer! God has used this teaching to touch lives in amazing ways. These incredible truths and vital keys come from hundreds of hours of sacrificial praying with the broken-hearted.

God heard and answered their prayers. Firstly, they discovered how vital the role of the human spirit is in bringing healing and secondly, how creativity can be powerfully used for even deeper restoration. This has changed forever how we teach and minister.

I will personally keep a copy of this book close at hand. It is full of revelation that will ensure many more lives will be miraculously impacted.

> "
> life had entered the core of my being

> "
> This has changed forever how we teach and minister

GOD'S CREATIVITY

Israel

Asia

Brush Lettering

England

USA

IN THE NATIONS

Felting

Asia

Netherlands

Scotland

Eastern Europe

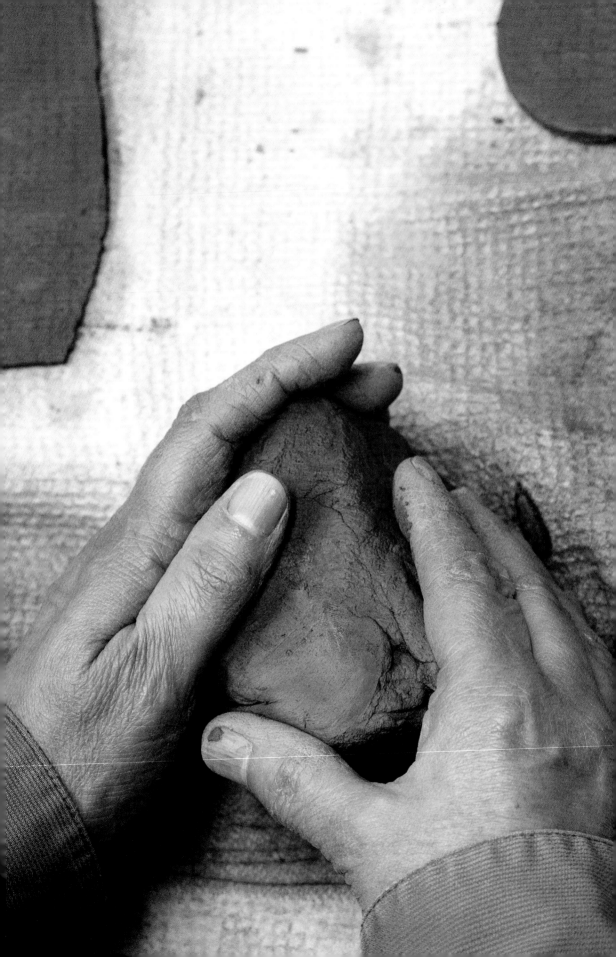

Part 2

Practical

HEALING THROUGH CREATIVITY

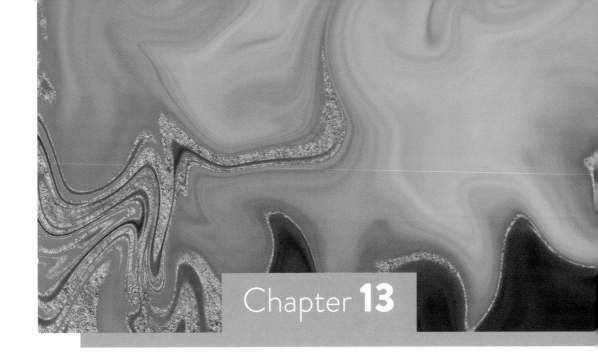

Chapter 13

CREATIVITY – SUMMARY OF HEALING PRINCIPLES IN PART ONE

In Part 1 of this book we saw how God's principles of healing through creativity provide the background to the true story of how this vision for healing was birthed, developed and is now bearing much fruit across the world. The principles, which are so solidly grounded in God's Word, the Bible, provide the keys to healing through creativity. Healing through creativity and having a relationship with the Creator cannot be separated.

God is Creator and We are Made in His Image

God is Father, Son and Holy Spirit

The three-fold nature of God is implicit throughout Scripture. We learn about the fathering love of our creator, the empowering of God's Spirit and the salvation that Jesus brought to reconcile sinful man back to a holy God.

> "I am the Alpha and Omega," says the Lord God, "who is, and who was, and who is to come, the Almighty."
>
> (Revelation 1:8)

> Jesus Christ is the image of the invisible God, the firstborn over all creation. For in him all things were created: things in heaven and on earth, visible and invisible, whether thrones or powers or rulers or authorities; all things have been created through him and for him. He is before all things, and in him all things hold together.
>
> (Colossians 1:15-17)

> In Him all the fulness of God was pleased to dwell, and through Him God was pleased to reconcile to Himself all things, whether on earth or in heaven, by making peace through the blood of His cross.　　(Colossians 1:20)

> As you therefore have received Christ Jesus the Lord, continue to live your lives in Him, rooted and built up in Him and established in the faith, just as you were taught, abounding in thanksgiving. See to it that no-one takes you captive through philosophy and empty deceit, according to human tradition, according to the elemental spirits of the universe and not according to Christ. For in Him the whole fulness of deity dwells bodily and you have come to fulness in Him, who is the head of every ruler and authority.
>
> (Colossians 2:6-9)

God is Creator and We are Made in His Image

Creativity is not only what we do, but it is an expression of who we are. God designed us as intensely creative human beings and intended our creative identity to be expressed in the following ways:

- In relationship with self, others and God
- Through body, soul and spirit
- Through freewill choice
- In time and space
- With boundaries and limits
- Through play and work
- Through bonding
- Through temperament and character
- Through imagination and expression
- Through physical and spiritual senses
- Through talents and gifts
- Through exploring and adventuring
- Through vision and invention
- With responsibility and accountability
- In family
- For fruitfulness (destiny)

The potential and need of all of the above, is contained within our human spirit from the moment of conception.

For our Creative Humanity to Grow Healthily, God Designed Us with Human Needs

These are legitimate needs which He planted in every one of us:

- Love
- Acceptance and belonging
- Safety and security
- Trust
- Value and worth
- Encouragement and affirmation
- Protection
- Discipline and guidance

We do not Live in a Perfect World

In fact, we live in a battlefield where, as a result of the Fall, there is much suffering and loss. What God originally intended for us in relationship with Him has been lost to one degree or another.

> " God saw the mess and He had a plan of redemption

God's enemy, Satan, brought about a plan of destruction, tempting humankind to cooperate with him in the sin of pride and rebellion towards God, which is now in the heart of humankind, leaving an inheritance of sin and death here on earth. We are living out the consequences of this distortion, but God saw the mess and He had a plan of redemption. Redemption is at the heart of who God is, and this redemption is being worked out through His Son Jesus for us all today.

Good News!

The good news of the coming of Jesus and His desire to heal is foretold in Isaiah 61:1-3:

> He [God the Father] has sent me [Jesus] to bind up the broken-hearted, to proclaim freedom for the captives and release from darkness for the prisoners; to proclaim the year of the LORD's favour and the day of vengeance of our GOD, to comfort all who mourn and provide for those who grieve in Zion – to bestow on them a crown of beauty instead of ashes, the oil of joy instead of mourning, and a garment of praise instead of a spirit of despair. They will be called oaks of righteousness, a planting of the LORD for the display of His splendour.

The Invitation

We are invited to receive life as our Creator God intended. Jesus said, "I have come that they may have life, and have it to the full" (John 10:10). These are the principles for receiving this new life:

- Jesus came to earth to restore and rescue. On the cross and through His choice to die and become a willing sacrifice on our behalf, He opened the way for us to come to God the Father in restored relationship.

- We are invited to receive free and full forgiveness for our sins through Jesus and to receive His righteousness.

- The way to God is through humbly acknowledging the need of Jesus in our lives to forgive, cleanse and change us. We all have pride, rebellion, stubbornness, as well as the more obvious sins. There is no-one outside the need of God's forgiveness.

- Our humanity needs help from the Holy Spirit, who brings the life of Jesus into our hearts and empowers us to overcome and shine as God the Father intended.

- There is contention and battle over us from the enemy of God, whom Jesus calls 'the father of lies' – he is the false father who comes to tempt and deceive us away from our primary source of goodness and life. The Bible describes him as a robber and a thief and says that there is no truth in him.

- Through His willing sacrifice, Jesus won the victory over Satan, sin and death. This victory is ours to appropriate as we walk in His ways, seek His face, learn from Him and trust Him and His Word. It is a journey.

- God has placed eternity in our hearts (Ecclesiastes 3:11). We are, first and foremost, spiritual beings and God planned for us an eternal future with Him. Jesus has prepared a place for all who believe on His name where one day we will be fully at peace and fully completed in our God given identity and destiny.

We are All Creative!

When God created the earth, He looked at what He created and declared that it was good. When He made humankind He said, "It is very good." Our humanity is not made bad, wrong or a mistake by the Creator, despite the sin which became entangled around us.

The Mess

The good news of Jesus' coming is that He came into the mess to rescue us. He knew it was impossible for us to climb out of the mess alone and make ourselves good enough, whoever we are. We each need to own and bring our individual struggle, mess and suffering to Jesus for His forgiveness, cleansing, comfort, healing and strength.

The Journey

We are on a journey, and it is through this journey that we experience the richness of relationship with God as part of His family. We are not alone. It is in the journey that our character changes and matures, and we see things from the perspective of God's plumb line.

It's not about the end result but about the journey

To try and separate healing through creativity from having a living relationship with the Creator God (through Jesus His Son, empowered by His Spirit), limits the touch and restorative handiwork of our loving God. His intention is for His people to enjoy redeemed, abundant life here on earth and then spend eternity with Him. We could apply some of the principles of creativity on our own, and indeed, most of us already do so to varying degrees. But God always has more for us in Him, and He invites us to seek His design for who we are so that we can enter into what He planned for us in the first place.

God invites us to seek His design for who we are

The Destination

God has a purpose for each one of our lives. The objective of all healing is not just to feel better, but to live a fulfilled life as God intended, unimpeded by the events of our past and the journey we have been on so far.

Healing through creativity touches right down into the very core of our being, that place where God inspires the desires of our heart. It is from here that new life begins to flow, and we enter into the joy of actually being the person God intended us to be, able to do the things that God in His love and merciful provision prepared in advance for us to do (Ephesians 2:10).

We are designed and loved

Chapter 14

CREATIVITY – HOW GOD WORKS THROUGH IT

God works through the vehicle of creativity, building a bridge (connection) from 'head knowledge' into the vital area of 'heart language', which for all kinds of reasons can become 'shut down', making it difficult for us to access who we are in our God-created identity. God uses the expression of creativity to bring us into life, both in a human sense and in relationship with Him.

Through creativity – God restores:
   The human spirit and soul

Through creativity – God brings forth expression of:
   Free will, opinions, emotions and decisions

Through creativity – God releases:
Potential with the ability to change, learn and grow

The joy of potential

Through creativity – God connects us:
To our own identity, who we are and who we are becoming

Through creativity – God brings bonding:
To ourselves, to others and to Himself

Through creativity – God teaches His principles of:
Responsibility and accountability, limits of time, energy and resource

Through creativity – God brings fulfillment:
A sense of achievement through experimentation, exploration, invention and skill

Through creativity – God redeems:
By building up and giving life back to hurting, damaged and empty places

God Works through His Creativity in us to:

Bring Freedom

- ୬ Freedom to be – no right or wrong, no expectation, just different

- ୬ Freedom to find yourself – own opinion and choices, individuality

- ୬ Freedom to give – something of me that I can give to someone else

- ୬ Freedom to receive – safely without fear or restraint

- ✦ Freedom to change – without fear and control
- ✦ Freedom to grow – blossom and flourish
- ✦ Freedom of spirit - to express, create, hope, envision, communicate and relate with God and others

Gently Break Down Hidden Walls of Invisible and often Subconscious Strongholds:

- ✦ Isolation
- ✦ Loneliness
- ✦ Intellectualism
- ✦ Perfectionism
- ✦ Lack of confidence
- ✦ False guilt

- ✦ Embarrassment and inhibition
- ✦ Inability to bond and receive love
- ✦ Blocked emotion and memory
- ✦ Sin
- ✦ Lost identity

Bring Connections to Mind Sets, such as:

- ✦ "I'm not that type – I'm intellectual."
- ✦ "I'm no good at this – it's not worth trying."
- ✦ "I always fail – it's not safe to make a mistake."
- ✦ "I must achieve – the result is everything."

- ✦ "My life is a mess – I don't go there."
- ✦ "I can't be spontaneous – I need to stay in control."
- ✦ "I can't cope with change – I stay with what I know."

Reduce Anxiety by:

- ✦ Unwinding tension and stress
- ✦ Bringing rest
- ✦ Calming nervousness
- ✦ Dissipating illusion through connection to truth
- ✦ Disempowering unhealthy controls

- ✦ Releasing Emotions
- ✦ Removing blockages to tears in surprising ways
- ✦ Freeing laughter
- ✦ Bringing connection to injustice and pain in healthy ways

- Giving a framework for expressing emotion in non-verbal ways
- Bringing release through 'letting go' in creative expression

- Explosions of negative emotion and mess being healthily discharged

Enable Us to Come as Children to the Father's Banquet to Receive/Experience:

- True guilt washed, cleansed and forgiven
- Rest
- Personal worth and value
- Unconditional acceptance and belonging
- New confidence
- Overcoming
- Joy and laughter
- Release

- Place of change and growth
- Safety to fail and be imperfect
- A new perspective
- A softened and yielded heart
- A deeper intimacy and trust
- Ability to receive conviction, loving correction and heart transformation
- Fruitfulness
- Family

"For I know the plans I have for you," declares the LORD, "plans to prosper you and not to harm you, plans to give you hope and a future." (JEREMIAH 29:11)

Ah, Sovereign LORD, you have made the heavens and the earth by your great power and outstretched arm. Nothing is too hard for you. (JEREMIAH 32:17)

Chapter 15

CREATIVITY – HOW GOD USES IT TO BREAK THROUGH INTO SUBCONSCIOUS AREAS

Coping with problems and difficulties is part of being human, and the learning curve to do so can be steep along life's way. It is in the subconscious area of our inner being that danger lurks. We may not be outwardly aware that how we behave and react can come from unhealed hidden places within.

Problems arise when the painful reality of these inner places does not just 'go away' but remains 'suffering' and produces mind sets and realities, which the person living everyday life has no cognisant connection to. Sometimes, those responses, reactions and behaviours from the subconscious place are thought of as being 'just me' and 'the way I am', when the truth is that these are painful places which need help and healing.

> He sees
> beyond the
> mess to the
> real person

This inner being is the place which God wants to reach with His love. Jesus came for us as people, and His focus is on finding us. He doesn't see us as a series of 'issues' to be dealt with but sees beyond the mess to the real person beneath. We can ask Him by His Holy Spirit to guide us into acknowledging, accepting and embracing the sensitive truths and realities of our inner being where the experiences of life have formed and shaped the person we are.

Freedom comes when we embrace truth in these innermost places (Psalm 51:6). The identification of wounding opens the way to receiving the Father's compassion and healing. Recognising and owning sinful responses and actions are equally releasing and healing. The Holy Spirit's work brings light and truth to the places where sin has been gripping like graveclothes, entangled around our God-given identity and frees us from condemnation (Romans 8:1). The enemy loves to capitalise on the sins and wounds in the subconscious places of our inner being, in order to bring further crushing to the true identity of the person God created us to be.

At any and every level, creative expression helps break through subconscious barriers, facilitating God's heart being able to bring powerful restoration. We may not be aware of the kind of cords that constrain us, like invisible chains holding us back from realising the potential God placed in us from the beginning of life. For this reason, it is particularly vital to bring ourselves to Jesus, allowing His grace to bring connection between our inner and outer being.

God's design is for our spirit, soul and body to be in unity and to work together in harmony. Because of the Fall we live with a certain amount of conflict (Romans 7:15-20), but it is not God's intention for us to be at war within ourselves. As one person expressed it, "Healing must be being the same on the inside as you are on the outside." Understanding ourselves and who God made us to be, is the beginning of healing, bringing peaceful harmony to the inner being.

My goal is that they may be encouraged in heart and
united in love, so that they may have the full riches of
complete understanding. (Colossians 2:2)

*Healing must be being the same on the inside
as you are on the outside*

Some Types of Subconscious Blockages and Controls

Fears and Anxiety

For the Spirit God gave us does not make us timid, but
gives us power, love and self-discipline. (2 Timothy 1:7)

Fears come in all shapes and sizes and are common, in one
way or another, to us all, e.g.:

- Fear of failure
- Fear of making a mistake
- Fear of people
- Fear of self
- Fear of wasting time, being a nuisance, in the way
- Fear of not getting everything right and perfect
- Fear of making a choice

- Fear of God being angry
- Fear of expressing an opinion
- Fear of responsibility
- Fear of change
- Fear of being ridiculed and mocked
- Fear of not pleasing people
- Fear of rejection

Fear, anxiety and insecurity stifles and controls life. God wants
us to have assurance of understanding (Colossians 2:2). If we
understand something, it goes a long way to undermining
paralysing fears. There is no security in this world alone, but
there is in belonging to Him and His family. His family is

designed to be a safe place where fears can be owned and addressed and brought to Him. He delivers us from fear (Psalm 34:4). Creative expression helps to touch the reality of subconscious fears and anxieties and enables us to face them and be set free.

Phobias and Obsessions

For some people, fears become complicated since they turn into phobias. A phobia is the desperate need to avoid something we are extremely fearful of and is often seemingly irrational, e.g. a phobic fear of enclosed spaces, or alternatively, of open spaces. However, there will be a rational root behind the fear.

An obsession, on the other hand, is the need to cling to something or someone in order to gain a sense of safety. It could manifest in behaviours such as obsessive thinking, list-making, handwashing, checking or hoarding etc, and it and it can be tied to a compulsive need to control food, possessions or circumstances.

Subconsciously, inner nervousness, anxiety and panic are at work feeding the need for the top layer of behaviour to be strongly in control, which in turn leaves no space for life to be lived freely. It is a treadmill of 'having to do' rather than 'able to be' – inner tensions hold spontaneity back.

These invisible cords of bondage can be broken through personal creative expression, especially when there is someone alongside to help that expression.

Compulsions

The Lord is near. Do not be anxious about anything, but in every situation, by prayer and petition, with thanks-giving, present your requests to God. And the peace of

God which transcends all understanding, will guard your hearts and your minds in Christ Jesus. (PHILIPPIANS 4:5-7)

Compulsive behaviour comes from a need to control circumstances and to feel safe. Creativity undermines the control, using play and elements of creative expression that have no right or wrong or which cannot be controlled. The Holy Spirit can bring revelation and freedom to where these controls are rooted and where fear needs releasing during the creativity time when there are less guards up.

Creativity undermines the control

Addictions

Love must be sincere. Hate what is evil; cling to what is good. (ROMANS 12:9)

Addictions are the outworking of deeper issues. God brings healing through creativity as a means by which the Holy Spirit can touch into areas where anxiety and controls are rooted. It can help emotional expression to be released in safety, thus reducing or even eliminating the inner drive for the addiction. Conviction, ownership and responsibility must also play their part, as with all aspects of healing, but particularly so with addictions.

Depression

It is impossible for God to lie, we who have fled to take hold of the hope set before us may be greatly encouraged. We have this hope as an anchor for the soul, firm and secure. (HEBREWS 6:18-19)

Depression is a broad term which encompasses a wide variety of symptoms, roots and fruits. Some of the issues listed above are likely to be present alongside depression. Being with others is often difficult for people with depression, and loneliness and isolation can be part of the problem.

God does know the depth of depression, and creativity can meet a person in depression in remarkable ways. It is not a therapy to make you feel good. Creativity is a means of bringing God's heart and His life-giving truth and comfort to crushed places on the inside.

Anger and Rage

In your anger do not sin.   (EPHESIANS 4:26)

Bottled up and dissociated anger and rage wreak havoc with our mental, emotional and spiritual life. They also rob us of relationships. But God is not afraid of anger. The Psalmist is very real with God in expressing anger (Psalm 13:1-4, Psalm 139:19, Psalm 17:8-13). Satan will always make us feel it is too big or out of control, and he would like that to be the case and to shame us in more sinful ways.

Through belonging to Jesus, He gives us victory over these areas. We need to entrust our emotional responses to Him in appropriate ways. Creativity enables the mess to be expressed in safety if we ask the Holy Spirit to help us.

Triggers

Hidden in the inner being can be 'triggers' which are associations with negative past events. On a simple level, the trigger could be the look and smell of something like custard, which instantly takes us back to the lumpy, cold custard we were made to eat at school! On a more serious level, triggers can connect our human senses to subconscious traumatic events – a noise, a smell, a taste, a familiar but disrelated sight, a sensation or feeling.

Creativity facilitates connection to the hidden trauma of negative life experiences which has often been carried for many years. It is a powerful vehicle for expressing previously blocked emotion and receiving God's comfort and healing.

Existing and Surviving

Existing and surviving can subconsciously become a way of life particularly if you have had to learn to push down feelings in extreme situations and carry on. God designed us to process and digest our responses and feelings. The human spirit needs space and time to do this, because this is where healing of our core identity lies.

Although, more often than not, we need to carry on with everyday life, with all its pressures and responsibilities, there comes a time when it is dangerous to override the inner being and not 'hear' what the heart cry on the inside is. Jesus has heard that cry and this is where He can bring His comfort, kindness, healing and change. 'Now to him who is able to do immeasurably more than all we ask or imagine, according to his power that is at work within us' (Ephesians 3:20).

We may have been overpowered by:

- Too much responsibility and expectation from a young age
- Deprivation
- Manipulation of emotions and thinking
- Absence of balanced discipline
- Role reversal (child parenting the parent)
- Absence of parental guidance and safety
- Cruelty and punishment
- Sexual abuse
- Trauma (circumstances of life)

God uses creativity to bring about redemption, something He wants to give back in the face of what has been lost. We may have lost ourselves along life's way, where circumstances became too much, and we were overwhelmed. Non-verbal creative expression helps release the inner being (and possibly child within, where the hurt and damage is). As Jesus helps bring the connection to these subconscious areas, He carries the burdens and releases joy and freedom into our lives.

Perfect love drives out fear. (1 JOHN 4:18)

Relational Issues

God created us with a need for bonding with others. He did not set us in life for isolation and complete independence. We are designed for a healthy mix of independence and dependency, which is inter-dependence. Bonding is a natural outworking of drawing close and to trusting others in life.

Bondage, on the other hand, is to be unhealthily tied in relationship. It is more of an attachment, than a freedom to give and a freedom to receive. Conversely, there is the possibility of the opposite problem where no ties of any description are made and are, rather, avoided at all costs.

Without a healthy bond, usually made in the womb with the mother, the prime source of nurture and nourishment, an inner emptiness can occur leaving a gap in our identity. Healthy bonding leads to the ability to trust and, if those principles are damaged or missing, it can lead to all manner of difficulties in relationships. Without trust there cannot be an authentic relationship. We harm ourselves without trust. This damage occurs in the subconscious place.

We all need a healthy trust in ourselves, in others and, most importantly, in God in whom our security ultimately lies. God is out of time, and He can effect profound healing using creativity to facilitate natural bonding experiences.

" without trust there cannot be an authentic relationship

In relationship with Jesus, we are brought into God's family as His children – we belong!

> See what great love the Father has lavished on us, that we should be called children of God! And that is what we are!
>
> (1 JOHN 3:1)

This truth is outworked to some extent here on earth amongst the family of God. We are brothers and sisters and have a Father who loves us, knows us and plans for our good. The family of God is designed to be a healing place not a divisive one, and it is here there is much healing work to be done, which begins with us as individuals.

Family brings enrichment and bonding

Creativity helps us to let go of barriers in relationships, such as, dominance, judgement, transference of guilt, legalism, passivity and religiosity.

> For he himself is our peace, who has made the two groups one and has destroyed the barrier, the dividing wall of hostility. (EPHESIANS 2:14)

It is God's blessing that we are set in His family, where we can learn, change and grow, each in our own unique and individual personhood. Everyone is at a different place on their personal journey and we can each help one another along the way. This is God's plan, which we see in Jesus's prayer for us in John 17, that we may be one, and in John 13, where He says the world will know we belong to Him by the love we have for one another.

Having others close to us, who can help with the release of our creativity and consequent walk in God's truth, is a desired blessing in life. We are all designed to be imparters of life, both in the giving and receiving.

Chapter 16

CREATIVITY – HOW GOD USES IT TO BRING HIS HEALING, RESTORATION AND TRUTH

There are many ways in which God brings His healing into our lives through the expression of creativity – so many, in fact, that it is hard to define them as separate entities because one blessing simply flows into another, and another until the whole person is blessed.

For example, creative expression may be a way of facing sin issues that need to be confessed and forgiven. But this in turn brings restoration to our human spirit, which then changes our disposition and can lift us out of depression and restore our mental health! So, while in this chapter I have listed some of the many ways God can bring healing and restoration through creativity, the potential for many different consequential blessings is limitless!

Types of Healing and Restoration Brought Through Creativity

Restoration of the Human Spirit

> The LORD is close to the broken hearted and saves those who are crushed in spirit. (PSALM 34:18)

Scripture makes it clear we are created spirit, soul and body. It is possible for the human spirit to be crushed, which results in loss of identity and potential. Creativity and inspiration are sourced in our human spirit, and God wants to bring His restoration and healing where there has been crushing.

Feeding the human spirit with life

Restoration of Identity – Being Found and Known

> You have searched me, LORD, and you know me. For you created my inmost being; you knit me together in my mother's womb. I praise you because I am fearfully and wonderfully made. (PSALM 139:1, 13–14)

Some people have lost themselves

Loss of identity can come in many ways, and some people have lost themselves and do not know who they are. Scripture makes it clear that God does know us and that it is His plan to find us and give us fulfilment and life. Creativity gives the Holy Spirit the time and room to connect us to lost and buried places within. It helps us own ourselves and not to hate or hide places in us that we are ashamed of.

Restoration of What has been Lost (Bereavement and Loss)

> To proclaim the year of the LORD's favour and the day of vengeance of our GOD, to comfort all who mourn, and provide for those who grieve in Zion— to bestow on them a crown of beauty instead of ashes, the oil of joy instead of mourning, and a garment of praise instead of a spirit of despair.
>
> (ISAIAH 61:2)

Bereavement and loss are part of life and we all have the human need to feel and express bereavement and loss. It should not be overlooked. God is the God of all comfort (2 Corinthians 1:3). Creativity allows time and space to express meaningful ways of letting go and grieving.

Mental Health

DEPRESSION

Depression can be beyond words and drains motivation. It comes from a crushed human spirit which is intended by God to be the life-source of health and strength. God knows how to lift the spirit and bring hope into the hopeless, lost places. He brings life to the dead!

He reaches into the lost places of our hearts

Creative expression without words, possibly using the messy paints, can bring about a non-verbal way of reaching into crushed places of the human spirit. Expression of any kind helps disempower depression. The crushed human spirit can begin to breathe, and this may come through hearing music, writing, talking or listening to inspired songs. It may come through touching something of God's character in nature by walking, painting, sailing etc. These things bring

Jesus close and are in harmony with receiving the comfort of His Word.

MOOD SWINGS

Trusting the Holy Spirit to help bring forth the expression of feelings in a creative way, can release the truth of God to bring balance and release into subconscious areas where controls are hidden.

PERSONALITY PROBLEMS

Creative expression facilitates God finding and restoring the lost inner child. The Holy Spirit can use it to help bring connection to self, valuing of self and acceptance of self.

DISSOCIATION

Dissociation creates unreality, which is fiercely guarded since it brings disconnection to painful truth. However, connection to the reality of suffering is, ultimately, the way to peace. Running away makes matters worse. God can use creativity to bring His truth and comfort, instead of the false 'fix-its' of dissociation and denial which in the end bring torment.

INNER VOICES

As false shame and false guilt are identified and embraced, the need for inner voices is disempowered, and instead God's truth is imparted. The enemy will always seek to whisper lies and deception into our inner being. Through creative expression which can be in many different ways, Jesus draws close and releases us from condemnation, which is the work of the enemy.

> finding and restoring the lost inner child

Behavioural Dysfunction

Love is patient, love is kind. It does not envy, it does not boast, it is not proud. It does not dishonour others, it is

> not self-seeking, it is not easily angered, it keeps no record
> of wrongs. Love does not delight in evil but rejoices with
> the truth. (1 Corinthians 13:4-6)

Often there is an inner child who has suffered deprivation, abuse, cruelty, neglect, been overlooked or spoilt, or the circumstances of life, e.g. extended or traumatic sickness, which may have caused a gap in development. God is a redeemer and He wants to restore and give back where suffering has taken place, and to wash and cleanse the guilt and defilement of behavioural dysfunction. He also wants to bring safe discipline into our lives bringing growth, accountability and good boundaries. Various types of creative expression and bonding can help develop maturity and strength.

Restoration of Brokenness

> The Spirit of the Sovereign Lord is on me, because the
> Lord has anointed me to proclaim good news to the poor.
> He has sent me to bind up the brokenhearted, to proclaim
> freedom for the captives and release from darkness for the
> prisoners. (Isaiah 61:1)

The Lord is close to the broken hearted (Psalm 34:18). He hears and He knows their cries. God will use our creativity to come close, whether it is through music, personal expression or through bonding within His family. He plans for good and to give an opportunity to receive good things from His hand. He wants us to know He is close, and His comfort is not just words but also practical and real. Expression through poetry, writing, painting, music etc. help with identification, expression and connection to the painful areas God wants to touch and heal.

True Sin

> Therefore, there is now no condemnation for those who are in Christ Jesus, because through Christ Jesus the law of the Spirit who gives life has set you free from the law of sin and death.
> (ROMANS 8:1-2)

We are all sinful and it is healthy to acknowledge this and to want to change. Our need is of light and conviction which come from the Holy Spirit who shines truth into our hearts. Creativity can be a means of helping us connect to our hidden desires, responses, bitterness and our heart intentions, such as:

UNFORGIVENESS

> Bear with each other and forgive one another if any of you has a grievance against someone. Forgive as the Lord forgave you.
> (COLOSSIANS 3:13)

God brings healing through creativity as it can highlight the need to both receive and give forgiveness. Those who have hurt, betrayed and abused us and the memories alongside can be touched and connected to. Bitterness might need to come out, perhaps in a messy painting-type way or expressed in writing and later placed in a bin as a practical way of release to God. Jesus alone can take the weight of the wrongs we have done, and the wrongs others have done to us. Forgiveness often involves the powerful use of writing or an act of release in a creative way.

HATRED

> But the fruit of the Spirit is love, joy, peace, forbearance, kindness, goodness, faithfulness.
> (GALATIANS 5:22)

Hatred towards self and towards others brings destruction. It is important to seek the Holy Spirit's work of conviction and help in releasing these powerful strongholds. Owning these truths and giving them to God can sometimes be facilitated through writing or with paint in the messy room.

MANIPULATION

> If you hold to my teaching, you are really my disciples. Then you will know the truth, and the truth will set you free.
>
> (JOHN 8:31-32)

Recognition of the way we control by manipulating another person, their emotions, feelings or beliefs, into what benefits us, is important. Shame can be a strong means of keeping us from confession and allowing deceit to keep us blind. Holy Spirit inspired creativity, however, is a powerful connector to truth and, if we are willing, allows the Holy Spirit to show us the truth about ourselves, which will result in enormous personal release and freedom, and have its outworking for others too. We are empowered to change and lose the need to manipulate.

a powerful connector to truth

LACK OF SUBMISSION

> Let everyone be subject to the governing authorities, for there is no authority except that which God has established. The authorities that exist have been established by God. Consequently, whoever rebels against the authority is rebelling against what God has instituted.
>
> (ROMANS 13:1-2)

Independence can be a prime excuse never to come under another person's authority. It is a prideful position. Inspired creativity can bring Holy Spirit conviction of the truth that authority is God-given, and that teamwork and advice, correction and accountability and input from others are all essential parts of peaceful living. Creativity can help bring a truth home, allowing the Lord to heal fears and help us give way to living as God intended in His family without the prideful friction caused by "I know best" and "I'll do it my way."

PASSIVITY

Passivity is a form of rebellion. The refusal to enter into relational activity, coupled with allowing others to take responsibility on our behalf, can rob us of fruitfulness. Passivity stands in the way of adventuring, changing and growing. God brings healing through creativity which can help us to mature and grow on the inside, especially when it is with others who are able to reflect truth back to us. It is good to have a safe place to begin to enter into new things and take up rightful accountability and responsibility.

ATTITUDE

The glasses through which we view life can be greatly influenced by deep inner beliefs about ourselves and the world around us, and these glasses produce attitudes and prejudices which can, in turn, rob us of truth.

Our lives, with our beliefs, need to be anchored in who God is and His truth, which is a plumb line guiding us into security and safety. We also need others around us who can bring a balance of truth and perception. God brings healing through His family and in many forms of creative expression, including teamwork.

Isolation, frustration, jealousy and independence can be exposed and then brought to Jesus for His cleansing and healing. The Holy Spirit can bring about a change in these core beliefs towards ourselves and others, confronting and connecting us with conviction to a freeing truth. It may be to dispel false guilt, melt a bitter attitude or to soften our hearts towards another person etc. Not least, a false attitude towards our own self, and even towards God, may be changed.

God Uses Creativity, It Begins and Ends with Him

Creativity is meant as an aid and facilitator to the work of the Holy Spirit, bringing conviction of sin, freedom and healing. The team works alongside, supporting and encouraging an individual to work with God, allowing Him to bring truth into the situation and achieve breakthroughs in an uncontrived and personal way.

> And over all these virtues put on love, which binds them all together in perfect unity. Let the peace of Christ rule in your hearts, since as members of one body you were called to peace. And be thankful. Let the message of Christ dwell among you richly as you teach and admonish one another with all wisdom through psalms, hymns, and songs from the Spirit, singing to God with gratitude in your hearts. And whatever you do, whether in word or deed, do it all in the name of the Lord Jesus, giving thanks to God the Father through him."
> (COLOSSIANS 3:14-17)

How Creativity is Used in a God-Given Way to Bring God's Healing

- It is a servant to the message – it brings God's life to His children.
- It is not an end in itself – there is no focus on result or end product, although this could be the outcome.
- It is a facilitator for God to work – releasing subconscious and hidden controls.
- It is God's gift to build up lives and put good things in.
- It is a powerful connector to Father God.
- It is a family environment, bringing about God's principles of bonding and sharing.
- It has a broad spectrum, so God's principles can be

used in many different settings.

- It is a reflector of the nature and character of God, so brings Him close.

- It is like an appetite - it needs awakening so that the Holy Spirit can work.

- It is not taught but caught – it builds a bridge from the head to the heart and helps remove cerebral reliance on God.

- It releases faith and trust in God.

- It is not just about 'doing crafts' (as some people think creativity is), although God can use craftwork, in the sense that He is the Master Craftsman.

- It does not necessarily have a definite aim or goal, i.e. production. It is more about 'being' than 'doing' and finding God in the experience of 'just being'.

- Through intercessory prayer, it releases an anointing of the Holy Spirit on the experience and the individual person's unique personhood.

- Affirms the person's own conviction that God is working in their life, which brings peace.

- Diminishes and even takes away fears, panics and behavioural dysfunction, if there are those around who can bring God's assurance and comfort.

- Validates pain and genuine struggle as it releases God's heart, He is close to the broken-hearted.

- Invalidates apathy, passivity and self-pity, which are graveclothes entangled around wounds. It prods the places necessary to move us out of stupor and into life as a child of God not an orphan.

- Encourages coming into the light where the safety of Jesus is, rather than hiding away.

- It releases healthy Holy Spirit conviction of sin, rather than condemnation from the enemy and self or others.

- It disempowers false guilt and shame, condemnation and self-hatred. The Holy Spirit can move in ways, which touch these places without restriction, and into the heart areas where the core issues are.

- It helps affirm a person's own likes, dislikes, choices,

feelings, opinions – these are precious to God.

- ✿ It releases encouragement and advice – to change, try something else, adventure, experiment or explore.

- ✿ It entails sharing who you are, fun things, struggles, giving, receiving, mistakes, muddles and messes. In sharing the life of God together, there is a strengthening which breaks down the isolation and lies of the enemy. God's family is designed to be a strength to build one other up. 'As each part does its own special work, it helps the other parts grow, so that the whole body is healthy and growing and full of love' (Ephesians 4:16 NLT).

- ✿ It brings about God-given bonding, joining and growth.

- ✿ It facilitates God's gifts of time and space and freedom of personal choice.

- ✿ It exemplifies God's principle of 'no favourites' – in the family there is safety to be unique, embracing one other, relaxing, having fun, letting go of masks – it is inclusive to all. No one is outside of having been made in God's image, even though we have all received levels of distortion through the fall. God is there in our struggle and loss.

When is Creativity not 'Healing Through Creativity' as Expressed in this Book?

- ✿ When it is akin to a test.

- ✿ When it is a job, or about producing something as a performance.

- ✿ When it is disjointed from the message.

- ✿ When it is prescriptive.

- ✿ When it becomes a way of 'venting' anger as opposed to releasing it to God.

- ✿ When the creative gift or activity becomes an idol or worshipped.

- ✿ When it is separated from God's nature and character as Creator and Father.

- When it is seen as a substitute for traditional prayer and Bible reading.

- When it leads into idolatry or purely a selfish pursuit, rather than leading us to serve and give to others out of gratitude for all that has been given to us.

- When it distorts, diminishes or mocks beauty.

Qualities of a Creativity Team

- Those who know and love the Lord Jesus.

- Spiritual mothers and father figures who are able to nurture others.

- Those with homely, welcoming, embracing hearts for people.

- Those who are willing to share of themselves.

- Imparters, mentors and encouragers.

- Non-judgemental and non-condemnatory people.

- Those with the ability to teach a skill, and be under pressure without reacting.

- Lovers of people.

- Kind, sensitive and generous natured people.

- Hard workers.

- Teachable people who are under the authority of a church body or organisation.

- Preferably trained in prayer ministry and/or pastoral work.

- Those who have ability in a particular creative field e.g. sewing, pottery, woodwork (no need to be a professional!).

- Ability to draw alongside without dominating or controlling another.

- Good team players – willing to fit in, be flexible to a changing agenda and be there for the good of the whole.

- Confidential and trustworthy people.

- Willing to be flexible and releasing.
- Those able to share their own personal journey with God, with others and impart faith and hope.

Chapter 17

CREATIVITY – **CREATIVE ELEMENTS IN THE JOURNEY OF HEALING**

The following pages feature some of the different creative experiences that God has used on our *Healing Through Creativity* courses, to minister His love and healing into people's lives. But this is not a comprehensive list, and for each person there are different ways in which God can work. For example, my husband would include fishing on his list. He finds getting out in the middle of a loch with just him, the surrounding beauty, the art of fishing and, of course, God, an incredibly restorative experience.

He would also include restoring something to its original beautiful condition on his list of creative joys, as well as reading and doing jigsaws!

Clay & Pottery

> Yet, O LORD, you are our Father; we are the clay, and you
> are our potter; we are all the work of your hand.
>
> (ISAIAH 64:8)

Clay is a powerful means of connection and engages our senses both physically and spiritually. It brings connection to God. One particularly broken person put it this way:

> When I was on the wheel, the teacher put her hands onto mine to guide them. I came with a deep fear of anyone touching me. I mistrusted everyone. Through the teacher's kind and gentle approach, I felt a safety come over me. I knew that God was using this person to break down and melt my fears as I allowed my hands to mould the clay with hers guiding me, God was enabling me to trust Him.

Moulding clay releases spontaneity and imagination, as there is often no right or wrong way with it. Some people like to simply play with the clay, finding a freedom in not having to perform and produce.

Imagination free to go wild

At times, it doesn't go as planned and God so often speaks powerfully into a person's broken heart through these seeming calamities, releasing emotions and bringing connection to a very real struggle in their life.

One lady spent a very long time trying to mould a heart shape. It kept going wrong, so she repeatedly squashed the clay back into a ball and tried again. Finally, in her frustration and disappointment, she turned to God, asking, "Why can't I do this?" He answered her heart cry, saying, "This is what you've done all your life – you've tried to change and mould your own heart. Let me help you."

God brought connection to the years of striving, and as the emotion was released, she invited Him to help her this time, to mould a new clay heart. This time. not only was the result beautiful, but the Lord had met her in the place of her

> "...you've tried to change and mould your own heart. Let me help you."

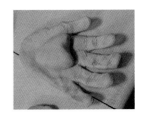

very real struggle in life and set her on a new path with Him.

Something therapeutic is released in engaging with clay. Touching and feeling this earthy medium brings a life of its own. The idea of moulding something out of nothing heralds new life.

Learning a skill can be healing. Some people have never received kindness and patience, or experienced another person giving of their time to carefully show them how to do something. Subconscious messages many have received, of, "No good!" or "Failure!" are like invisible cords and bonds, that begin to be released.

> "No good!" or "Failure!" are like invisible cords and bonds, that begin to be released.

learning a new skill

Another person wrote this:

> For a long time, I have been creatively active, but after the Creativity Course something changed: I found I was more patient towards myself and able to work at sculpting something from clay for a longer time, being more attentive. I was so encouraged to finally be free to make 'mistakes', step by step making it more beautiful, bringing in details. In fact, it is only because I had the courage to start the process, knowing I was free not to have to succeed the first time, that I have ended up making something I like much better than anything I've done in the past, something that needed more time and attention than just doing something quick in a moment. This has been so rewarding for me!

God loves building something good into our lives. He does not just address our sin and leave us stuck in our pain and suffering. Making pots, bowls, jugs and more at the potter's wheel is fun and fulfilling, and much is taught in the process, that is not just about the end result!

GOD

IS

MY

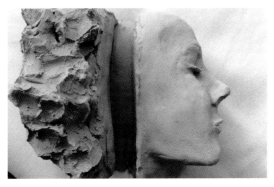

MAKER

Textiles

> For you created my inmost being; you knit me together in my mother's womb ... My frame was not hidden from you when I was made in the secret place, when I was woven together in the depths of the earth.
>
> (PSALM 139:13 AND 15)

These aspects of creativity are not just for women! Many men enjoy this type of creative expression and some are particularly gifted in these areas. There is something of the heart of God about threading a needle and making something out of cloth, or weaving, knitting or felting different colours together, which speaks of how God puts us together. There is a designer to one degree or another in all of us.

Making various textures available including, for example, velvet, hessian, silky, woollen, cotton, fluffy, bright and bold, pastel and muted, patterned and plain. An array of fabrics, yarns, ribbons and trims call out to be touched and felt, chosen and used to make something. It could be something useful, for example: a book cover, a bag, a hanging heart-shape, a small item of clothing, a decorative item, a rug, a scarf, a piece of jewellery, a blanket, hat or picture.

Weaving or felting can be crafted to make a bag, a rug, scarf or wall hanging. Knitting can be worked to make a small garment, a brooch, or just a pattern, or squares to make blankets. The array of colours in the wool alongside the blends are a joy to the eyes.

All these things can come out of the imagination, our own vision or a pattern. They can be quirky, made just for the fun of it, useful or meaningful or a mixture. The important thing is that there does not necessarily have to be a right or wrong, since it is the journey of learning and experimenting which is joyous in itself.

" it is the journey of learning and experimenting which is joyous in itself.

Sewing

Having a 'Mum' at the sewing machine brings back memories for some. It can be a difficult reminder of school and how the teacher pronounced failure. One lady shared with me about the perfectionism of her mother, who made her sit for hours getting everything absolutely right, and at the end told her, "You will never be any good with this."

For others, there is an emptiness and a longing for the Mum who was absent, never there, never entering into creative pleasures with them. For yet others, the sewing workshop is simply a wonderful reminder of days long gone when there was time to play and experiment. The joy of re-discovery, with time just 'to be' releases stress and anxiety locked underneath in subconscious areas. Mind sets regarding sewing can also be broken, e.g. "It's a 'women's thing.'" Thankfully nowadays these stereotypes are being broken, and the inclusion of both men and women in any aspect of creativity is welcome. We all have expressions to offer.

Old mind gets broken

Sewing can include the smaller handsewn items or the bigger items: keyrings, brooches, book covers, bags, cushion covers, banners, quilts, items of clothing and the list goes on!

There is something about sewing which speaks of God intimately holding us, guiding us and taking time to shape and make something beautiful of our lives.

Weaving

Many men as well as women have enjoyed weaving the coloured threads in and out to build up a body of cloth. Each creation has its own meaning because we put something of ourselves into the process. We may keep the finished piece as a reminder of touching our own choices and desire, or perhaps give it to someone as a meaningful gift. Our guests tell us how they have met with God and heard Him speak during the process of taking time to weave a piece of cloth, which possibly goes on to be made into a rug, a handbag, scarf, wall hanging or other kind of gift.

Giving God and ourselves time in something creative, like weaving, is helpful in stopping our daily routines of 'having to do' rather than 'be', and from there, we can find we have heard His voice and known His presence.

Felting

The felting process is one which requires a great deal of finger and arm strength to mould the wool fibres together with soap and water. This takes time, energy and patience! Discovering the unprescribed result is fun! God uses this to speak of His patient way with us.

It is impossible for two finished pieces to be the same, because you cannot control the outcome, it is largely experimental. As the colours blend and hold together, shapes are forged, making the end result into a piece of beautifully blended wool, which can be used for practical things or simply as a collage or piece of jewellery.

"

As the colours blend and hold together, shapes are forged

Another type of felting is needle felting, which involves using strands of felting wool and using a needle to press them into a prepared surface to make a picture. This is very popular since it doesn't require the same amount of physical effort and good results are produced fairly quickly. It is an excellent group activity which brings bonding and joy and is helpful in overcoming fears and learning a new skill.

The delight people have in felting is immense. To be able to make something worthwhile from strands of coloured wool in a fairly quick period of time is fun. Our guests often share how using their hands to work the felt with the soap and water has brought aspects of God's nature and character to them in personal ways.

The wool itself speaks of Jesus as the Good Shepherd of the sheep. His sheep hear and know His voice. How brilliant of God to make sheep, whose wool bless us human beings in so many ways, not least in keeping us warm.

Knitting

Sitting together in comfy chairs and knitting breaks down barriers and encourages a relaxed atmosphere and flow of bonding. Many share how being together as a little group doing something for pleasure, has helped them begin to open up and communicate. Laughter often emanates as both men and women enjoy this aspect of creativity, helping each other with techniques and, of course, the inevitable dropped stitches!

Some tell us that the knitting process itself, releases tension and the expression of emotions, as they experience connections to unresolved areas within themselves which need working through, the actual act of knitting helping them to work out feelings and emotions.

God uses everything: the unravelling, a dropped stitch making a hole, mistakes in the pattern etc to bring out frustration and anger, tears and pain. In picking up stitches it is an encouraging reminder that with God when things have gone wrong in the past, it is not hopeless because He can go to those lost places within and bring comfort and healing.

*Untangling the wool and knitting –
it brought such peace*

Somehow, God uses the physical working with textiles to bring a powerful connection to an inner reality, and to work His restoration. Sewing, weaving, felting and knitting speak of the threads of our lives being held by God and a purpose being worked out by Him. During the time spent engaging in this type of creative activities, many give stories of how God spoke to them. They often experience a clear connection to their own life in relationship with Him.

Jewellery Making

In Scripture, God speaks of those who belong to Him as 'His precious jewels' (Malachi 3:17).

A small child will learn and enjoy threading beads. Jewellery is something we like to wear and adorn ourselves with. In essence, it adds sparkle and life to our personality. Some wear jewellery that is highly crafted by artisans, but for others it is homemade and just as precious in its meaning and enjoyment.

Having boxes of beads in a wide variety of shapes, colours and textures is a great way to start creative juices going! Ideas begin to flow for beads to adorn the dullest of things, and to be put together to make something exquisite, like a butterfly or a 3D element to adorn a piece of art or sewing work.

The shapes, colours, textures are a feast!

Making jewellery as a gift is very popular. If there are diamonds, gold and silver (not real of course!) in the choice, these are the first to disappear. They speak of value. There seems no end to the ways that jewels can be used creatively as a decoration.

Collage and Craft

Collages are a good way of expressing through nature. Going for a walk to collect 'natural treasures', such as fir cones, leaves, flowers, twigs, pebbles, seashells and feathers etc, bring restoration and healing deep inside through the natural world. Imagination can run riot with nature in a multitude of ways.

If, for any reason, you do not have access to the natural world or the right timeframe, the use of old magazines with all the colours and gifted photographical images they contain, also bring the outside world close. We touch our own identity, our opinion, choices and responses, "Oh! Isn't that lovely? I like that!" or, "Ugh! I would never buy that!" "Wow! How stunning!" etc. Touching your own opinion and personhood is very important, it is a way of valuing yourself and helps with bonding to your own self.

The use of words and photographs cut out from magazines: people images, work images, textile images, food images and much more, help with expression. On our *Healing Through Creativity* courses, we use these images to help people search for ways God might be speaking to them, to help them express their own likes and dislikes, and to build something of how they view their own identity.

A great depiction of individual creativity can go into collage-making, with the use of natural resources, such as food products, like flour, pasta shapes etc.

Making Cards

> *you cannot fit anyone in a box!*

A plethora of coloured card, patterned papers, paints, pens, crayons, stickers, sequins, glue, lettering, ink stamps and pads and an abundance of all manner of bits and bobs. They all get the imagination working, and whether working to a pre-designed template or from nothing, designs emerge. These can come out in quirky, arty, expressive or beautiful ways, enough for us to realise you cannot fit anyone in a box!

Making a card prompts holding another person in mind and facilitates God's healing in the area of bonding with another through giving something of yourself, which makes the card all the more meaningful at the receiving end.

Colouring In

This has been a childhood pleasure for many and is now being resurrected in adult form! There is something relaxing in spending time colouring in, which at the same time can bring connections on the inside. Sitting colouring in, diverts our thoughts, and perhaps gives God space to bring His thoughts into our minds because we are relaxed. It can also be a social activity which is less intimidating than just sitting with others doing nothing.

Some of the colouring books which feature words of Scripture and images of creation are an excellent means of touching our human spirit.

Writing and Journalling

To get something we are thinking out onto paper is exceptionally freeing. It helps us see where we have come from, how we feel and what we might aspire to. Writing and journaling can be a means of pouring out expressions of anger, jealousy, longing, gratitude, mess and sin. There is a great release in being able to be real with yourself.

For some people, writing poetry expresses freedom in a way nothing else can. We hold writing workshops on our *Healing Through Creativity* courses, where our guests are encouraged to just begin to write and not to try to work out what to say. It is truly amazing to see how the Holy Spirt enables people to express themselves, and many are surprised at what they have written! Humour and hope are often expressed as the Holy Spirit brings inspiration.

Journalling is a brilliant way of describing a journey with God, and for looking back and seeing how far you have come along the way. We can be reminded of how struggles have been overcome, how God speaks to us and receive strength to keep moving forward.

Watercolour Painting, Acrylics, Inks, Oils, Crayons or Other Media to Create Pictures – Pencils, Granite for Drawing

I have set my rainbow in the clouds.   (GENESIS 9:13)

God created the rainbow, He placed it in the sky to speak to us of His promises and covenant. He is the author of colour, created for our joy! He could easily have made the world in black and white, and functional, but because He is beautiful, He placed His beauty in creation with colour, depth and meaning.

An artist's full pallet and all the possibilities that arise from it, are only a fraction of the artistry and colour of God. Since we are made in His image, we carry within us the desire to reflect the Artist! Drawing and painting bring wonderful expressions of the world we live in, all unique to the individual artist.

I remember my art teacher telling us that we needed to remember to put the shadows in our paintings, otherwise they would be flat and lifeless. How true this is of life too.

We all have shadows but to dismiss these things is to live our lives in a degree of unreality; in short life is not real. We need shadows to bring out the colour and light.

God can use painting and drawing as a means of reflecting back to Him, who He is and who we are in response to Him. Various aspects of creating pictures hold the key to healing principles:

Using colour is a means of releasing choice. The mixing of colours to find an unexpected outcome brings out the journey of experimentation.

Having a vision (ideas and experimentation) and using colour and paint to achieve can produce fantastic results, whether these are skilled artwork or not! In fact, the 'surprise factor' is often the best way.

A seemingly negative emotion, such as frustration, can be the key to positive results. Frustration is a necessary part of learning and growing, e.g. a child learning to ride a bike first wobbles and even falls off until the practice brings its reward.

Watercolour painting has its own way of taking things out

of control. The water merges with the paint in any way it falls and runs. 'Happy accidents' occur and often make for an interesting painting, or even make the painting! We can learn that mistakes lead to successes and undo control and fear. In fact, watercolours, encaustic art or any creative activity that is out of our control, whilst challenging can be very helpful to an anxious and controlling person, because it holds the potential to free up those inner messages which drive the desire to control both circumstances and other people.

Something expressed on paper helps bring connection to our own personhood. Once painted, drawn or written, it is 'out there' and this can help break down controls and fears that have been blockages to our own personality and expressing our thoughts, opinions and feelings outwardly for others to see. Getting something out and onto paper can be a helpful key to overcoming fear, especially fear of failure or being ridiculed.

Light, shade and reflections are part of God's character, and through them He can speak to us of how He brings life even in the middle of seeming darkness.

Painting releases non-verbal expression, which is healthy, especially if we are a very cerebral type of person. God hears our hearts and does not need our verbal expression alone.

Fun and Laughter – Paper Aeroplanes, Building Bricks, Train Sets, Toys, Games, Jigsaws, Sand, Water ...

> When the LORD restored the fortunes of Zion, we were like those who dreamed. Our mouths were filled with laughter, our tongues with songs of joy. (Psalm 126:1-2)

Children grow with an unabandoned expression of fun. A baby, if encouraged, will reflect a smile and laughter from a very early age. Smiling and laughing are signs of wellbeing and pleasure. God designed us this way to bring about bonding with others and to bring goodness into our lives.

We are all different personalities, but we do not grow out of our need to laugh and have fun which is a restorative value from the heart of God.

During our *Healing Through Creativity* courses we have made room for areas of life which evoke fun and laughter and may bring back a long-lost joy. God uses simple activities like folding and flying paper aeroplanes together as a small group or playing with building bricks, train sets, toys, games and jigsaws, in wonderful ways to bring about connections, bonding and spontaneity, while tensions are subliminally released and 'guilty' mindsets undone: "This is a waste of time!", "Not allowed!", "How very childish and unnecessary!", "I don't do play" or "You're making a fool of yourself."

A very serious-minded man arrived on a creativity course. It turned out that his parents had struggled to bring him up as an only child, and at school he had been bullied into an isolated way of living. Hence, he had difficulty in relating to God in any other way than through spiritual truth and belief. To put it simply, he was 'stuck in his head', and although he could put all of us to shame with his spiritual knowledge, real life was passing him by.

He was determined his problems were spiritual ones and I could see this was the only way he really knew how to relate. We strongly encouraged him away from this particular line of thinking into seemingly unspiritual answers. At first, he could not see the point and resisted but playing and laughing with others was God's best medicine for him. Isolation began to melt, and the unseen healing work of relational bonding was taking root. A starved need was being met and, along with it the enemy's hook was being removed.

Through laughter, we receive from another person and bond with them in a shared experience. Laughter releases emotion and tension. It lightens life and undermines striving, hardship and religiosity.

Freed to laugh at myself

Playing with non-threatening elements, like sand or water, enables a person to express themselves, often bringing back

> "How very childish and unnecessary!",

thoughts and emotions, something deep that has been buried and lost along life's journey.

Play has no right or wrong, no expectation, no rule or plan. Each component of play brings a different dimension, connecting us to the ability to 'just be' rather than 'do and achieve'. Play also undermines perfectionism and the need to always be in control.

285

Wood

The majesty of a mature tree is indisputable. God speaks of who He is through trees in a multitude of ways, and there is no doubting that as human beings, we love wood – the smells, the textures, the colours and especially the designs of the natural grain of the tree.

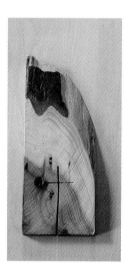

Blessed is the one who trusts in the LORD, whose confidence is in Him. They will be like a tree planted by water, that sends out its roots by the stream. It does not fear when heat comes; and its leaves are always green. It has no worries in a year of drought, and never fails to bear fruit.

(JEREMIAH 17:7-8)

But I am like an olive tree flourishing in the house of GOD; I trust in GOD's unfailing love for ever and ever.

(PSALM 52:8)

They will flourish like a palm tree, they will grow like a cedar of Lebanon; they will bear fruit in old age, they will stay fresh and green, proclaiming, "The LORD is upright; he is my Rock, and there is no wickedness in Him.

(PSALM 92:12-15)

Working with wood brings a special connection to the brilliance of God as Creator in creating trees. Jesus Himself, was a carpenter and what a natural He must have been as He fashioned the wood for use.

Carving and sanding down wood is a satisfying process. It speaks of how God fashions us with great patience and ingenuity, and that He has us on a journey which takes time. There is a sense of fulfilment in rubbing down the rough edges and giving it a polished surface, bringing out the unique pattern of the grain), releasing the distinctive aroma of fresh-cut wood and forming something beautiful to use or for ornamental purpose.

Wood can be fashioned to produce a piece of furniture, a utensil, an ornament, a toy, or in the wider sense, can be used for a group of people to work together to build something like a fence, a bridge, a boat, den or shed etc.

Working with wood is skilful, but it is also for those who simply enjoy touching it, smelling it and seeing its beautiful shapes, grains and patterns. Delight and joy are palpable in the woodwork room! All kinds of visions from name plates to fish shapes, crosses, coasters, sheep, flowers, jigsaws and more emerge.

Tactile abundance touched deep places

A lady who came on one of our courses, bravely daring to push against the boundaries of her fear, sat nervously at the fret saw, slowly and carefully cutting out of a piece of wood, the word, Jesus. When she eventually finished, she was thrilled with her work, but just as she had set it on the side for the varnish to dry, someone accidentally knocked it, and it fell to the floor. She was horrified to see her wooden 'Jesus' broken into two pieces.

These are the very situations, through which God so often does His deepest work, and as a team member turned to see what had happened, without a second thought, out of her mouth came the words, 'That's your Jesus, broken for you!' God brought amazing redemption right into that critical moment. That broken Jesus suddenly had a depth of meaning for the lady, speaking right into her fears, in a way that the unbroken piece would never have done.

Water

> Jesus stood and said in a loud voice, "Let anyone who is thirsty come to me and drink. Whoever believes in me, as the Scripture has said, rivers of living water will flow from within them."   (JOHN 7:37-38)

> "Whoever drinks the water I give them will never thirst. Indeed, the water I give them will become in them a spring of water welling up to eternal life"   (JOHN 4:14)

Water brings life to the earth, and Jesus describes Himself as a drink that never runs dry. When using water in creative settings, it brings its own spiritual drink and the presence of God.

In nature, whether we are blessed to be near a river, a moat, a waterfall, the seaside, a fountain or just in the rain, God can use this to draw us close to Himself and speak to us of His immeasurable strength, majesty, power or provision, and not least, His saving power for all our needs.

The swimming pool at Ellel Grange and the swimming baths near our centre in Scotland, have provided people with the opportunity to immerse themselves in water. As one person put it, "The water around me showed me God truly is holding me." Floating in water can be a way to allow God to impart trust, rest and a letting go into His arms.

There are many ways water is used in a creative way to bring about healing. For example:

- æ Learning to swim and being set free from fear of water
- æ Playing and splashing with abandon releasing tension
- æ Swimming or thrashing water can be used by the Lord to release emotion, particularly anger and pain
- æ Being part of a group in water brings fun, play and bonding

Nature

> For this is what the LORD says – he who created the heavens, He is GOD; he who fashioned and made the earth, he founded it; he did not create it to be empty, but formed it to be inhabited – he says: 'I am the LORD and there is no other.'　　　　　(ISAIAH 45:18)

It is hard to know where to begin in looking at the ways God brings healing through the natural world. It would take many books! However, in the smallest way, the creativity of nature is God's blessing and gift. Creator God has placed within nature so many restorative properties for our physical healing, but nature also heals the soul and spirit. We speak about how our spirit 'lifts' at the sight of a wonderful view, for example:

- ❧ Nature evokes all our senses of smell, taste, sight, hearing and touch, thereby touching us in deep ways.
- ❧ Being outside, moving and walking, breathing in fresh air, feeling the earth beneath our feet, hearing the birds sing, absorbing an expansive view or even the tiniest corner of nature, causes inspiration to arise within us.

Stones, leaves, seeds, sticks, flowers, grasses, feathers, cones, shells, sand and how much more are collectors' items for creative use! There is no need for creativity to be expensive as ideas flow plentifully when God releases our imaginations to play, have fun and simply create something out of nothing. These are often the best of creative times.

Creative Walks

> The LORD is my shepherd, I lack nothing. He makes me lie down in green pastures, He leads me beside quiet waters; He refreshes my soul. He guides me along the right paths for His name's sake. Even though I walk through the darkest valley, I will fear no evil; for you are with me; your rod and your staff, they comfort me. (PSALM 23:1-4)

It is helpful to have an inspirational person, who can help a group identify and relate to nature and share how God is with us and speaks to us through His creation and we can speak to Him. Everyone, at some time or another, goes through a valley and experiences the need of rest along the way. I love the way Creator God uses His creation all the time to speak to us of who He is and how He will meet with us and help us.

Opening people's eyes to the Lord is a gift, awakening awe in the Creator and arousing inspiration in the way His imagination and mind must have been working when He carefully crafted every intricate part of His creation – butterflies, flowers, insects, how He made every blade of grass unique, how there is order, how there is relationship and how vital even the smallest piece is to our earth etc.

We bring joy to the heart of God when we take in His provision of beauty – a sunset or sunrise, the mountain grandeur, streams and rivers, the power of waves, the ebb and flow of the tide, the animals, insects, flowers and trees. Every nation holds its own identity of beauty.

Energy and Movement

> Do you not know? Have you not heard? The LORD is the everlasting GOD, the Creator of the ends of the earth. He will not grow weary; and his understanding no one can fathom. He gives strength to the weary and increases the power of the weak. Even youths grow tired and weary, and young men stumble and fall; but those who hope in the LORD will renew their strength. They will soar on wings like eagles; they will run and not grow weary, they will walk and not be faint.   (Isaiah 40:28-31)

As human beings our energy is limited, it is a limited resource. It is also a resource that can be crushed. The Bible tells us that 'God is love' (1 John 4:8), and love is energising: when we are loved we are strengthened, energised and motivated, and when we pour our love out to someone else, we use our energy to do so.

In a practical way, God intends energy to be a blessing in many different spheres of our lives, not least through creative expression and giving of ourselves in healthy ways that facilitate healing.

There are many diverse ways that God pours His strength and energy into us through His love, and we in turn can give it back to Him and are energised to give out to others, for example, to walk and run, kick a ball, swim, ride a bike, dance, exercise, etc. brings a release of endorphins, but these are also means of releasing negative feelings and emotions.

Sport is God's creative design for a healthy outlet. It releases energy and takes us away from the intensity of everyday hassles and brings an antidote to pressure. It engages our brain but, at the same time, also takes us away from overthinking and intellectualising.

Sport exercises the body, it is fun, it holds a challenge, it brings healthy bonding and, in right balance, brings lightness to life and teaches us how to cooperate and work with others for the good of the whole. Teamwork and sport are God's ideas. We all need a challenge, and sport is a perfect way to bring healthy challenge into our lives. Challenge produces the character of patience, perseverance and endurance.

God wants to give back and build into our lives good things and to bring us the energy of love. This does not happen in a vacuum and it is as we gain an understanding of our creative need to personally receive and to express ourselves, that we can receive love and with this, the energy and motivation for life.

Dance

Let them praise his name with dancing and make music to him with timbrel and harp.   (PSALM 149:3)

Wearing a linen ephod, David was dancing before the LORD with all his might.   (2 SAMUEL 6:14)

Dance brings about an outward expression of an inward truth. It engages the whole of our body, soul and spirit. There are many connections made through dance, with our own self, with others and also with the Lord.

Dancing can be an act of worship towards the Lord bringing His love and presence close (Exodus 15:20, 2 Samuel 6:14). The whole of our body, soul and spirit are offered to Him.

an outward expression of an inward truth

Dancing with banners, flags or ribbon streamers creates an extension to worship. The energy of the flags and streamers in the wind and their flowing, rippling movements add a powerful dimension. The type of banners and the types of music accompanying the dance can bring strong healing messages to hidden inner depths.

Dance takes the dancer into the freeing elements of space, time and energy, which God can use to bring healing.

Drama

Acting a part and allowing ourselves to enter into how another might feel or what another might say, behave or respond can bring a deep connection and awareness to our own personality and how we might think, have an opinion, make a choice or a desire that might be buried. Drama also engages us body, soul and spirit and involves bringing about expression of thought and emotion.

Music

> Shout for joy to the LORD, all the earth, burst into jubilant song with music; make music to the LORD with the harp, with the harp and the sound of singing, with trumpets and the blast of the ram's horn—shout for joy before the LORD, the King. (PSALM 98:4-6)

Music, they say, is the sound of heaven! If ever we have evidence that we are spiritual beings, music tells us so. It has no function to keep us alive, except to raise our spirits and souls. Music brings an expressive overflow to our personhood, whether we are into classical music, jazz, opera, popular or anything else in between.

Singing, playing a musical instrument or joining a choir or orchestra, can all bring us great fulfilment and joy, not to mention training in a skill and teaching us how to be harmonious. The following ways touch the human spirit:

- Singing hymns with meaningful words to melody lines
- Singing worship songs
- Singing children's songs
- Hearing or playing musical instruments

The saying, "music to my ears" is full of meaning. Music brings an awakening of our spiritual senses and connects us to emotion and spirituality beyond that which is attainable any other way. God created music as a means of bringing worship to Him. Worship through music, feeds us with strength, is uplifting and brings God close to us in intimate ways. Music is a means of receiving healing and comfort. It is heaven's gift brought down to earth.

Noise and Silence

Both of these extremes are part of our human experience. Silence for some people would be frightening, and yet it is in silence and quietness that we can hear ourselves and also God.

In quietness and trust is your strength.   (ISAIAH 30:15)

On the other hand, at times we need noise, however loud, or even a whisper to be awoken to life's joys and challenges.

There is a huge variety of healing needs amongst us all. A person who has been kept silent in life will need freedom to make a noise. Conversely, a person who has lived in a noisy environment will need permission to be quiet and still.

Do-It-Yourself (DIY)

> I have filled him with wisdom and understanding, with knowledge and all kinds of skills – to make artistic designs for work in gold, silver and bronze, to cut and set stones, to work in wood, and to engage in all kinds of crafts.
>
> (Exodus 31: 3-5)

It can be quite easy to go and buy something readymade from a store to give as a gift, but for a variety of reasons this is not always possible and, not least, the expense. However, when we make something, such as a cake, a jar of jam, a painting, a piece of furniture or something decorative for the home etc. for someone else, we are giving something of ourselves which holds great value. It involves the giving of time, skill and energy, which blesses another and builds them up in value.

It connects us to the values in God's heart of love, which is sacrificial and giving, to benefit the whole.

It connects us to the values in God's heart of love

Cooking

> Bless the LORD ... who satisfies your mouth with good things."
> (Psalm 103:1 and 5 NKJV)

For many of us, food is a favourite pastime. Most of us have to limit what we would like to eat! Cooking is a gift and a cook is usually everyone's favourite person! When asking people why it is that they like to cook, their replies are many and varied: experimenting, having a vision, tasting, smelling, feeling, creating something which gives pleasure to others! Food touches the heart!

Gardening

> Now the LORD GOD had planted a garden in the east, in Eden; and there he put the man he had formed.
>
> (GENESIS 2:8)

> They will plant vineyards and drink their wine; they will make gardens and eat their fruit.
>
> (AMOS 9:14)

Experiencing something growing out of a seemingly insignificant tiny seed and a vision being implemented is hugely satisfying and rewarding. There is joy in feeling the soil, the leaves and roots and not least taking in the fresh air and space. Gardening is God's idea. When we watch over a helpless seed and plant and nurture it until it comes into full bloom, it speaks of the Divine Gardener. We touch His heart and the way He puts the plants in suitable places for them where they will flourish, just as He wants to do with our lives. He enjoys gardening with us! He invented it!

Science, Technology and Engineering

> Great are the works of the LORD; they are pondered by all who delight in them.
>
> (PSALM 111:2)

Scientific research and exploration provide endless opportunities for creative thought, imagination and discovery. The study of science and technology is a never-ending adventure, since here on earth it is impossible to get to the end of the knowledge which God has hidden within the whole of His creation. There is always more to discover.

Adventures and surprises

The power of engines is breath-taking. To envision and make something, which ultimately leads to the release of power, is exhilarating. Even a small child receives abundant joy when a clockwork toy engine is wound up and travels on a track!

Travel and Outings

> How many are your works, LORD! In wisdom you made them all; the earth is full of your creatures.
>
> (PSALM 104:24)

New sights, new experiences, adventures and being out of routine, is a means of receiving God's restoration in our lives. God's gift to us is the world in which we live, with all its amazing diversity, learning and fun.

Work

> I know that there is nothing better for people than to be happy and to do good while they live. That each of them may eat and drink and find satisfaction in all their toil— this is the gift of GOD. (ECCLESIASTES 3:12-13)

Work is God's design for making things happen. Without work, we would not be able to live. Our daily jobs are one kind of work, but there are different and creative ways in which work outside of daily routine, can bring blessing to ourselves and others.

Being part of a team, doing something together for a common goal is God's plan. We are wired that way and it brings us health and blessing.

Messy Painting

Being free to make a mess is a powerful means of connecting to inner struggles, pain, and sinfulness. As a non-verbal means of communication, there is nothing better. Messy painting encourages the heart to speak its own language. It gives the Holy Spirit the freedom to bring a hidden reality out into the open. When the truth from God's heart meets that hitherto hidden truth about ourselves, it is then that a journey to freedom really begins to take place. Truth is healing and brings peace, however painful those inner feelings were.

> You desire truth in the innermost being.
>
> (PSALM 51:6 NASB)

Then you will know the truth, and the truth will set you free

(JOHN 8:32)

"

we cannot drag ourselves out of our own messes

The miracle of the coming of Jesus is that He came into the mess of the world. He knows we cannot drag ourselves out of our own messes and we cannot clean ourselves up. It is a beautiful work of His Spirit on our behalf.

Messy painting can also be a means of having fun or connecting with our own opinions and expressions. We can find out in an unthreatening way what kind of colours and shapes and movements we like or dislike. There is no right or wrong with messy painting, which can make it a non-threatening creative activity.

"

God finds us in the midst
of pain and sin

Making a big mess and even putting hands and feet in the mess has been tremendously releasing for some of our guests.

Conclusion

The elements described in this chapter are all creative ideas for the way God can bring His healing and restoration, remembering that He is close and speaks through all the many things He designed and created to bring us His life, rejuvenation and antidote to stress. The above are just a few of the myriad ways through which God uses creativity to bring healing and enable us to take important steps on the journey with Him.

I pray your eyes have been opened to ways in which God can speak with you and enjoy those times with you. A parent's highest joy is watching their children enjoy the things they have provided and entering into the experiences of life they too have had. God made parents this way because He, as our Father God, has made us to enter into all He has provided, and it gives Him great joy when we do so. Whatever way you choose to enjoy creative expression, God is enjoying it with you. It blesses His heart in just the same way as any human father enjoys seeing his kids doing things that he has taught them to do.

Chapter **18**

ILLUSTRATIONS AND STORIES OF HEALING THROUGH CREATIVITY

On the following pages are some illustrations and stories of those who have experienced God's healing power, through attending our *Healing Through Creativity* or *Bridge from the Head to the Heart* courses. In very individual ways, they depict a common theme that God the Creator, as Father and Jesus our Saviour, bring about a breakthrough when people experience His Holy Spirit through creative expression.

I hope these written and photographic 'snapshots' help to bring insights and encouragement into the way God heals through creativity.

Thank you
For making me feel welcome
For a lovely room, some lovely room mates
And a bath!
Thank you
For never telling me to calm down
Never squashing my laughter
Never expressing disapproval
Thank you
For so much choice but no need to only choose once
So much organisation without ever organising us
So much order but we never had to clear anything up
Thank you
For letting me play
For not worrying about the mess
For demanding nothing and giving so much
Thank you
For protection, and covering,
For subtle ministry to those around,
For joining in
Thank you
For giving so that I could receive

Freely you have received, freely give. Go in My name and because you believe, others will know that I live!"

(MATTHEW 10:8)

◆ ◆ ◆

I have found the 'me in me'

I have spent my whole life striving to please people, to win their approval and I thought my worth was in producing. I became strongly rebellious about everything I made. During *Healing through Creativity*, God spoke to me, "I do not want you to do, I want you to be." This has been the hardest week, but through the option to 'just be' I have found the 'me in me' which had become lost under all the production and striving. I am so grateful to Jesus for finding me.

306

◆ ◆ ◆

Healing through Creativity brought me healing in relationships. Thank you, Father, for finding the deprived, starving, hurting one, that she is growing, and now relationships which I thought were all pain, can be good and fun. Through this I am stepping out into new life.

◆ ◆ ◆

I cannot express my thanks enough for the creativity ministry of Ellel and for the team. I needed so much to allow myself emotional expression. There have been tough moments and tears, but these have helped me accept me and to learn about Jesus. I have been released to have fun and paddle in the stream! Jesus released laughter and fun in me. Healing has definitely taken place.

◆ ◆ ◆

> I am stepping out into new life

NOT FOR YOU

Sober, small, simple.
Don't think big.
Don't dream big.
One born for a penny,
will never be a pound.

Not for you
Others may flag,
    but that is not for you.
Others may dance,
    but that is not for you.

Others may sing,
    but that is not for you.
Others may stand on the podium,
    but that is not for you.

But
What is happening now?
There is a creative weekend at Ellel.
The Lord has prepared a banquet for me,
with so many beautiful workshops that I have
    trouble choosing.
May I do all of that, Lord?!

Wow, in freedom and security,
    I am allowed to flag,
    I am allowed to dance,
    I am allowed to sing,
    I am even allowed to stand on the podium.

Like a child, I enjoy, even though it is sometimes
    awkward and not perfect.
I enjoy these gifts so much, Lord!
You say, 'This is for you!'

◆ ◆ ◆

Healing for me came through there being no agendas
and time out 'just to be'. This was so healing for me. I am a
single mother and my life is full of struggles to make ends
meet. I had become a 'human doing' and did not know
how to let go or relax. Through *Healing Through Creativity*,
God touched me deeply on the inside releasing stress and
anxiety.

◆ ◆ ◆

I was in bondage to fear and became a perfectionist. I
wanted to run away at first, but the team gently helped me
to take steps to overcome my fear of failure. I knew something inside me had to let go. After trying a few workshops,

I knew God was on my case! By the end of the weekend, God was unravelling areas of my life and miraculously re-ordering and putting me together. The knitting, spinning and felting workshops helped me so much.

◆ ◆ ◆

My life of addictions ate away inside. I could not see the relevance of just playing and doing things which seemed disconnected to my condition. God had other ideas, and as I pursued trying out woodwork, then messy painting, I felt strongly that something was happening deep on the inside. My depression had worsened over recent times, but God reached something deeply buried. I received a wonderful healing and release.

God reached something deeply buried

◆ ◆ ◆

PHILIP'S STORY

I approached creativity with a distinct lack of interest, disliking painting and drawing and regarding my efforts as worthless. I like structure; having an end result to focus on. I don't like mess. So, when it came to messy painting I 'girded my loins' and went for it, not expecting anything useful to come out of it. I could then tick it off and say I'd done it and move on. I didn't expect much to come out of it for anyone else either. Those that might get something from it I would regard as 'fluffy' and on the weak emotional scale!!

A couple of ideas come to mind of what I could try and produce, but I sensed they were my own thoughts, so discarded them. I tore off some paper haphazardly and felt drawn to red, green and black paint, and someone brought some white. I was co-operative, but still unwilling. I didn't know what to start with, but soon felt it needed to be a hand, so I covered my hand in red paint and started with that even though it felt rather yucky.

The rest followed naturally without any need to think it through. My picture had a red hand in the middle, signifying me. Then five red hands surrounding 'me' which I realised signified everything major I had done in my life. I poured black paint onto the centre hand (me) and knew I had to make that radiate out to the other five hands. The sinfulness of my life had affected not just me but everything I had done. I picked up the white paint and made a cross in the centre and knew that had to radiate out to completely cover the blackness of sin in the other five 'hands'. Finally, green, representing new life, reached into the other hands (radiating from 'me'), and then beyond them and out of the confines of the page.

I knew God was telling me that it was done. There was nothing I needed to try and dig up to fix. The cross had covered it all. His new life (green) was taking me beyond everything I had ever accomplished before, and it was going to continue expanding until the day I died. This was not just the past, but also into the future as there was much more blessing still to come. It really blessed me.

I was impacted by the profound effect messy painting had for others too, and particularly challenged by those, who like me, had approached creativity very negatively. I could not deny how God used it and realised it was so very important.

The next day, with pen and paper I drew one brick, which became a wall with a black hole in it. My life before Christ. I felt led to draw arrows into the black void and label each how I felt about painful things in my life, particularly involving my parents. Just doing that and seeing the words on paper touched me as I faced up to those feelings.

I knew the cross had filled that void and drew a picture of my relationship with God. I was a plant with a flower filled with seeds, turned to the sun (Father) and receiving His love. Holy Spirit was the rain nurturing me. Jesus was the farmer close to me with a watering can in one hand

> "
> I knew God was telling me that it was done

(fertilising me and feeding me) and pruning shears in the other (cutting out what would otherwise hold me back). He was loving me in all of these things, and I wrote that it was as if I was the only plant in His garden and I was so precious to Him. All that further emphasised to me that all was ok and I just needed to rest in His love.

◆ ◆ ◆

THE WALL

Hiding. Hiding away in fear.
What of? Why?
Am I enough? Am I too much?
Hide your true self – you're not acceptable.
Present a mask.
Not too much trouble, don't cause a fuss,
Don't tell people what to do – they won't want
    to know you.
Not the real you.
So, build up the wall.
Stop people getting in. Stop the bad stuff in
    you getting out.
Build up the wall. If you get close to the top and risk
    spilling out – build it up higher.
You have to. The real you isn't acceptable.

*But my child, I love **YOU**, just as you are.*

You can't, no you can't. How can you love this
    demanding mess?
I've let you down, pushed you away.
I know you must know what's inside – You know everything.
But if you REALLY knew you'd agree –
I'm not worth it.
Not worth Your blood.

Not worth Your tears.
Not worth Your time.
Not worth Your love.
Others are better. Go and heal them.
Don't waste your time on me.

*But my child, I love **YOU**. I love all them as well,*
    but I love you.
I care for you.
I wept for you, I intercede for you, I bled, and
    I died for you.
Not who you could be if only you worked harder,
    *but for you **now**.*
In the midst of the mess, all the anger and tears, I looked
And I saw all the pain, all the hurt, all the ways that you
    sinned, all the sins against you,
And I loved you.
I chose you and you are mine.
So, I turned and walked resolutely to the cross.
I heard all your protests and reasons why not and I
    went anyway –
'cos I know the TRUTH.
You are mine and I want you.
Even if no one else does, I want you – so I died for you.
To reconcile you to your true Father.

But what do you mean? - I don't have to impress?
How can this be?
From the very beginning I had to prove I was worth it.
I was only allowed to live as I wasn't disabled – a burden
    and price too high to pay.
So, I made sure I wasn't a burden too great
Hide away, hide away,
Do it yourself
Don't cause a fuss, be good enough, don't be too much.
Now You say that's all lies? So how should I live?

Leaning on me – Your Father and Lover

But how does that work? What do I do?

You be.

I be?! Who should I be? And how do I do being then?

You don't do, you be. You be being you.
I made you unique, so play at being you.

I don't **know** who that is.
I've lost who I am.
I don't know how to play at being me.

Hush my child, don't get worked up.
I'll teach you again how to play my way.
You have known before but the pressure to do was
    too much for you to bear.
Now that is gone. So be.
But about this wall – it has to come down.

Come down?!! No, it can't!! How could that be?
It's my only protection against being me.

Exactly my child, it stops you being you.
Let me bring it down and I'll protect you.

But what of the mess? All it's holding within?
What will people see?
How do I know if they'll like the real me?

That is not your concern, let me be the judge.
I like you, I love you – let that be enough.
I won't turn away if I find something wrong,
But will lovingly restore you to my perfect plan.

Jesus, I long and I choose to trust You.
Help me submit to what You want to do.
So, take down that wall, one bit at a time,
Let the contents spill out
With all of that mess,
For I know in **Your** arms is my only true rest.
Be at rest, O my soul, in your true Father's arms,
He likes, loves and accepts you, His beloved child.

◆ ◆ ◆

God wanted to deal with a lot of emotional stuff buried inside. I went to the swimming pool, and it was as though the Holy Spirit became the physiotherapist. It was an amazing time. My body began to move in places where I had not been able to move it previously. I have been unable to do certain things in my profession because of this. I knew He was going to deal with spiritual things and emotions but hadn't realised He was going to touch me physically.

◆ ◆ ◆

This week has really changed the way I think. I now believe that everything is worthwhile instead of hopeless. I discovered I had terrible control over myself, events and others. In the mess room, I allowed the Lord to dig deeper and I made a lot of mess. He showed me my identity as a daughter of the King, and now He is in control. I know who I am, and the burdens have gone, I am at peace.

◆ ◆ ◆

Even though there were so many people around, I asked God why I felt so lonely, and He said I had put up so many walls that people cannot get close because of my self- protection. When we sang the line in the butterflies children's song, 'He gave me Jesus and He made me His child' I actually believed it. So today I know God loves me, and I am His child. I feel I have been replanted in the good soil of Jesus Christ.

◆ ◆ ◆

MARTIN'S STORY

I was deeply touched by the reminder that we didn't choose God, but He chose us, He wanted us, it was His decision to give me life, to create me in my mother's womb. He didn't wait from a distance until I decided to follow Him, He initiated our relationship as my Creator!

To express my new understanding creatively and see what God would add to it, and moving out of my comfort zone, I chose soap stone. God guided me in choosing a small piece and carving out a little baby. As I filed and polished, He said: "Just as you're shaping this stone, I created your body, soul and spirit." Then in messy painting, I dared to use my hands to apply a black background, enjoying going beyond the edges of the

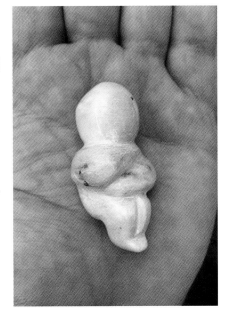

paper. I put a red area right in the middle, which mixed somewhat with the black layer beneath. I wanted to paint a beam of light, but to prevent it mixing, I had to wait. I came back several times to check whether the paint had dried, and God said, "I also had to wait for the right time."

I painted the beam with white and yellow and finally a little baby at the end of the beam. As I sat, looking at the painting, I felt God wanted me to lie down but I was reluctant, thinking I would draw too much attention from others. But the message got clearer, "Let go and lie down". Finally, I did, and the Lord showed me that He created me using my loving, but imperfect parents.

For a number of years, I have been diagnosed with Asperger's Syndrome, just as my father. I have become increasingly aware of my struggle to live life as if I have no deficiencies. But as I laid there, God said to me: "Please stop with your coping mechanisms and trying to fix it yourself, I want to fill in the gaps. You don't have to be perfect, just let me be perfect in you."

◆ ◆ ◆

Unfurl your rainbow banner in my life, dear Lord
And let me dance for you in jewelled colours.
Let my winter turn to Spring and glorious summertime
And let me raise the ruby glass of your new wine
To my parched lips
And taste new life
At last.

◆ ◆ ◆

During the teaching, I began to realise my true identity. I
had been a workaholic, achieving too hard, loving others
but not myself. In the messy room, I opened up the empty
hole and asked Jesus in. During the ministry night I realised I had forgiven others but had not forgiven myself. As
I placed my stone representing forgiveness of myself at
the cross, God helped me grieve deep loss. I learnt not to
push down and deny the hurt in me, and since then I have
opened up to share with others. I know He still has more
amazing things for me as I become more complete as His
child.

> I had forgiven others but had not forgiven myself

◆ ◆ ◆

The course brought connection with my heart, my mind and
my childhood identity, as well as to other people. It was
a breakthrough to accept my birth and I actually received
joy to celebrate my day of birth. Other people's love and
encouragement helped me receive friends and to talk with
people more again. I actually dared to be late and not
perfect! I accepted myself as being quite humorous and
took small steps in being "me."

Dancing to give of myself to Jesus rather than to attract
others attention was a revelation. I have seen attention as

something dangerous, never wanting to be noticed. So much in this course has helped me.

◆ ◆ ◆

As a child, I was very artistic and was greatly encouraged both at home and at school in drawing and painting. I particularly wanted to carve but this was never an option. Over 25 years, I have read many books, collected lots of wood and bought many tools, but I could never take the plunge to begin carving – the thought terrified me!

What a freeing experience this course has been! I was encouraged and helped and have actually completed my first carving – relief! I know the Lord has done a new work in my life and I fully intend to walk in that. Thank you, Lord for freeing me from failure and for the Ellel team in their obedience in being channels of healing and wholeness.'

◆ ◆ ◆

Creativity connected me with the little girl inside me, who never felt she was valuable or lovable, and fought against love, because it made her feel vulnerable, insecure and unprotected. I didn't like her and didn't want her in my life. She had a wounded heart, which I tried to ignore because of the pain it caused me every time love touched my heart.

So, I didn't allow myself to receive, by heart, any love. It was all in my head, but my heart was desperately longing to be able to receive God's love and the love of my family in Christ.

Through creativity, the Holy Spirit helped me express the truth that I wanted to believe in my heart, but yet only existed as head-knowledge. During the process, I experienced the love of God become stronger than all my fear and shame. This revelation made me jump into my Father's arms, trusting that His love was strong enough to catch

"
The love of God become stronger than all my fear and shame

me and hold me tight. I asked Jesus to help me love and value the little girl inside me, in the same way He loves and values me. The gentle touch of my Father's love to the wounded heart, released tears of pain and grief that had been buried over many years. He found His lost pearl! I found my lost pearl too, and my true identity as daughter of my heavenly Father, who loves me and is proud of me.

◆ ◆ ◆

THANKS BE TO MY GOD

Searching, searching for oh so long
Just wanting to truly, truly belong
Endless pain, torture and fighting
I couldn't carry on and wanted to die
But, Lord, you were always there (though I did not know it)
You listened to me and heard my cry
You lifted me up
And put the right people in my path
And you didn't stop there, Lord
You helped me fight against the enemy's wrath
Family and friends I have anew
As I am learning, Lord, to trust in You
Thank you, Father, that You love me so much
Your warm embrace and your heavenly touch
Praise You, Lord, and have Your way
As I am Yours and here to stay
At the foot of the cross I pour out from within, at Your feet
What comfort, peace and joy to know
You will never leave me nor forsake me, until
Paradise when we again shall meet

SHARON 2017

◆ ◆ ◆

I can't express my thanks enough for the creativity ministry at Ellel and for the team. The continuity of the team has helped tremendously for me to learn about trust, interacting with others and building relationships. Creativity really is helping with my understanding of everything and with the acceptance of emotional expression and my journey with God.

◆ ◆ ◆

It was lovely to get under the banners and learn to dance, and I was amazed that I didn't fall over. It was so releasing and wonderful. The tears started to flow, and the Lord Jesus moved deeply in me, it was a wonderful experience.

◆ ◆ ◆

Through many failed marriages, I had a deep sense of being rubbish. I believed something was deeply wrong with me. I didn't realise I was very angry, and it was in the mess room attempting a nice picture that the anger rose up in me and was released when I went outside and tore it up. It was how I felt: anger towards myself and then anger towards those who had hurt me. I felt a fresh start and went back in, and to my amazement painted a beautiful and delicate flower.

◆ ◆ ◆

I was encouraged to join in messy painting. I chose yellow paint and covered a large sheet with this – no idea why at the time. Some black flies started to land on the yellow sheet which bothered me. A friend nearby suggested God was joining in and decorating my yellow paper with nature. Suddenly I was furious and upset. It was as if God was spoiling my yellow – I decided to join in and added lots of black handprints and blobs – I was very angry.

The immediate realisation, I had, was that I wanted everything in life to be nice and 'yellow' – but the black happened and in fact made my life real. Overnight I kept pondering this and found I was connecting to a very deep sense that God could not be trusted and spoiled things in my life. This was a shock to me as I thought I really did trust the Lord.

The next morning during worship we sang, "You are a good, good Father." I just broke down I could not sing that. A reassuring word spoken over everyone during the repeat of the song, was especially helpful to me. I received it very personally: God wanted to reassure us that connecting with the 'messy/bad' me, did not negate the reality of the 'me' who loved and served Him – He saw and validated the sacrifice, love and work done for Him and that this was still true and real.

It was Father God I had the problem with, not Jesus or Holy Spirit. So, I wrote to Him exactly how I felt, and from this I had a deep sense that even Jesus had felt forsaken by Father God on the cross, but that history showed this was not the truth.

Since then I have had a sense of something settled inside, something I had not realised was not settled before, as far as relationship with Father God is concerned. I have a new sense of peace and certainty in my reliance on Father God and an awareness of His presence that I had not had before. Also, I have not had a headache or migraine since that weekend.

◆ ◆ ◆

WONDERS OF GRACE

When darkness and fear surround me
And hope is almost gone
I reach deep down inside until I find you
Your grace lifts me up and carries me on ...

When Gods family turn me away ...
Leaving rejection and hurt to knock at my heart,
Cast away, confused, misunderstood ...
Who is there, Lord?
No one but you and your boundless Grace ...
When the journey has been so long
My soul so parched from your love ...
Who else is there? I ask myself
Only you, Lord, and your abiding Grace ...

What keeps my feet upon the path?
Though my sandals have worn thin?
I look up, it is you, Lord,
Your amazing Grace carries me on.

Such humility, such gentleness is in your face
It is you, Lord, I long to embrace
How can I not see you, Jesus, the scars, the pain?
How precious is your Grace that leads me on.

Is the journey worth walking when I feel so lost?
Yes, a little flower within lifts up its weary head
There is only you, Lord, I love
I thank you for your faithfulness
It is Your Grace that walks me on.

I cast myself before you again and again,
You lift me up and dust me off.
One glimmer of hope, one touch of your embrace
Picks me up and fills my heart with faith.

How precious is your endless love?
Tears too painful to cry, lost in the maze of my heart,
I look up and ask you to find me, Lord, hold me tight
Until the time my tears can flow freely with yours
Endlessly away, covered by your Grace.

◆ ◆ ◆

God is here. I thought I would be ashamed to stand with
tears in my eyes, but He said, "No, you do not have to be
ashamed." My father was very strict. I had to learn swimming,
and I did not like it at all. Whilst here I have enjoyed swimming
in the pool. I felt God around me as I played with ducks, like
a child of 6 years old. It was such a good experience. Yester-
day evening I felt very contented, just happy to sit in the dining
room, fear and striving gone. I know the main thing is to 'be,'
to be loved by God and to love Him and then to bless others.

◆ ◆ ◆

I was not allowed to express any emotion ever. I wasn't allowed to cry or express feelings about what was done to me. It
had gone so deep down. I found it so powerful to get hold of
some paint and use it whatever way God directs. I was able to
express myself and speak out all my feelings - such a release.
God was healing years of rejection through powerful prayer in
the messy room. I feel secure, a new security I've never known
before. I am not expecting the blow to fall. I am not expecting
the rejection to come. Praise God, I'm so grateful.

◆ ◆ ◆

It was at the creativity course that I experienced real joy for the
first time in my life. The Lord gave me joy! So, I have come on
Bridge from the Head to the Heart which has far, far exceeded
all my expectations, giving me yet more deep joy in my heart.

> " I experienced
> real joy for the
> first time in
> my life

◆ ◆ ◆

During worship, I longed to pick up a banner, but I didn't have the courage, fearful of what people would think. However, the next day, as the worship began, I dared to shakily pick up a gold banner, I felt the anointing of God, he filled me with courage and as I worshipped I felt a new freedom like I had never felt before. It felt completely natural, like an extension of my body. My spirit soared, I couldn't believe the peace I felt, I could use the banner as an expression of my love and gratitude to Him, as well as a way of expressing anger or sadness and pain, and then His peace would come.

Later, on the Creativity course, I struggled to know what to do, as I didn't think of myself as particularly creative, and when they mentioned sewing, I immediately thought I'd never go there! I had previously tried to use a sewing machine but as I'm lefthanded found it was the wrong way around, so difficult and frustrating. I didn't see how God would help me to make anything good or desirable to Him in there. However, God had other plans!

I wandered around, praying, and found myself in the sewing room. I came across a delicate pink tulle and some gold material and felt God wanted me to make a banner. I argued with myself, although part of me wanted to try to make it, I knew I would need a lot of help. But the sewing lady reassured me, and I cut the tulle. It was difficult to use as it was quite slippy, but God said I needed to be patient and take my time, He would help me, and He wanted me to enjoy it. I finally managed to pin it in place, and it was sewn together. I cut out gold butterflies to represent new life in Jesus, and sewed them on, they looked like angels! It was frustrating as I couldn't sew in a straight line and they looked jagged, but God showed me that my life has never been in a straight line, and though the jagged times were hard, those were the times I needed Him and called on Him most.

I used my banner during the next worship time, and felt His love and joy fill me. I started a procession around the conference room and to my amazement, others were so encouraged that they picked up banners from the back and joined in! We were all laughing, and singing, and praising Jesus, and I sensed that He was with us, enjoying our worship. I heard Him say, "This is why I have called you to banner worship, I want you to lift my name high, and encourage others to seek me in this way so that they can find freedom from the things that hold them down."

> " I cut out gold butterflies to represent new life in Jesus

◆ ◆ ◆

THE HUSBAND'S STORY

When my wife suffered a miscarriage, she was utterly devastated, so even though it felt like the world stood still for me too and I could hardly breathe, I held myself together and stayed strong. But I later became overwhelmed by fear and began to suffer panic attacks, which steadily worsened, with extreme anxiety and serious depression. I went through a long series of sessions with a psychiatrist and therapy groups and was prescribed a lot of medication. When it looked like I was making small steps to recovery, it all felt apart again with terrifying suicidal thoughts.

My wife became pregnant again but within a year of his birth I was admitted to psychiatric hospital. The closed unit was so dark and cold, and I became more and more anxious and fearful. I felt so lonely, so guilty, a bad husband and Daddy. I felt miles away from God: guilty, unwelcome, unworthy, with a huge fear of eternal punishment. I didn't have the deep secure knowledge that I was really saved, and that God really, really loves me! I longed for it sooo much, but just couldn't capture it, and I was slipping further and further away from Him.

In a desperate way, I reached out for God's healing. During the *Creativity* weekend God took me on a deep journey of healing, beginning with the trauma of my wife's miscarriage. My wife and I really know that our 'unborn child' went directly to his or her heavenly Father. My wife made a drawing of our child, and gave our unborn a name, so that she could give them a place. Throughout that desperate time, I didn't have a clue what was going on and was plagued by thoughts like "Healing is not for me, I'm too sinful", "This is what I have to carry on my own", "How and when will I ever hear God's voice ... or receive healing?" Through the teaching and creativity, expressing feelings, especially grief, I can now clearly see that God was never mad at me and never left me, even though I was trying to hide myself from Him (because of deep fear of His punishment).

Life now, is getting better and better. I enjoy my role as a father so much, I'm so happy and blessed with my son, who is almost three, I never have panic attacks and I enjoy

> Life now, is getting better and better

going to the zoo, on vacations and to visit family with my wife and son. The Lord has really given me back my joy, my dignity and my purpose. He's helped me to grow stronger and stronger in Him, and I find my identity more and more in who I am in Christ. It's still a process, and it grows, as I am getting closer to Him. It's all about relationship with the Father through Jesus Christ, instead of what you have achieved. And at the *Creativity* weekend the Lord gave me back my passion, through leading me to write an amazing rap song, which I shared with the whole group.

> the Lord gave me back my passion

◆ ◆ ◆

THE WIFE'S STORY

Soon after the devastating miscarriage, my husband, Josh, began to have panic attacks, which progressed to depression. I became pregnant again, but it was a stressful time, not knowing how it would go. Josh was increasingly bothered by sleepless nights and anxious dreams. Finally, he broke. He was prescribed medication and the psychiatric team supported him, coming to our home, giving him structure each day and assessing how he was doing. I thought he would soon recover.

The low point was Josh's admission to a closed psychiatric ward. It broke my heart to leave him there, even though he believed it would help him to get rid of the negative thoughts. In addition, he was unable to take care of our 6-month-old son through fear of getting it wrong, and his wish to die was great.

For me, the bright spots were the weekends he went to Ellel: *Healing the Human Spirit* course, a *Healing Retreat*, and especially *Healing through Creativity*, I saw a glimpse of hope when he came home. He was enthusiastic. Despite the fact that it subsided, and the depression seemed to take over again, God had laid a new foundation. Slowly, he grew stronger and medication was phased out. He's not so easily distracted or confused by the opinions of others anymore. For me, it is a miracle where Josh is now. There are still challenges but it is going well.

It was special for us to attend *Healing through Creativity* together, so great to see God give Josh back his passion for words, rap, rhyme and the restoration of the image of God as his Father. There was also healing for me, I'd been in survival mode for three years, I was stressed out. I'd set myself aside for my family, to keep things going, take care of my son and Josh. But God showed me there is room for me, the passion to be creative. Through creativity He drew me to my own self, my own emotions, the pain, the hurt and let it come to the surface. He continues restoring me, Josh and our marriage. For me, it is certain, that I would not have come through this without God. I would not be where I am now. His mercy is enough. So true!

◆ ◆ ◆

COMPILATION

When Jesus rules your heart you become like Him.

God is my Daddy, He forgives sins.

When I give up control, God does the most amazing and unsuspected things in my life.

At last I am free of Satan's lies.

God has shown me through the use of paint, such truths that it has opened up a whole new dimension to life.

God has brought me from a place of feeling rejected by church to knowing and feeling accepted.

I have been set free from being so cerebral and analytical – this week has been purely 'being and enjoying. I'm getting hold of the idea that God want me to enjoy being me!

At last! God has broken through into the very core of my being – that part which has been locked away since before I was born. The course Bridge from the Head to the Heart has done exactly what it says on the label.

I now understand better why I have been like I have and what to do about it! The Lord did a lot of healing, it was very encouraging. Thoroughly enjoyed my time.

Jesus has brought more release. I am less inhibited. The flag dancing helped liberate me!

A whole team approach to building up people was great. I was able to overcome many past hurts and blocks to anything creative, there was so much support to get through. I will definitely recommend it to other frightened people. Thank you, Lord.

Chapter **19**

PRACTICAL PRAYERS

The Heartbeat of God

At the heart of *Healing Through Creativity* events is prayer. God as Creator invites us to come to Him through His Son, Jesus Christ, and because He has made us for relationship, He waits for us to invite Him into our lives. He will never override His principle in giving us freewill choice.

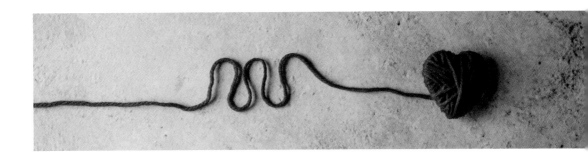

PRAYER

Father God, thank you for sending Jesus to save and restore me back to you. Thank you, Lord Jesus, for willingly shedding your blood and dying in my place so that I can receive forgiveness and cleansing from all my sin and be restored in relationship with my Heavenly Father. I ask you to fill me with your Holy Spirit so that I can receive your presence within me helping and guiding me in your truth. In Jesus' name, Amen.

Communication with God

God created us to walk with Him and to talk with Him. Prayer was never designed to be restricted to a church pew or a certain place but rather in a daily relational journey through the ordinariness of life. That is not to say that in the quietness of a place set apart, there is not a very real sense of the presence of God and a conduciveness to prayer in a powerful way.

PRAYER

Thank you, Heavenly Father, that I am your child (daughter/son). I come to you in simple trust, seeking your way in my life. I know that you plan for my good. In Jesus' name, Amen.

I hope this book has opened your eyes to wider and creative means of communicating with God in personal ways. We do not have to adopt a certain language other than the language of our hearts when we come to Him simply as His children.

We cannot enter a trusting relationship except by becoming 'as a child' (Matthew 18:3 and 1 John 3:1).

Cleansing

Guilt and shame bring defilement. When we are guilty of sin and are truly ashamed of our actions and thoughts, in order to be free, we will need to bring these in open confession to the Lord Jesus. It is sometimes powerful to have someone else alongside us to witness our confession (James 5:16).

 **PRAYER**

> Lord Jesus, thank you that your blood was shed so that I might be set free. I bring to you these deeply guilty and shameful places I have in my life and ask you to cleanse me from all unrighteousness. Amen.

It may be helpful to write a list, draw, paint or use some other creative means as a way of letting go, receiving forgiveness and allowing the past to be placed in God's hands.

Forgiveness

When we have suffered betrayal, an injustice, man's inhumanity to man or simply been wronged, even through sins of ignorance against us, we need to forgive those who have hurt us.

 **PRAYER**

Lord Jesus, I ask you to help me receive a melting in my heart towards those who have wronged me. I want to be able to forgive. Thank you that I have been forgiven and I now release those who have hurt me into the freedom of my forgiveness. In Jesus' name, Amen.

As an act of willingness to forgive, think about writing the names of those you need to forgive on a piece of paper and then tearing the paper up as you forgive or burning it in a fire. Remember forgiveness is a journey and there can be many times we need to express it anew.

Forgiveness – God's Master Key by Peter Horrobin (Horrobin P, Sovereign World, 2009) is a powerful book for those struggling in this area.

Battle

As has already been shared in Part 1, 'our struggle is not against flesh and blood, but against the rulers, against the authorities, against the powers of this dark world and against the spiritual forces of evil in the heavenly realms' (Ephesians 6:12). We should not be ignorant of the enemy and his false ways (2 Corinthians 2:11). We do not pray to the enemy, but we can stand in the authority that is given to us when we belong to Jesus Christ.

 **PRAYER**

In the Name of Jesus, I stand against the lies of the enemy and declare God's purposes over my life to bring freedom from all the works of darkness. Amen.

It is helpful to write a list of those things we consider false and lies, and perhaps on another piece of paper, those things which God speaks about us which are true and wholesome based on His created order. Finding a friend or someone you trust to share this, is bonding and builds faith and trust. The enemy seeks to keep us locked in his lies.

Restoration

Jesus came to heal the broken-hearted and bring His redemption and new life (Isaiah 61:1 and John 10:10).

 **PRAYER**

Lord Jesus, thank you that you paid the price to save and restore me. Please help me to silence the lies and accusations of the enemy and to receive your truth into my heart. Thank you that you made me in your image, and you are at work to redeem and restore my life. Amen!

Consider using creative ways to express emotions and to name them. Connecting to our inner being is always healthy and by inviting Jesus to be our Healer, the Holy Spirit can do a deep work of releasing things which have been deeply buried and which are locked in pain.

Finding Me

We are made in His image and beautiful to God (Genesis 1:27). He is always at work to find and rescue us.

PRAYER

Heavenly Father, thank you that you made me in your image and know me. I ask you to bring out in me all the beauty you intended. I ask you to refine and change my character to be more like you and to reflect who you are. Please bring out my gifts and talents for your glory, and to remove any blockages in connection to my true self. In Jesus' name, Amen.

Think of all the ways you are creative and how Father God loves to relate with you whilst you are engaging in just being you!

Relationships

We are not alone. God has set us in family (Psalm 68:6), and His desire is for His family to be one and undivided (John 17:21).

 **PRAYER**

Thank you, Lord Jesus, for the family of God, for
belonging and for the joy of relationship. Help me
to give my gifts and talents for the good of everyone
and not to hold myself back. I pray that I may be a
channel of your peace and goodness to others. Amen.

Think of ways you can give creatively to bless others, and in
doing so, you bless your Heavenly Father.

Intercession

Intercession is about standing in the gap on behalf of another.
In other words, being a bridge so that someone else might
find life and freedom. That bridge may be in traditional
prayer on their behalf or it might be in practical prayer
ministry.

 **INTERCESSORY PRAYER**

Lord Jesus, I stand on behalf of (insert the name
of person you are praying for) and I ask you to
bring freedom and healing into their lives. I ask you
to remove the blockages and obstacles which are
obstructing your light and truth reaching them. Amen

There are ways of being practical in intercession which involve
our creativity, in supporting, encouraging and strengthening
those in need.

Journalling

It can be very creative and freeing to keep a journal. Firstly, it is an outward sign of an inward truth. Things often come out in writing that are surprising. Thoughts emerge, feelings emerge too, and finally, ideas emerge. All these things add up to bringing a settlement, as the Holy Spirit is at work helping us to express what is on our heart.

To journal, also brings God's heart to us. In writing, we can record Scripture and bring this to life in a personal way. It may be that God wants to speak very clearly into our lives, and through the release of pen on paper those impressions and conviction come through onto the page.

Recording events and our journey in life is a way of releasing both positive and negative emotion in a safe way. It can simply be 'me time'.

 **PRAYER**

Heavenly Father, I ask you to use this journal as a vehicle to my personal relationship with you. Please awaken my creative juices to have thoughts and impressions which bring life to my inner being. I ask you to speak with me, in Jesus' name. Amen.

Lordship

We can belong to the Lord Jesus but still remain unyielded in the deep recesses of our hearts. He calls us to make Him Lord of our lives. In other words, to be willing to come under His reign and authority as King of Kings.

 **PRAYER**

Lord Jesus, I ask you to be Lord of my life – spirit, soul and body, my emotions, my thoughts, my choices, my behaviour, my gifts and talents and all of my creativity. Please set me aside for your purposes to love and serve you. Amen.

Use creative ways to express your walk with God, it may be making something, e.g. a cross, a bracelet, painting a picture or a card, or walking or climbing somewhere special. God loves it when we do things in relationship with Him. They also bring us powerful reminders and are a record to us of His faithfulness in our lives.

Praise and Worship

Praise is gratitude. Gratitude releases trust, it tells someone we trust them if we express gratitude to them for a gift or a task. A principle of prayer is that God releases His anointing and blessing through praise. It is through praise we tell Him He is a good Father and we trust Him.

Worship is likewise but in a different kind of way. Worship is not just about singing, although worshipful singing is a wonderful expression. Pure worship is the submission of our hearts. When we worship, we bow down, and in doing so, we tell God that He is trustworthy, He is greater and more powerful than any other. We lift Him up in our hearts and through our humility, the powerful grace and goodness of God is released into our lives.

PRAYER

Lord God, Creator of all things, we praise you for who you are. You are faithful, kind, true, an omnipotent, mighty God and we worship you. We bow down and give you all the glory, trusting you in our lives. In Jesus' name, Amen.

Dancing, singing, playing music, reading His Word, speaking, sharing and so many other creative expressions are part of us giving God all the glory, praise and honour due His name.

Group Work

It may be that you would like to use some of the principles in this book to help others in a group-type setting. Intercession is vital for the power of God to be released through creativity to bring His healing and transformation of lives. The emphasis should always be on the following:

- Praise and worship of Jesus, proclaiming His Lordship over the lives of everyone present and the event itself.

- Seeking the anointing of the Holy Spirit and the pushing back of all powers of darkness in Jesus' Name

- Asking Father God to come and meet with His children, to release joy, fun, laughter, pain and struggles

- Seeking the Lord for ways in which He wants to bring breakthrough's and healing help

- Walking in unity as the family of God

- Remembering life is a journey, it is not about the end result

- Asking the Lord for the gift of His encouragement, affirmation and safety into people's lives

- ✎ Keeping a prayerful attitude throughout the time, alert to the Holy Spirit's work

- ✎ Trusting Jesus to bring the Father's heart to His children

- ✎ Receiving the infilling and empowerment of the Holy Spirit

Chapter 20

THE MASTER CRAFTSMAN AND HIS GLORY

To conclude our understanding of healing through creativity we need to come back to our Creator God. We can do no better than reach out to the One who is the Master Craftsman, to touch our lives and bring out the very best within us. Creator God, who made everything beautiful in its time and season, is utterly faithful and completely safe. We can trust Him in each and every circumstance of life.

Plans for Good

Nothing compares with God's artistry, His originality and His handiwork. The rainbow, the butterfly, the olive tree, the sun, the moon and the stars, animals, people – indeed, the whole of the natural world displays His Glory and His ways.

If you have ever been to a butterfly house, you will have seen exquisite butterflies of every size and shape. On a recent trip to Asia a friend videoed the most exquisite butterfly I have ever seen. Its huge wings were decorated with stunning colours of purple, striking blue and gold. Then, as we watched, the butterfly brought its wings together turning into what looked like a brown leaf, perfectly camouflaged against the matching leaves of the plant it had settled on! The whole story of the life of a butterfly, beginning as a caterpillar, then turning into a chrysalis, and finally, after a long struggle, emerging as a butterfly, is just one tiny depiction of God's immense creative design.

In a similar way, we too, can be on a journey with struggles, where perseverance and endurance are doing a vital work in changing us. It is often during these testing times, that something beautiful is being forged within. When we yield and submit to God's way in our lives, He is at work bringing about His purposes which will be for our good.

> "I know the plans I have for you," declares the LORD, "plans to prosper you and not to harm you."
>
> (JEREMIAH 29:11)

Safest Hiding Place

I have had the privilege of visiting African game parks, with all the excitement of finding animals, roaming completely free and wild. Any kind of creature may be lurking or hiding just inches from you! Yet, they are often hard to see because their camouflaged design makes them melt into the landscape. We needed to 'tune' our eyes to seeing beyond the obvious, it became a joyous, addictive search. I will never forget the thrill and heightened excitement of unexpectedly coming upon a lion lying hidden in the long grass!

There is no easy route to God, at times it seems He is not easily found. He requires that we seek for Him. But then, when we find Him, He covers us and hides us beneath His wings of protection. He is our hiding place.

> "You who live in the shelter of the Most High, who abide in the shadow of the Almighty, will say to the Lord, "My refuge and my fortress; my God, in whom I trust." For he will deliver you from the snare of the fowler and from the deadly pestilence; he will cover you with his pinions, and under his wings you will find refuge.' (PSALM 91:1-4 NRSV)

> **"**
> He covers us and hides us beneath His wings of protection

Standing in Awe

We live in a time-dominated world that is shaking all around us. Nothing is certain in life here on earth. Creator God, however, is eternal and beyond the limitations of time. His hand of certainty stretches from eternity into time, reaching out to those He created and loves, intending we should find Him, love Him and live in relationship with Him. He is a Holy God who invites and urges us to follow Him by faith.

Scripture challenges all of creation to see the hand of God in everything that He made and warns us not to dismiss the truth about Him that is evident for all to see.

> "For what can be known about God is plain to them, because God has shown it to them. Ever since the creation of the world his eternal power and divine nature, invisible though they are, have been understood and seen through the things he has made. So they are without excuse; for though they knew God, they did not honour him as God or give thanks to him, but they became futile in their thinking, and their senseless minds were darkened. Claiming to be wise, they became fools; and they exchanged the glory of the immortal God for images resembling a mortal human being or birds or four-footed animals or reptiles." (ROMANS 1:19-23 NRSV)

It is a sobering truth, but absolutely vital for each one of us to understand, that outside of God, we are lost without an anchor and without a purpose. Left to human devices, destruction is at work everywhere you look. Almighty God is loving and kind, but He is also a Holy God who has not left us without warnings to heed in His Word.

I had no idea what to expect when we first visited the Niagara Falls in Canada. As we walked along the road towards the falls there was no visual evidence of what was about to be revealed. Then, suddenly, it seemed, we were there. The first realisation of the enormity and magnificence of Niagara Falls was the deafening thunder coming from millions of gallons of water cascading into the abyss below. Then there was the spray, which drenched you, as if you were in a downpour of rain. It is no exaggeration to say that my breath was taken away by a force of nature so massive, that there were no adequate words to describe what we were seeing. All you could do was try and take in the enormity of this spectacular display. Every inch of my humanity felt so small by comparison.

Standing there beholding the majesty, beauty and grandeur of the falls, I was in total awe. And I needed the language of worship to describe what Creator God had made. This experience helped me to describe the way we should approach God. As we come close to Him, dare to approach Him and to allow Him to come close to us, it should be with 'awe' and 'wonder'. Although He is divine and all-powerful, He stoops to take each one of us by the hand. Having a holy fear of a Holy God brings health and wholeness. We become masterpieces in the hands of the Master Craftsman, reflecting His meticulous design, order and care for those He loves.

> We become masterpieces in the hands of the Master Craftsman

A Grateful Heart

When we truly understand who He is and what He has done to rescue us, worship rises from a grateful heart. Worship, as we have seen, is submitting, bowing down and giving way to someone we trust. As we trust God as Father, Jesus draws us close to Himself.

> "You are worthy, our Lord and God, to receive glory and honour and power for you created all things and by your will they existed and were created." (REVELATION 4:11)

As we give ourselves to God in gratitude and trust, His life, healing and creative energy flow into us.

> But whenever anyone turns to the Lord, the veil is taken away. Now the Lord is the Spirit, and where the Spirit of the Lord is, there is freedom. And we all, who with un-veiled faces contemplate the Lord's glory, are being trans-formed into his image with ever-increasing glory, which comes from the Lord, who is the Spirit.'
>
> (2 CORINTHIANS 3:16-18)

The Glory

Where better to finish this book than to contemplate God's Glory and understand something of the meaning that there is in His creation. If we look, we will find and see Him, not just with our physical eyes, but with the eyes of our spirit. We will be moved to express worship to Him through the creativity He has placed in the heart of every one of us. Wonderful though creation here on earth is, it is not the end, it is only a reflection of what is yet to come!

> For now we see in a mirror, dimly, but then we will see face to face. Now I know only in part; then I will know fully, even as I have been fully known.
>
> (1 CORINTHIANS 13:12 NRSV)

What no eye has seen, nor ear heard, nor the human heart conceived, what God has prepared for those who love him.

(1 Corinthians 2:9 NRSV)

Jesus has opened up the way for us to receive the gift of eternal life prepared in advance for us, in a place where there is no more suffering and no more tears. We will not have to contend with sin and evil anymore, no more battle with Satan and his kingdom of darkness.

And here on earth, we are privileged to have the best creative gift of all. For, Jesus left His Holy Spirit to fill us and empower us. It is through the Holy Spirit that the very best of who we are, can shine with the beauty He placed within each one of us. We will find that as we yield to Him, laying aside our own agendas, He will bring about a plan for our lives which will exceed all our expectations.

We hold within us something of the glory of God, because He made us in His image, and we give Him all the glory, for He (Father, Son and Holy Spirit) is a Holy God and worthy of our praise and worship – both now and for ever and ever and ever!

> a plan for our lives which will exceed all our expectations

The Word became flesh and made his dwelling among us. We have seen his glory, the glory of the one and only Son, who came from the Father, full of grace and truth'.

(John 1:14)

"You are worthy, our Lord and God, to receive glory and honour and power, for you created all things, and by your will they were created and have their being."

(Revelation 4:11)

And my God will fully satisfy every need of yours according to His riches in glory in Christ Jesus. To our God and Father be glory forever and ever. Amen.'

(Philippians 4:19 NRSV)

Further Help

Intercession & Healing: Breaking Through with God
(Horrobin F, Sovereign World, 2008) – for practical ways to
help people through prayer

Forgiveness, God's Master Key
(Horrobin P, Sovereign World, 2009)

Journey to Freedom series of books
(Horrobin P, Sovereign World, 2018)

Healing from Accident, Shock and Trauma
(Horrobin P, Sovereign World, 2017)

Shepherd Love: His Heart Towards Me
(Smith P, Hartfield Publications, 1996)

Shepherd Walk: His Heart Towards Me
(Smith P, Hartfield Publications, 2005)

Jacqui Grace's Christian Colouring Books
(Just Cards Publishing)

Healing the Human Spirit
(Hawkey R, Sovereign World, 2019)

*Sarah - From an abusive childhood and the depths of
suicidal despair to a life of hope and freedom*
(Shaw S, Sovereign World, 2009)

The books by Jacqui Grace may be ordered from
www.justcardsdirect.com

All the other books, and many more on different
aspects of healing, may be obtained from
www.sovereignworld.com

ABOUT THE AUTHOR

Fiona Horrobin is married to Peter, the founder of Ellel Ministries. Between them, they have four married children and nine grandchildren. Fiona has pioneered the work of Ellel Ministries alongside Peter and has over thirty years' experience teaching and praying for people from a wide range of backgrounds and across many nations. She has taught on many different aspects of the healing ministry.

It was through ministering to the broken-hearted that Fiona discovered the keys to healing that flowed out of creative expression. Through discovering their creativity, people were getting deeply in touch with their Creator and experiencing His healing love.

Fiona's passion for seeing God heal the hurting and seeing their lives restored then led her to pioneer the vision for *Healing Through Creativity* courses within the work of Ellel Ministries. The lessons learned have proved dynamic and relevant to people from every culture and all the nations – from China to Africa and Australia to North America and especially including the formerly devastated nations of Eastern Europe.

It was through this work that Fiona also had a personal breakthrough in her own life and discovered her talent for art and painting. Her first book on *Healing and Intercession* was also the fruit of many years of practical experience of seeing God at work bringing healing and restoration to people's lives.

For details of
Healing through Creativity
events and courses
please go to

ellel.org

Creativity is included on many other Ellel Ministries
courses and retreats and you are warmly invited to
browse the website to discover which may be of
particular interest for you or those you know.